Teaching, learning and assessing science 5–12

Teaching, learning and assessing science 5–12

Wynne Harlen

P·C·P
Paul Chapman
Publishing Ltd

Paul Chapman Publishing Ltd
A SAGE Publications Company
6 Bonhill Street
London EC2A 4PU

SAGE Publications Inc
2455 Teller Road
Thousand Oaks, California 91320

SAGE Publications India Pvt Ltd
32, M-Block Market
Greater Kailash -I
New Delhi 110 048

British Library Cataloguing in Publication data

A catalogue record for this book is available from the British Library

ISBN 1-85396-448-4
ISBN 1-85396-449-2 (pbk)

Library of Congress catalog card number available

Typeset by Dorwyn Ltd, Rowlands Castle, Hants
Printed and bound by Athenaeum Press, Gateshead

Contents

Introduction

The second edition of this book was written in response to the developments following considerable change that took place in the early 1990s in the status of science in the education of children in the age range 5–12. At that time the importance of science as part of basic education was being recognised in many countries through the development of national or state-wide curriculum guidelines or standards, some statutory and some bolstered by programmes of assessment and testing. The effect of expecting, if not requiring, that science be part of every child's basic education from an early age was to draw attention to a wide range of issues relating to providing it. These issues ranged from the nature of children's learning in science to the problems of teachers who were ill-equipped by their own education and training for teaching science. Consequently the last seven years have seen increased research aimed at illuminating these issues and developments for supporting teaching. The resulting developments in understanding and in provision for teaching, including the opportunities opened up by the use of information and communications technology (ICT), are reflected in the changes made in producing the third edition of this book.

Matters relating to assessment have been a particularly significant area of change, and this is acknowledged in the change in the title of the book. Inevitably much of this interest is the result of expansion in testing in science. These summative tests serve the purposes of accountability and evaluation within and across schools as well as providing information to parents and other stakeholders in children's learning. However, more important from the point of view of improving learning has been the appearance of clear evidence of the benefits to be had from using assessment formatively, as part of teaching, to help learning. This role of assessment, advocated for many years (e.g. Match and Mismatch, 1977), has been shown to have the potential for raising the levels of children's achievement.

The implications for teaching science of translating this potential into action are, however, quite profound. They include the need for teachers not only to be aware themselves of the course of development towards greater understanding and of ways of helping children along it, but to share these things with children and involving them in deciding their next steps in learning. This simply recognises that children are the ones who do the learning and the more they know what they should be aiming to do, the better able they are to take some responsibility for their learning. It requires, however, a radical change for some teachers in their view of their role and the role of the children in learning.

As in the case of earlier editions, this book falls roughly into two parts. The first is about learning, comprising Chapters 1 to 5; the second about teaching, Chapters 6 to 15. There is, perhaps, less change in this edition to the material in Chapters 1 to 5 than in the rest of the book. This reflects the research and development attention that has been given to assisting classroom teaching, in which an important part has been played by institutions such as the Nuffield Foundation and the Association for Science Education in the UK and the National Science Foundation in the USA. In this edition the two parts are bound together by the overall framework provided by the model set out in Chapter 1 of what influences the decisions made about teaching. Derived from evidence of classroom decision-making, this model suggests that how teachers understand children's learning and what they understand the goals of learning to be, frame their decisions about the provision of learning experiences. In turn the teacher's view of appropriate learning experiences determines the roles that he or she takes, the roles of the children, and the parts that materials and assessment play in the learning experiences.

As a first step in working through this framework, Chapter 2 sets out a view of science that reflects current thinking and underpins the goals of science education for 5–12-year-olds. These goals, which are consistent with but not identical to those identified in any particular national curriculum or standards, are followed through in the later discussion of progression, assessment and classroom activities and interactions. They include the development of scientific attitudes, which are constantly noted in research as important in learning, but which continue to be given sparse recognition in some national curricula. Chapter 3 provides an extended example of children's interaction with materials and each other during an investigation. Children's ideas about other topics, revealed by research, are reviewed in Chapter 4.

Both Chapters 3 and 4 provide evidence to support points made in later chapters, and Chapter 5 presents a model of learning drawing on this evidence. This model, although making the same statement as in previous editions about learning as change in ideas, is expressed in a different form than before, resulting from a continued effort to represent a complex process without oversimplifying. It is a further attempt to convey learning with understanding as demanding a close interaction of process skills and ideas. Ideas which are understood are those which the learners have worked out for themselves by using their own ideas, or ideas suggested to them, and by trying them out against experience. As a result the initial ideas may be modified, rejected or strengthened in the light of evidence. Which of these happens depends on *the way* the ideas are related to evidence as well as on what the evidence is, so the development of skills of selecting, applying and testing ideas is fundamental to the development of those ideas.

Chapter 6 takes up the next step in the model set out in Chapter 1, by considering the kinds of learning experiences that give opportunity for the learning described in Chapter 6. Some of the roles of the teacher and children in these experiences are discussed in Chapter 7, whilst Chapter 8 overviews the roles of assessment in education. In relation to assessment, the focus in this book is assessment *for* learning rather than assessment *of* learning. Four chapters (Chapters 9 to 12) are devoted to the different aspects of assessment for learning, which are all integral to teaching. They cover ways of gathering evidence about children's ideas, skills and attitudes, ways of interpreting this evidence to indicate where children are in the progress of developing these attributes and, most importantly, helping further progress. It is in the interpretation and use of evidence that formative assessment differs from assessment for other purposes. The possibility of summarising some of the evidence gathered for informing teaching and using it for reporting progress is discussed in Chapter 13, on summative assessment.

The selection of resources for learning science, including the use of new technologies, is the subject of Chapter 14. Chapter 15 deals with matters of planning and monitoring provision for science throughout the school. A major trend in recent years has been the extension and better definition of the role of subject leaders within schools for 5–12-year-olds, where teachers are generalists, not specialists. So the science subject leader is likely to be expected to take responsibility at the school level for devising, supporting and monitoring a school programme which promotes continuity and progression. The role also includes attention to professional development in science for colleagues, an area where new technologies are beginning to play a part.

In summary, this book attempts to provide a theoretical underpinning for the suggestions that are made about the experiences that promote children's learning in science and what teachers can do to provide these experiences. It seems important to me that we should be able to justify what we do in classrooms in terms of how children learn and of helping them achieve worthwhile learning. But there are no easy answers and so it is essential for the reader to review critically the ideas in this book and their implications for practice. To help this process there are points for reflection at the end of each chapter from Chapter 2 onwards. Sources of further information about some of the points raised are also suggested. The ideas and information offered here will no doubt be overtaken by new thinking as we continue to strive for more effective ways to help children to learn with understanding. If what is here helps to stimulate this thinking, this book will have achieved its major purpose.

Wynne Harlen,
Edinburgh
September 1999

Acknowledgements

We are grateful to the following for permission to quote copyright material; Oxford University Press, Inc.; Education Queensland and the Australian Council for Research in Education; the Centre for Mathematics and Science Education, Queensland University of Technology; the Association for Science Education. While every attempt has been made to contact copyright owners, in some cases it has not been possible to do so. For any such oversights we apologise and ask that parties concerned contact us so that the situation may be rectified in future editions.

1

Teaching science 5–12: why and how

This chapter is about the reasons behind why and how we teach science. Although we no longer have to justify why we teach science from the start of formal schooling – and, indeed, often include relevant experience in pre-school education – it is important to keep the reasons in mind to ensure that what we do serves the intended purposes. So we begin with a brief reminder of the important reasons for including science in the curriculum for 5–12-year-olds. We then turn to reasons for teaching science in certain ways. Evidence from classroom observations is used to propose a framework for decision-making about the kinds of learning experiences that are provided for children and the roles of the teacher, the children and the learning resources in these experiences. The key factors in deciding these things, it is argued, are the kinds of learning that are valued and the understanding of the goals of science education, which incorporate a view of the nature of science.

This decision framework provides a loose structure for the rest of this book. Thus the description of its main components serves as a rough guide to the subsequent chapters.

The value of teaching science 5–12

The case for beginning science in the pre-secondary years has been accepted universally for some years now (Morris, 1990). There is hardly a country that does not include science in its pre-secondary school curriculum and it is probably only necessary here to summarise the main points of the case:

- Learning science enables children to develop understanding of the natural and made world around them, so that from the start of their formal education, they build up ideas that gradually become broader as their experience and exploration of their environment expands.

- In order to deal with the rapid changes that result from scientific and technological advances, all citizens of the world need to be scientifically literate. The phrase 'scientific literacy' indicates a broad basic understanding and competence in science rather than a detailed grasp of every principle and extensive factual knowledge. Being scientifically literate can be thought of as being 'at ease' with key scientific ideas and skills. It is as necessary in society today as is being 'at ease' with numbers, with percentages, with rates of change (numeracy) or with various forms of language (literacy). There is further discussion of the meaning of scientific literacy in Chapter 2.

- Children develop ideas about the world around them from their very first days and this is continuing during the primary years whether or not they are taught science. But without intervention that introduces a scientific approach in their exploration of the world, the ideas that they develop may be non-scientific and may obstruct later learning. There is ample evidence (some reviewed in Chapter 4) to show that these ideas are the result of thinking and reasoning and as such make sense to the children. However, this thinking and reasoning is not scientific (that is, not rigorous in the collection and interpretation of relevant evidence) and the ideas do not accord with the scientific view. A major role for pre-secondary science is to reduce the gap between the children's own ideas and the scientific view by engaging children in explaining and testing their ideas through systematic enquiry. Ways of doing this are discussed in Chapter 11.

- The earlier children experience scientific activity for themselves, the more likely they are to develop positive and thoughtful attitudes towards science as a human activity, instead of uninformed reactions to the popular image of science. Attitudes to science develop in the pre-secondary years, earlier than attitudes to some other school subjects, and children need to experience science activity for themselves at a time when attitudes are being formed which may have an influence for the rest of their lives.

The basis of classroom decisions

The list above sets out some *potential* benefits; whether or not they are realised depends on what we take to be education in science. So we do need to be able to justify, to ourselves as well as others, what we teach and how we teach it. Teachers should be able to say why they are teaching something in terms that go beyond 'because it is in the book or curriculum' or 'because they have to know it for the test'. They should also be able to say why they are teaching it in a certain way, for there are many ways of teaching any subject and *how* children are taught is just as important to what they learn as is the content.

This book is about a particular way of teaching towards particular goals of learning, and so the justification for these needs to be spelled out. All other matters follow from this.

Within the constraints imposed by time and other resources, teachers make decisions relating to children's learning experiences to be consistent with their views of what it is important for them to learn and their view of how children learn. Evidence for this has come from classroom observations and discussions with teachers. Asked why they teach in a certain way, the answer is likely to be 'because this helps the children learn' and is implicitly based on a view of how learning takes place. Decisions about matters such as whether the children work in groups, whether these are friendship groups or based on ability, whether low-level noise is permitted in the class, whether children can move round the class without asking permission, whether they have materials to explore or learn from books – these decisions are justified in terms of supporting learning of the kind that the teacher values. Where this is not the case, and teachers have to adopt procedures decided by someone else, they may be dissatisfied that they are not able to achieve the learning that they value.

Two classrooms

This was illustrated by recorded discussions with teachers who organised their classrooms in very different ways (reported in Match and Mismatch, 1977). Teacher A had the children sitting in rows, all facing the blackboard, working in silence, mainly from books. In discussion she explained why:

> Well, you see, the main thing – I can't stand any noise. I don't allow them to talk in the classroom . . . I mean they go out at playtime, they go out at dinnertime and so on. But actually in the classroom I like them sitting in their places where I can see them. And I teach from lesson to lesson. There's no children all doing different things. You know, it's formal . . . and of course I like it that way, I believe in it that way.

Asked about the use of materials other than books teacher A confirmed that all the learning was from books, the blackboard or from her because 'that's the way they learn'.

By contrast, Teacher B, who taught the same age group, 10–11-year-olds, and had a similar number of children in the class (32) had the desks in the classroom arranged in rather irregular groups. She spent most of her time moving round the groups and allowed the children to talk whilst they worked on a variety of activities. She explained:

> I hate to see children in rows and I hate to see them regimented. At the same time, you know, I often get annoyed when people think that absolute chaos reigns, because it doesn't. Every child knows exactly what they have to do . . . it's much more – you could say informal – but it's a much more friendly, less pressing way of working and you find the children do . . . it's nice for them to be able to chat with a friend about what they are doing . . . I mean, adults do when they work. As long as I get the end result that's suited to that particular child I don't mind, you know. Obviously if a child's not achieving then I do go mad because at nine, ten and eleven, they should know they've got a certain amount of work to do and the standard one expects of them.

A general framework for classroom decisions

Although the above extracts were recorded in 1976, discussions with teachers today indicate a similar consistency between classroom arrangement and teaching procedures and the beliefs of teachers about what is needed for learning. Put more generally, the point being made is that the views of learning and of the goals of learning provide the rationale for decisions about learning experiences and how these are provided in the classroom. These things also influence decisions about how children's learning is assessed and how the effectiveness of the teaching is evaluated. These relationships are expressed diagrammatically in Figure 1.1, which is adapted from a model, or framework, proposed by Harlen and Osborne (1985).

In Figure 1.1 the two-headed arrows indicate that there should be consistency between the things in the linked boxes. The broken lines suggest feedback from both formal and informal evaluation of procedures and outomes, making the model dynamic rather than static. If this model is indeed general, then it should describe the implications of any view of learning and of the outcomes of learning. So, for example, if the view of learning were to be that it is a matter of memorisation (rote learning), then:

- the 'learning experiences' box would indicate that children were to be exposed to accurate information, presented in well-defined and limited 'packages' that are each to be mastered before proceeding to the next
- the goals of learning box would indicate knowledge of scientific facts and procedures

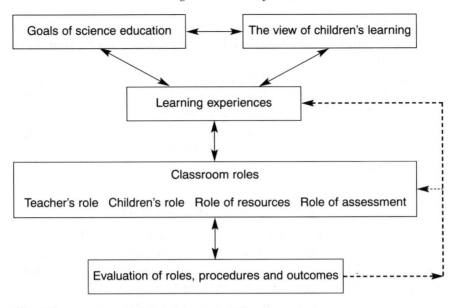

Figure 1.1. General model of decisions about classroom practice
Source: Adapted from Harlen and Osborne (1985)

- the children's role would be to memorise and recall
- the teacher's role would be to give clear expositions of information and ensure children's attention to it
- the role of resources would be to assist in conveying information and to hold attention
- the role of assessment would be to identify when each 'package' of information has been mastered
- the evaluation criteria would be the extent to which the procedures had successfully exposed the children to the information.

Applying the model to teaching science for understanding

The view of learning developed in this book is quite different from rote learning. It aims for understanding and is grounded in the view that this is to be developed from within the learner rather than transmitted from outside. Understanding means that knowledge extends beyond isolated facts, that the learner can link together items of information and use these links in explaining particular events. Knowledge which is understood can be applied in situations not previously encountered, whilst knowledge learned by rote and not linked into other experiences can be recalled only in situations closely resembling those in which it was learned. (This is not to deny a role for memorising facts, but is an argument for linking these with other facts or experience to produce ideas that have wider application.)

The framework in Figure 1.1 can be used to summarise the main features of the approach to teaching and learning science for children 5–12 which underpins this book. The model elaborated in this way serves as an organising framework for the rest of the book and as a guide to where particular topics are taken up in more detail in the later chapters.

The goals of science education

The outcomes of science education as a whole are skills and concepts that enable understanding of scientific aspects of the world around. The skills include those involved in identifying and interpreting relevant evidence, and the concepts include ideas of science and ideas about science. The outcomes of learning at a particular stage have to be considered in relation to what is appropriate to the experience and ways of learning of children at that stage. In the early stages of learning, the goals of science activities are to help children:

- to construct effective and useful ways of making sense of scientific aspects of their environment
- to develop effective ways of learning through enquiry
- to understand the nature of scientific activity and its strengths and limitations.

(Chapter 2 considers the goals in more detail.)

The view of learning

This is what is now widely known as a constructivist (or generative) view of learning. Its central feature is the recognition of the role of learners in actively constructing ideas or concepts rather than absorbing them passively from teachers or other sources. In constructing meaning, a learner uses the ideas or concepts already formed from previous experience and attempts to make sense of new experience in terms of these existing conceptions. These tentative ideas about explaining new experience have to be tested out, sometimes mentally and sometimes through a combination of mental and physical activity in the form of an investigation or experiment. The way in which this testing of possible explanations is carried out involves mental processes, which therefore play an essential part in developing understanding in this view of learning. (These points are taken up in Chapters 3, 4 and 5.)

Learning experiences

In the context of 5–12-year-olds learning science, building understanding has to begin with the objects and events familiar to them. From the ideas used in understanding specific aspects of their environment ('small' ideas) more widely applicable ones ('big' ideas) are created by making links between ideas from related but different events. The bigger ideas have greater power (because they help to explain more events); these bigger ideas are themselves linked with others in forming broad theories or principles.

The process cannot proceed in the opposite direction, since the broad theories are necessarily highly abstract and, indeed, meaningless if they do not evoke the many real situations which they link together. Thus, for example, if children develop, through investigation and observation, an understanding that there is interdependence among plants and animals in their own environment – their back garden, the park, the stream or the hedgerow – they may eventually understand the reasons for protecting the rain forests. But if the big issues relating to this conservation are the starting points, they may be understood at no greater depth than slogans and the relationships never more than superficially grasped. Moreover it helps understanding if learners can reflect on what they have learned and the way in which they have learned. From these arguments it follows that experiences that will lead to learning are those that:

- are within the reach of the children's current ideas and ways of processing
- can be linked to their previous experiences
- stimulate children to explore and interact with living and non-living things in their environment
- enable them to test their ideas for explaining phenomena or events that are new to them
- give them access to alternative ideas which can also be tested
- help them to develop the skills needed to test ideas scientifically
- give them control of making sense of new experience
- encourage reflection on how their ideas and skills have changed.

(Chapter 6 discusses the kinds of learning experiences that are suited to children at different stages and Chapter 15 takes up the role of the whole school in providing them.)

Classroom roles

Teacher's role

In the most general terms, the teacher's role is to enable children to build effective ways of investigating and understanding the scientific aspects of their surroundings. In order to do this, teachers need to have a clear idea of the goals of learning and of the path of progression towards those goals. They also have to have the skills to find out where the children start from and knowledge of ways to help them make progress, including sharing with the children the goals of learning and helping them to assess their own work and progress. This knowledge and skill supports the teacher's role, which is to:

- find out the children's ideas and use these as a starting point for building towards more effective, scientific ideas
- promote interaction of the children with the materials and resources through which they can develop understanding
- help children to develop the skills needed to test out ideas scientifically
- provide children with access to alternative ideas to their own, including the scientific one
- help children reflect on their ideas and on their ways of thinking
- monitor progress and reflect on the effectiveness of the learning experience provided.

(These points are taken up specifically in Chapter 7 and in Chapters 9, 10, 11 and 12, whilst all other chapters have some bearing on the teacher's role.)

Children's role

The active involvement of the children in their learning is an essential feature of a constructivist approach to teaching and learning. This means that they have to be both mentally and physically active and also that they engage in reflection about what they are learning. Even very young children can take part in discussing how they are exploring as well as what they are finding. Thus their role in learning is to:

- engage in investigations and enquiry into events presented in the classroom and in the world around them
- become involved in developing ideas and skills that help them make sense of their environment
- reflect on how their ideas and skills have changed as a result of their activities
- begin to identify what they have learned from particular activities

• assess their work and take part in deciding how to improve it.

(Chapter 7 deals with these matters.)

Role of resources

Resources include physical materials for investigation, equipment used in investigation, books and other sources of information, which have an essential part to play in learning science. Their role can be summarised as:

• providing opportunities for children to investigate and manipulate things in their environment
• stimulating interest and provoking questions that children can attempt to answer by enquiry
• providing the means and the evidence for children to test ideas
• providing information to help children construct useful ideas.

(Matters relating to resources are discussed in Chapter 14.)

Role of assessment

There is an important formative role for assessment in all learning and teaching, but particularly when the approach is to help children construct their ideas. It is essential for teachers to know the starting points in terms of the children's existing ideas and skills so that they can provide appropriate experiences that promote change and development. Assessment of this kind is integral to teaching and is concerned with helping learning, not with assessing outcomes or with labelling children's achievement. It involves children, so that they can judge their work and be helped to recognise the next steps they need to take. Thus in this context assessment has the role of:

• supporting learning
• identifying children's ideas and skills
• giving both teacher and children information about progress
• providing the basis for action to support further learning.

(Assessment for this formative purpose is discussed in Chapter 8, and Chapters 9, 10, 11 and 12 are concerned with using assessment to help children's development. Assessment for summarising and recording progress is part of Chapter 13.)

Evaluation criteria

Evaluation involves making judgements about the effectiveness or quality of what is being evaluated. Feedback of these judgements to those able to change the situation gives evaluation a formative role in learning. Thus it is important always to be asking the questions: 'Do the children have the opportunities that are intended?' 'Are they learning in a way consistent with the view of how learning takes place?' 'Is the teacher taking the role intended and using resources and assessment to support the learning experiences?' and so on.

However, the judgements depend on the criteria being used. For example, someone observing teacher A's class (p. 3) using the criterion that an effective classroom organisation is a formal one where children work individually and silently, would judge that class to be effectively organised, whilst judging teacher B's class to be ineffectively organised. The judgements would be reversed if the criteria were that an effective classroom organisation enabled children to work collaboratively and share ideas. The criteria to be applied in the context of a constructivist view of teaching and learning would be, for example, that:

- children are engaged in inquiry in new situations, raising questions and attempting to answer them
- children are questioning ideas (their own and others) and testing them against previous experience and against new information
- children are basing their conclusions on evidence and are prepared to change their ideas in the light of evidence
- children are reflecting on how they have tested ideas and how their testing can be improved
- teachers are aware of the children's ideas and are providing opportunities for them to consider and test alternative ideas including the scientific view
- there are sufficient resources available and children are using these effectively
- teachers are using assessment formatively and involving children in assessing their work and deciding how to improve it.

(Matters relating to evaluating children's learning opportunities are included in Chapter 15.)

Summary

This introductory chapter has sought to provide:

- a brief summary of the case for teaching science to children in the 5–12 age range as a reminder that we must ensure that how and what science is taught should serve these educational ends

- a framework, or model, for making decisions about how and what science to teach
- an overview of the implications of embracing a constructivist view of learning
- some signposts to parts of the book where the discussion of particular aspects is taken up in more detail.

All matters discussed here are taken further in later chapters, where ideas for further reading are suggested.

2

The goals of science education

What learning do we want to achieve through science education? This is a big question but a fundamental one, given that the answer will help determine, in large measure, how we teach as well as what we teach and when we teach it. The answer at any one time depends on *priorities*, for there is never enough time or enough resources to teach all that it's possible or desirable to teach.

The changes made in the various drafts of the science National Curriculum for England and Wales since 1989 are evidence that views of what should be taught can change. But the differences should not be exaggerated. In practice there is considerable consensus across the world and over the years in national curriculum statement or guidelines both about the breadth of different outcomes that should be embraced and in the particular concepts, skills and attitudes that are felt to be important. Indeed, some would say, as we will see later, that there is too much continuity over time and not enough rethinking of what is relevant to the world today, rather than yesterday. Certainly it is fitting, as we enter a new millennium, to consider the matter of what learning it is important for future citizens to acquire through their school education as a whole and the contribution to this of science education for children aged 5 to 12.

We begin with the broader question: what is the contribution of science to the education of future citizens? The answer is influenced by consideration of the needs of the individual, the needs of society and the nature of the subject.

The value to individuals and to society

For the individual, learning science can:

- sustain and develop curiosity and a sense of wonder about the world around

- provide information that can lead to understanding that helps decision-making about matters relating to health, diet, lifestyle, etc.
- enable informed participation in debates about major issues such as environmental preservation, genetic engineering, the use of energy
- give access to ways of investigation and inquiry that are based on evidence and careful reasoning
- provide satisfaction in finding answers to questions through one's own mental and physical activity.

The values for the individual merge into those for society, since a modern industrial and democratic society needs citizens who have:

- informed views on matters such as pollution, biotechnology, species conservation and so on
- widely applicable skills,
- flexibility in thinking and respect for evidence
- the willingness and ability to continue learning.

In the twenty-first century, few will be able to lead a useful and satisfying life without being able to adapt to the accelerating changes in types of occupation, ways of living and in the requirements of any particular job or profession. Clear evidence of this is seen in the emphasis given in upper secondary school courses to the development of key, or core, skills. These are generally taken to be problem-solving, communication, numeracy, using information technology and working with others. Requirement to develop these skills is gradually moving down to earlier stages of education, in response to recognising that they can be more satisfactorily developed the sooner the process begins. So we should be looking to ensure that education at all levels makes a contribution to these vital skills.

Science education for all

Science education in school has to serve both the purpose of preparing future scientists and technologists and of providing all citizens with sufficient knowledge and understanding of the world around so that they can operate effectively and make sensible decisions about science-related issues that affect all our lives. Although in the curriculum for 5–12-year-olds there is no distinction between these two, nevertheless there is a tendency for the requirements of later stages of education to press down on the earlier stages. To date the need to educate future scientists has dominated the secondary science curriculum, perhaps because those who determine the curriculum tend to be, or to accept the views of, those who studied science at tertiary level. This situation has been widely criticised and curriculum developers are now being urged to consider as a priority the contribution that science education should be making to the education of everyone, irrespective of whether they continue study of science beyond the end of compulsory schooling.

The findings of two groups, who have recently considered what the contribution of science to the education of all should be, give some ideas of how this perspective might change the goals of science education.

One of these groups was of UK science educators who considered 'the form of science education required to prepare young people for life in our society in the next century' and published their findings under the title *Beyond 2000* (Millar and Osborne, 1998, p. 1). They expressed the outcome of their deliberations in terms of the need for a science curriculum which is 'seen primarily as a course to enhance general "scientific literacy" '. The meaning and implications of this were exemplified rather than being worked out in detail by the members of this group. They emphasised the need to build gradually, throughout education from the age of 5 to 16, 'general understanding of the important ideas and explanatory frameworks of science'. They suggested that these are best communicated in the form of 'explanatory stories', because:

- These stories emphasise that understanding is not of single propositions, or concepts, but of inter-related sets of ideas which, taken together, provide a framework for understanding an area of experience.
- They help to ensure that the central ideas of the curriculum are not obscured by the weight of detail. Pupils and teachers are then able to see more clearly where ideas are leading, and how they are inter-related – and so be able to work together towards clear targets.
- They provide a better portrayal of the sort of understanding we would wish young people to obtain from studying the science curriculum than do lists of separate knowledge statements – and hence a better pointer to the kinds of assessment approach which might be suitable.

(Millar and Osborne, 1998, p. 13–14)

This group also emphasised the development of an understanding *of* science, which should come from:

- evaluating, interpreting and analysing both evidence which has been collected at firsthand and evidence which has been obtained from secondary sources

- hearing and reading stories about how important ideas were first developed and became established and accepted
- learning how to construct sound and persuasive arguments based upon evidence
- considering a range of current issues involving the application of science and scientific ideas.

The second group which was considering what science education should aim to provide echoed many of the points made in *Beyond 2000*. This was an international group set up by the Organisation for Economic Co-operation and Development (OECD) to advise on the development of tests for the Programme for International Student Assessment (PISA). The PISA project was set up to conduct surveys every three years, beginning in 2000, to assess the 'extent to which the educational system in participating countries have prepared 15 year-olds to play constructive roles as citizens in society' (OECD, 1999, p. 7). The interest was in the outcomes rather than the curriculum processes, although some information is collected by questionnaire about students' exposure to learning experiences relevant to what is tested. Surveys look at achievement in reading, mathematics and science. In each case what is assessed is described in terms of 'literacy'.

The group deciding the framework for 'scientific literacy' defined it as: 'the capacity to use science knowledge, to identify questions and to draw evidence-based conclusions in order to understand and help make decisions about the natural world and the changes made to it through human activity' (OECD, 1999, p. 60). To take this to a more detailed level meant answering the question: what are the outcomes of science education up to the age of 15 that every citizen needs? The group identified science processes, science concepts and situations (or contexts) in which the processes and concepts are used. The process skills identified were:

1 Recognising scientifically investigable questions.
2 Identifying evidence needed in a scientific investigation.
3 Drawing or evaluating conclusions.
4 Communicating valid conclusions.
5 Demonstrating understanding of science concepts.

Although only the last item in this list explicitly mentions scientific concepts, it was recognised that science knowledge is needed for all five processes. Only when used in relation to science content does a process such as 'drawing or evaluating conclusions', for example, become a *science* process skill. Consistent with the definition above, the group considered that scientific literacy would be indicated by using these processes and applying science concepts in relation to issues that citizens of today and tomorrow need to understand and make decisions about. Nine such 'areas of application' were identified:

> Health, disease and nutrition
> Maintenance of and sustainable use of species
> Interdependence of physical/biological systems
> Pollution
> Production and loss of soil
> Weather and climate
> Biotechnology
> Use of materials and waste disposal
> Use of energy
> Transportation

(OECD, 1999, p. 65)

Thus the science concepts that are assessed, and considered to be useful outcomes of science education, are determined by the relevance to these real-world issues. The situations, or contexts, in which they are encountered – both in life and in the test items – can affect us as individuals (food, use of energy), as members of a local community (water supply, air pollution) or as world citizens (global warming, loss of biodiversity). It was also thought important to include a 'historical context' reflecting the way scientific knowledge evolves and affects social decisions.

The focus of both the *Beyond 2000* and the OECD/PISA groups was the whole science education of 5–16-year-olds, but what they have to say is relevant not only to the secondary school curriculum but to the age range 5–12 where, after all, the largest part of science education takes place. We take up the implications of this later in this chapter after first completing the discussion of relevant factors, by looking at the view of science that reflects current thinking.

The nature of scientific activity

In *Beyond 2000*, leading science educators in the UK reviewed the science curriculum in the UK and concluded that:

> The current curriculum retains its past, mid-twentieth-century emphasis, presenting science as a body of knowledge which is value-free, objective and detached – a succession of 'facts' to be learnt, with insufficient indication of any overarching coherence and a lack of contextual relevance to the future needs of young people. The result is a growing

tension between school science and contemporary science as portrayed in the media, between the needs of future specialists and the needs of young people in the workplace and as informed citizens.

(Millar and Osborne, 1998, p. 4)

The modern view of science is quite different from the one that sees it as yielding ultimate truths and providing proofs of objective theorems. It sees the characteristics which, in combination, define science as essentially these:

- Science activity is about *understanding,* that is, arriving at possible explanations of and relationships between observed events which enable predictions to be made.
- Science is a *human endeavour,* depending on creativity and imagination, and on skills of gathering and interpreting evidence: it has changed in the past and will change in the future as human experience and understanding change.
- The understanding, the theories, at any particular time are subject to change in the light of new evidence and so must be regarded as *tentative* at all times.
- The physical world around is the *ultimate authority* by which the validity of scientific theories and principles is to be judged. Whatever logic there seems to be in hypothetical explanations or relationships, they are only useful in so far as they agree with reality.

Each of these points is now briefly elaborated. In this discussion we take the opportunity to distinguish science from its closest neighbours – mathematics and technology. There are many reasons to combine teaching and learning in science and technology and in some aspects of methematics. But it is still important for a teacher to know how the learning contributes to knowledge and understanding in each of these subjects.

Science as understanding

In both learning science and doing science the aim is to understand. In practice this means that we have to have an *explanation* for what is known and that predictions made on the basis of this explanation fit the available evidence. In arriving at an explanation – a theory – a scientist uses existing ideas, makes predictions based on them and then makes observations to see whether the predictions fit the facts. For a theory to be worthy of the name, as Stephen Hawking points out, it must satisfy two requirements: 'It must accurately describe a large class of observations on the basis of a model that contains only a few arbitrary elements, and it must make definite predictions about the results of future observations' (Hawking, 1988, p. 9).

If the observations do not fit, the theory has to be changed, assuming that the 'facts' are not disputed. When Copernicus' model (theory) of the universe put the sun at the centre of planets moving in circular orbits, this was a great improvement on the Ptolemaic model. However, the predictions it gave about the movement of the planets did not coincide with how the planets were observed to move. Johannes Kepler then modified the theory, proposing that the planets' orbits were elliptical, not circular. Newton elaborated the model, providing an explanation for the elliptical orbits in terms of the 'law of gravitation', which gave predictions fitting the observations well – that is, until the technology existed that revealed previously undetected phenomena. Then it was Einstein's theory which fitted the events better.

These changes exemplify the gradual development of understanding, where each step is taken from the position reached by a previous one. A scientist does not come to a new phenomenon, or revisit a familiar one, without ideas derived from what is already known. In the same way, a pupil learning science has ideas derived from previous experience which are brought to bear in making his or her personal understanding of events and phenomena. These ideas are tested out against the evidence and modified so that they fit better that which has been observed.

While there are, of course, many differences between the ways of working of the scientist and of the child learning science – to be explored in Chapters 3 and 4 – they are both aiming for understanding and there are broad similarities in the way that understanding is developed. These similarities are certainly enough to support the claim that learning science and doing science are basically the same activities.

The relationship between science and technology

The concern with understanding, which is characteristic of science, enables it to be clearly distinguished from *technology*. Technological activity is closely connected in practice with scientific activity. Both are relevant in the education of young children but one should not be mistaken for the other. Technology is about solving problems by designing and making some artefact, whereas science is about understanding. They are, however, more closely related than this simple statement seems to suggest. In the pursuit of scientific activity, problems are often encountered which require technology, as, for example, in devising ways of observing (a microscope results from the application of technology to such a problem) or in handling data (a computer). At the same time the solution of problems by technology involves the application of concepts arrived at through science (the understanding of reflection and refraction of light in the case of the microscope, for instance).

Technology is also involved in the solving of problems in other areas of the curriculum outside science. While closely related, even at the primary level, science and technology are quite distinct. There is more to science than solving practical problems and more to technology than applying science concepts. Moreover, as Layton (1990) argues cogently, scientific knowledge has to be 'reworked' before the technologist can use it. Scientific knowledge is expressed in terms of theories which are general and widely applicable, while technology requires knowledge that is particular, specific and tailored to the particular situation.

Science as a human endeavour

It is implicit in what has just been said that scientific ideas originate in the way human beings make sense of their experience. So it is perhaps surprising that science is so often depicted as being some kind of objective picture of the world 'as it is', as if facts and theories exist in the objects or phenomena themselves to be teased out by those clever enough to do so. An unfortunate consequence of the term 'discovery learning' is that it gives this impression. We can agree that the answers to how things work do reside within them in that they are to be found by investigation and experimentation, but there is an important difference between regarding the process as 'finding *the* explanation of what is happening' and 'finding the best way for me to explain what is happening'. The difference is not trivial, for the latter formulation admits that there may be other ways of explaining things.

There is an intriguing question here about just how major changes in ideas come about. How did Kepler come to hit upon elliptical orbits as providing a better model than circular ones? How did Newton arrive at the universal theory of gravitation? In Newton's case we have the apocryphal story of the falling apple, but it still leaves a big question as to how any thinking about an apple was connected with the solar system. Biographies sometimes help to provide an explanation of an event, but inevitably they present it with hindsight, from the position of knowing that the new idea was in fact a useful one. From this perspective the new idea always appears so obvious that it seems surprising that it was not thought of before. At the time, however, it probably emerged from creative reflection, even day-dreaming, rather than rational thinking. Creativity and imagination have played a part in the successive changes which have led to our current state of understanding. The ideas, which appear sometimes to 'come out of the blue', have been seized upon and selected from others by a mechanism which Einstein described as 'the way of intuition, which is helped by a feeling for the order lying behind the appearance' (Einstein, 1933).

Science includes much more than controlled experiment, objective measurement and the careful checking of predictions. It depends on these but just as much on creative thinking and imagination; a truly human endeavour. Learning science through experiencing it this way is more likely to appeal to, and excite, children (and future citizens) than learning it as a set of mechanical procedures and 'right answers'. In particular it is more likely to appeal to the female half of the population who currently often feel excluded from science because of its masculine image.

The tentative nature of scientific theories

Reference above to the successive models of the solar system and theories of the universe provide an example of how certain ideas have changed. We can confidently add 'and will change', for there is no reason to suppose that this process will not continue. Einstein would have been the last to claim that he had arrived at some kind of final word on the subject. Many many examples of changes in ideas in other branches of science could be cited. Without labouring the point, what these changes mean is that, at any particular time in the past – or indeed in the present – the only certainty is that the current theories, although believed to be the most perfect insights, are only passing stages in human understanding.

The consequence of recognising this is that any theory must be regarded as subject to change and therefore as only tentative knowledge, for the chance of finding evidence which disagrees with it is always present. Even though a theory may provide predictions which accord with all existing evidence for centuries (as Newton's did) there is always the possibility of further observations which do not fit (as indeed eventually happened in Newton's case). Hawking expresses this with clarity and authority:

> Any physical theory is always provisional, in the sense that it is only a hypothesis: you can never prove it. No matter how many times the

results of experiments agree with some theory, you can never be sure that the next time the result will not contradict the theory. On the other hand, you can disprove a theory by finding even a single observation that disagrees with the predictions of the theory . . . Each time new experiments are observed to agree with the prediction the theory survives, and our confidence in it is increased; but if ever a new observation is found to disagree, we have to abandon or modify the theory. At least that is supposed to happen, but you can always question the competence of the person who carried out the observation.

(Hawking, 1988, p. 10)

If this applies to the theories of scientists, how much more seriously must it be taken in relation to the individual theories of learners? At any particular time learners' ideas are those which best fit the evidence available, but soon there are likely to have to be changes in the light of further information or observations. However, if we see for ourselves the evidence which brings the need to change, there will be no confusion but greater clarity. If children are taught science in a way which reflects the tentative nature of all theories, it will seem natural for them to adapt their own ideas as new evidence is presented. It is only when others tell them to adopt different ideas for which they as yet see no reason, that confusion is likely.

Reality as the ultimate test of scientific theories

It may seem obvious that, if science is about understanding the world around, then its theories must be judged by how well it does this. In practice, however, testing how well a theory fits is not always easy. Evidence may not be available, or may be contested, as Hawking noted, or may depend on such complicated mathematics that few people understand it.

In the history of science there are many examples of factors other than the fit with evidence being used to assess a scientific theory. It took a hundred years for the ideas of Copernicus, that the earth and planets moved round the sun, to be accepted even though this model fitted the observations far better than Ptolemy's model of the universe, mainly because the latter's earth-centred model had been adopted by the Christian Church. There are contemporary examples of theories based on cultural mores which are preferred to scientific theories in certain societies. The extent to which science is culturally neutral is the subject of current, and complex, debate.

So the statement that reality is the ultimate test of a scientific theory is not as uncontentious as it may at first seem. It raises the question of 'whose reality' for one thing. But, while not assuming a single view of science, the statement does help to distinguish the broad area of science from other disciplines. For example, in *mathematics* the ultimate test is the internal logic of numbers and relationships. There is no need for the predictions from mathematical theories to relate to reality (non-rational numbers are an example), in sharp distinction to the theories of science.

The goals of science 5–12

Now that we have looked at contemporary views of science and at what it is considered that science education should aim to provide by the age of 16, we turn to the question of what this means for the goals of science education 5–12.

It is helpful to recall the value of teaching science in the primary school years listed at the beginning of Chapter 1. These include both laying a foundation for later learning and enabling children to understand the world around them in their daily lives. Thus the ideas, skills and attitudes that we seek to help children develop should support both their ongoing and their later understanding.

The discussion of the nature and outcomes of scientific activity leads to the view that in order to build understanding at any level it is important for learners to be able to:

- raise questions that can be answered by investigation
- develop hypotheses about how events and relationships can be explained
- make predictions based on the hypotheses
- gather relevant evidence to test the predictions: planning
- gather relevant evidence to test the predictions: observing
- interpret evidence and draw valid conclusions
- communicate and reflect on procedures and conclusions.

These things involve processing ideas and information and so they are described as 'process skills'. Closely related to the *ability* to use these skills is the *willingness* to use them. This means willingness to question preconceived ideas in order to test them, to regard ideas as tentative, to change them in the light of evidence. It is important also to add a moral value of sensitivity for the environment, both natural and made, in the course of investigating it. Therefore the goals of science education should include fostering the attitudes and values of:

- curiosity
- respect for evidence
- flexibility in ways of thinking

- critical reflection
- sensitivity in investigating the environment.

These process skills, attitudes and values are reflected in most curriculum goals in these or similar terms. There is also wide agreement that they have a particularly important role in science for the 5–12-year-olds, since exploration, seeing for themselves and active learning are essential to learning at this stage. Thus, when we come to consider the content of science activities it is necessary to ensure that the ideas involved are ones that are investigable and accessible to children by using process skills. This does not mean that we are only concerned with ideas about things children can physically touch and manipulate. Many ideas will be, and should be, of this kind, but it is not necessary to exclude ideas about events in children's experience which cannot be manipulated, such as ideas about the sun, moon and stars and about the weather. Children can develop these ideas by collecting information through careful observation and recording, seeking ideas from books and other resources to explain the patterns they observe and checking predictions against further observations.

It is also important to keep in mind, as mentioned earlier (p. 7) that the development of 'big' ideas has to begin with 'small' ones. Therefore we will not be teaching young children directly about, for example, the global impact of deforestation, but this will start if they investigate soil and observe what happens when streams of water flow through it.

Bringing these points together, we can identify criteria for deciding ideas that should be given priority in science 5–12. These should be ideas that:

- help children's understanding of everyday events and their experience of the world around them
- are within the grasp of children in the age range 5–12, taking into account their limited experience and mental maturity
- are accessible and testable through the use by the children of science process skills
- provide a foundation for further science education that will develop their scientific literacy.

Applying these criteria takes us a first step towards identifying the ideas that should be goals of pre-secondary science. These should be ideas about:

- living things and the processes of life (characteristics of living things, how they are made up and the functions of their parts, human health, etc.)

- the interaction of living things and their environment (competition, adaptation, effects of pollution and other human activities, etc.)
- materials (their variety, properties, sources, uses, interactions, conservation, disposal of waste, etc.)
- air, atmosphere and weather (presence of air round the Earth, features of the weather, causes of clouds, rain, frost and snow and freak conditions, etc.)
- rocks, soil and materials from the Earth (nature and origin of soil, maintenance of fertility, fossil fuels, minerals and ores as limited resources)
- the Earth in space (sun, moon, stars and planets, causes of day and night and seasonal variations)
- forces and movement (starting and stopping movement, speed and acceleration, simple machines, transportation, etc.)
- energy sources and uses (sources of heat, light sound, electricity, etc.)

Summary

This chapter has discussed the role that science education has to play in enabling young people to become informed and thoughtful citizens of the twenty-first century. It has presented some current thinking about:

- the goals of science education, reflecting new emphasis on education for scientific literacy of all, regardless of whether they will study science beyond the end of secondary school
- the nature of scientific activity.

It has set out the first steps in identifying the process skills, attitudes, values and ideas that science 5–12 should aim to promote. The question of progression in the development of these things will be taken up in Chapter 6 when we look at learning experiences appropriate at different ages and stages. That discussion will be illuminated by the study in the next three chapters of the process of learning, and the ideas that children already have about scientific aspects of the world and bring to the classroom.

Points for reflection

- What view of science is communicated through the national curriculum, standards or guidelines?
- How important is it for science activities for 5–12-year-olds to reflect a view of science as being about understanding, being

tentative, being the result of human endeavour and being concerned with the use of evidence?

Further reading

Hodson, D. (1993) Teaching and learning about science: considerations in the philosophy and sociology of science. In D. Edwards, E. Scanlon and R. West (eds) *Teaching, Learning and Assessment in Science Education.* London: Paul Chapman Publishing and the Open University.

Ratcliffe, M. (1998) The purposes of science education. In *Association for Science Education Guide to Primary Science Education.* Cheltenham: Stanley Thornes.

3

Children learning

In this chapter and the next we look at how children approach the task of making sense of the events and phenomena that they encounter in the classroom and beyond. We begin here with evidence in the form of extracts from a verbatim transcript of a video recording of groups of 11-year-olds working on a problem of why blocks of different kinds of wood floated at different levels in water. Commentary on the actions of the children in the first two groups leads to hypotheses about how they try to make sense of their observations. Evidence from other groups is used to test these hypotheses, and some general themes about children's approach to understanding through active investigation are suggested.

Children observed

The children were working in groups of four or five. Each group was given four blocks of varnished wood of similar size and shape but different density and labelled A, B, C and D, a bowl of water, spring balance, ruler, and an activity sheet as shown below:

1. Float your blocks on the water Look carefully at the way they are floating.
What do you notice that is *the same* about the way all the blocks float?
What do you notice that is *different* between one block and another about the way they float?
Get one person to write down what you notice, or make a drawing to show how the blocks

3. Now discuss all the things that are the same about the blocks. Get one person to put down a list of things that are *the same* Now discuss all the things that *are different* and make a list of them.
For each thing that is *different* about the blocks you should put down what you found about each block.
Discuss with your group the best way to do this.

are floating.
Check that you all agree that
the record shows what you see
Put the blocks in order from
best floater to worst floater.
2. What other things are the same
about the blocks?
What other things are different?
Think about their size, their
mass, colour and anything else.
Weigh and measure them.
Make sure you keep a record of
what you find.

4. Now look at your results of
things that are different.
Do you see any patterns in the
differences?
Write down any pattern you
find.

Group 1: 'It's the varnish'

The first group of five will be called group 1. They are all girls and
the extract starts when they have just begun to digest the task:

Jenny	Yes, one person to write down
Anya	I know why – it's the varnish
Cheryl	Just a minute! How do you know it's the varnish when we haven't even looked at it?
Anya	Yes, but look, they . . .
Felicia	That one (putting block A into the water) Does it float? (all bend down to have a good look at the floating blocks)
Manjinder	Yes, half and half
Others	Half and half
Jenny	(Beginning to write this down) Right! (Felicia, Manjinder and Anya each pick up one of the remaining blocks)
Felicia	Shall I put B in?
Manjinder	I'll put C in
Anya	I'll put D in
Cheryl	Leave this A in there
Jenny	Now put B in there

Group 2: 'A sinks half-way and floats half-way'

Meanwhile a second group, of four boys (Ahmed, Richard, Pete and
Femi) and one girl (Rachel), have started in a similar way, putting
one block in at a time, and so far A, B and C are floating in the water.

Five heads are crowded round the bowl and before D is put in one of the boys says:

Ahmed	C's nearly all gone, so D must sink
Richard	D must sink
	(block D is then put in and floats very high in the water)
Pete	Ah, D's floating on the top
Femi	D's the best floater
Pete	Now why is D the best floater?
Ahmed	Got more air in it
Richard	Got more air
Femi	. . . air bubbles
	(Ahmed takes block D out of the water to look more closely at it)
Ahmed	It's lighter
Richard	It's the lightest
Rachel	It's balsa wood
Pete	(taking the block from Ahmed) Yes, that *is* balsa wood
Rachel	Balsa (taking block and putting it back in the water) (meanwhile Ahmed picks up the spring balance as if to suggest weighing but puts it down again as the attention of the group turns again to the other blocks in the water)
Pete	Now which is floating the worst?
Richard	This one – C
	(he picks C out of the water and hands it to Femi) Now feel that one
Femi	That's
Richard	That's terribly heavy
Pete	That's why it's still floating – all wood floats – but, if – the heavier it is the lower it floats
Femi	Yes
Richard	Yes, but it still floats
Femi	(taking B out of the water) B's pretty heavy
Pete	(picking up pencil to begin making a record) So A . . .
Rachel	– A is sort of –
Femi	A is half way down, and B's . . .
Richard	B sort of flops. It's half-way –
Rachel	– down at one side
Pete	(concerned to have an agreed record) So how shall we describe the way A floats?
Rachel	A equals about half

Ahmed	A sinks half-way and floats half-way
Femi	I think . . .
Pete	(writing) A is medium weight. Block A
Rachel	No, A block –
Ahmed	(to Pete) Yes, block A
Pete	(speaking as he writes) Block A
	(Ahmed turns to Richard while Pete writes and points to blocks B and C)
Ahmed	(to Richard) They're both the same
Richard	(to Ahmed) They're not, that one's lopsided
Pete	(speaking as he writes) . . . is medium . . .
Femi	(joining in with Richard and Ahmed) It's probably because of the varnish it's got on it
Rachel	(also joining in) Right
Pete	(summarising what he has written) So, block A is medium weight and so
Femi	B
Richard	B's lopsided
Pete	(still writing) . . . and so it . . .
Femi	Yes, B's the worst one
Richard	No, C's the worst one
Pete	(reading what he has written and regaining the attention of the others) . . . so it floats with half the wood under the water
Femi	Yes – about that
	(there is a pause, they all look again, putting their heads as low as possible to place their eye level near the water surface)
Femi	Use a ruler – are you sure?
	(he goes to fetch a ruler)
Femi	Here's a ruler

Commentary

Before going any further there is enough here in these children's activity to raise several points about the children's own ideas, mental skills and attitudes as they explore the material given to them. Right at the start Anya throws in what appears to be a wild hypothesis: 'It's the varnish'. There is no evidence for this, as Cheryl immediately points out to her, but it does show a desire to explain. In this case the 'explanation' is a low-level one, stated in terms of an observed feature (the varnish) without any attempt to propose a link between the supposed cause and its effect, although this may have been tacitly assumed. Cheryl's intervention indicates an attitude of willingness to use evidence. They then proceed to gather that evidence by putting the blocks in the water systematically. Their first 'result' is a rough one, 'half and half', but it is recorded at the time.

The second group is also making statements ahead of observation at the start of the quoted extract. They have already put three blocks in the water and noticed a pattern (quite accidental) that each one floated lower in the water than the last. Block C has been observed to be 'nearly all gone' and they predict 'so D must sink'. They accept the evidence when they see it, however, and find that D floats higher than any other block. So they are quite willing to change their ideas in the light of evidence. Immediately there is some further hypothesising as to why block D floats best. The initial hypothesis, about air inside it, is overtaken by one finding support within the group, that D is lighter. (Perhaps to the children these are not alternative hypotheses but different ways of saying the same thing: things with more air in them are lighter than things with less air.) They also use their previous knowledge to identify block D as balsa wood.

At the point where the floating of block D seems to have been explained by its being 'the lightest' there is in fact no evidence of this at all. The children have not yet even 'weighed' the blocks in their hands in any way which would have allowed comparisons to be made (although they do this soon after). The process of interpreting observations is clearly way ahead of actually making the observations in this case. But a realisation of the lack of evidence for their statement may be what makes Ahmed pick up the spring balance. He does not persist at this point, sensing that the group interest has passed on to other things, but much later (in the continuation, to come) he is the one who does introduce the balance and initiates the weighing of the blocks.

The hypothesis about the weight of the blocks of wood being related to the way they float seems to direct the next section of their work. Notice how Richard, when he identifies block C as the worst floater, hands it to Femi and says 'Now feel that one'. He is referring to 'feeling' the weight and the observations he is making about the wood are clearly focused and narrowed down by the idea he has in mind. Pete puts the suggested relation clearly, 'the heavier it is the lower it floats', after reminding himself, from previous knowledge, that 'all wood floats'.

Pete then directs his attention to writing down what they have found (he is the recorder). But is it what they have found? What he writes is 'Block A is medium weight and so it floats with half the wood under the water.' Their observation was about the floating not about the weight; in fact they have no evidence about how the weight of A compares with that of other blocks. The statement recorded seems to have given an assumption the status of an observation and made their observation (of the floating) into an explanation for it. The ideas they have, based apparently on no more than jumping to conclusions, have influenced the process of gathering information. But they are still exploring the blocks, the water and the equipment, and as long as the real things are in front of them there is the opportunity for them to reconsider and test out their ideas.

Group 2 continued

While Femi was explaining to Rachel why a ruler was needed, Richard was looking closely at block B floating in the water:

Richard	I can't understand why this is lopsided
Rachel	Well, look, see, it goes down that side
Richard	Yes, that's what I mean, I can't understand it
Pete	(who has not noticed this lopsided debate, having been busy writing the record, finishes writing about A) Now how is B?
Richard	Lopsided
Ahmed	Lopsided
Pete	(taking B out of the water) Now B is . . .
Rachel	Hang on a minute (she takes block B from Pete)
Pete	Now is B heavier than A, or lighter?
Rachel	Let's see if it's . . . (she uses the ruler to measure the thickness of the block at all four corners; all the others close round to see what she is doing)
Richard	(answering Pete's earlier question) Sort of lopsided, Pete
Femi	Lopsided
Rachel	(after finishing the measuring of B) Yes, it's the same length all the way down, but it's lopsided
Pete	(picks up blocks A and B, weighing them in his hands) Now which one is heavier, do you reckon?
Ahmed	(reaches for the spring balance again) Try this
Pete	(picks up the pan to use with the spring balance) If we try this, we can use this – who knows how to set up something like this?

Femi	Well, you put it on the hook
	(he hooks the pan on to the spring balance)
	. . . now you can weigh something on it
Richard	(who has put blocks A and B back in the water and is looking at block B)
	Lopsided, in'it?
Pete	(picking block A out of the water) Now shake all the water off. Try A first
	(Rachel holds the spring balance while Pete puts block A on the pan)
Rachel	Just put it on
Pete	Now what's it come up to?
	(he ducks under Rachel's arm so that he can put his eye right in front of the scale)
Femi	(also closing one eye and peering at the scale) . . . about sixty
Richard	(also trying to look) . . . about sixty-three
Pete	Is there something we can hang it on, 'cos if you hang it on your hand you're likely to bounce it about

They then seek and find a way of steadying the spring balance. In the course of this they notice the zero adjustment, take the block off and use the zero adjustment and then discuss the reading of the divisions of the scale. From this point their investigation takes on a much more businesslike air. They are not content with the rough 'feel' of the weight nor with describing the floating as 'half-way' for they begin to measure the parts of the block below the water. Pete finds a neat way of recording this by drawing the blocks upside down like this:

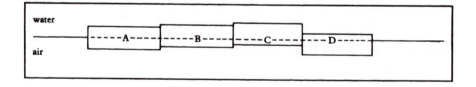

so that it is easy to see the direct relation between the length of the submerged part and the weight of the block.

Commentary

The group showed what seemed to be a considerable progression in the way they approached the task. Starting from rather gross qualitative observations, of both the weight and the floating, they proceeded to use measurement to refine their observations. It appeared that this early period of rough observation was one of working out for themselves what the problem was. Once they defined it in their own minds they tackled it in a more systematic and precise manner. This took some time (about 30 minutes) in this particular case, probably because the task had been presented to them on a sheet; it was not of their finding. It took time for them to become interested in it and make it 'their own'. When children work on problems they have found for themselves there is no need for this period of 'coming to terms' with it. When they take on problems given to them, and they are generally very willing to do this as evidently happened here, time may be needed for rough exploration before they begin to grasp what is needed and to apply mental skills and ideas at the more advanced level of their capabilities. This is not unlike the scientist who takes rough measurements to 'get a feel' for the problem before setting up conditions for more precise measurement.

The observations, and later measurements, of this group were very strongly focused by their idea that the floating was related to the weight of the blocks. This idea was introduced early on, it was not something they 'discovered' by induction from their observations. It was, in fact, stated before enough evidence had been collected to support it and became the framework for the observations and measurements they then made. It seemed that there was an immediate attempt to find a relationship that might explain initial observations and that later observations were focused by the desire to test this relationship. In the process another relationship might be suggested which was then tested. Thus all the observations were made for a purpose and not just to gather a range of different kinds of information which later would be put together to find patterns and relationships. It is entirely reasonable that this should be so, for without a purpose it would not be possible to decide what information to gather. The idea was in the children's minds and their investigation was carried out to test it.

So far, from this analysis of the observations, we might hypothesise that the children's approach was to find evidence to test the ideas that they already had about why the blocks were floating differently. They had the idea first and *then* gathered evidence including measurements. The ideas did not *come from* the evidence but preceded it and indeed determined what they looked for and measured.

To see if this applies to others than just this one group, here is another group working on the blocks activity and apparently making much more open-ended observations.

Group 3: 'They're magnetic when they're wet'

There are five girls, Kay, Lisa, Mena, Nicola and Ann (who is the recorder). We join them after about 20 minutes of exploratory activity with the blocks, when Ann has just summarised what they have so far done and is rereading the activity sheet to make sure nothing has been omitted:

Ann	(reading) What do you notice about the way they float? (answering herself) Well, we've found out that they all . .
Nicola	. . . don't sink (brief laughter at this jokey statement of the obvious)
Mena	I know what it is, none of them float lopsided
Nicola	(who has taken two blocks out of the water and is holding them touching each other) They're magnetic!
Kay and Mena	(repeating what Nicola has done) Yes, they're magnetic
Mena	And if you put them in like that, they go flat, look (she puts the blocks into the water with the largest face vertical and they settle with this face horizontal)
Kay	And D goes flat
Mena	Test with D and B
Lisa	They're getting water-logged now, aren't they?
Mena	This one goes flat last I think
Nicola	Hang on, let's put them all in and see which goes flat last (they do this)
Mena	C
Lisa	C
Kay	No, it may have been B
Mena	I think it shouldn't be that, it should be D
Lisa	That one's the heaviest, so it should go over first because it's heaviest (Four pairs of hands go into the bowl, placing the blocks in vertically)
Mena	I think B should go over first and D should go over last
Nicola	Why?
Lisa	(to Ann) And they're magnetic
Mena	Yes, they're magnetic when they're wet (to Ann, who has been writing all this down) Write that down. They're really magnetic
Lisa	(reading from the worksheet) What other things are different?

Mena	Yes, look, the colour. The lightest in colour is the lightest in weight (Mena and Nicola take up the blocks and 'weigh' them in their hands)
Nicola	. . . and the darkest in colour is the heaviest in weight
Kay	Yes, the darkest in colour is the heaviest
Nicola	Yes, you know it's like white is very cool and dark is very hot
Mena	Yes, you see this is the lightest and it floats the best and this is the darkest so it doesn't float so well
Nicola	The lightest is . . .
Ann	(leaving the report-writing) Let's put it against the side (she picks up the two blocks in question, the heaviest and the lightest and directly compares their dimensions) You see, they're all the same size
Lisa	(pointing to the heavier one) It hasn't got so much light in it
Nicola	They're magnetic as well
Mena	That's probably only chance
Lisa	If you get them really wet and then put the sides together
Mena	(puts two blocks side by side) No, hang on – no, they are – even though they're shorter, this one's wider
Nicola	They're all the same size, then
Ann	The darkest is the heaviest and the lightest is the lightest
Lisa	Look, get them all wet (dips two blocks in the water and holds them with the largest surfaces together)
Nicola	(does the same as Lisa, holding up one block with another clinging beneath it) Yes, they do, look. They're definitely magnetic
Mena	You've got to get them really wet
Kay	Try C and D
Nicola	Try the heaviest and the lightest (they try various combinations and find that the heavier block falls off when hanging beneath a lighter one)
Mena	The heaviest ones don't work very well

Kay	A heavy and a light work, but not two heavies
	(a moment or two later they start weighing and
	measuring each block; Kay holds the spring balance)
Nicola	Put D on first
Ann	We can see that they're the same length
Nicola	Put D on, then we'll measure them all with the ruler
	(Kay puts D on the pan)
Nicola	That is
Lisa	(interrupting) But we should dry them all off first
	because the water may affect them
Mena	But they're water-logged already
Kay	Here you are, here's some dry towels
Lisa	The water may affect them. The water will affect to – er
	– thing
Kay	(pointing to the wet balance pan) This is wet – better
	dry that
Lisa	But that's going to be the same in all of them – so it
	won't matter
Ann	(still measuring with the ruler) They're about 12 cm

(Some time is spent taking measurements of the blocks. They decide to find the average dimensions, for some reason, and Lisa sits aside from the rest of the group doing this. The others stand round the bowl apparently doing nothing in particular, but they are in fact watching the movement of blocks 'stuck' to the side of the bowl. The movement is very slow . . .)

Mena	They'll never come off
Kay	I know, I'll give it a little jog and see which comes down
	first
	(both bang the sides of the bowl)
	They're not going to come down
Ann	This one should come down first
Kay	Yes, that one came down when I pushed (on the sides)
	but that one was harder to push down
Ann	So D came down, then A
	(goes to record this. Nicola takes her place and
	continues to experiment in the same way, with Kay)
Nicola	We got to find patterns, what patterns have we got?
Kay	Well, we've got two dark ones and two light ones
Nicola	That's not a pattern
Kay	I know but . . .
Mena	We've got to find out what sort of pattern the weight
	goes in – there may be a pattern in the weight

Nicola	Start with D, then A, then C, then B (weight order)
Ann	Press them all down to the bottom and see which comes up to the surface . . . I should say D should come up first
Ann	One, two, three, let go!
Nicola	D, A, C, B, so that went in the heaviest order, because we found that B was the heaviest and D is the lightest
Kay	. . . and D came up first
Ann	. . . so it came out right, so we know our facts are right

Commentary

There are more widely ranging observations made by this group than by group 2 and some attempt to explain each observation. Not all the ideas are tested, sometimes because other observations divert their attention, and the validity of many of the tests could be questioned. At the start of the extract the girls are following up their observation that if the blocks are placed in the water with the largest face vertical they do not float that way but turn over and 'go flat'. They have noticed a difference in the time taken for the blocks to 'go flat' and, at least in Mena's view, this is connected with the weight of the blocks. They decide to test all the blocks together rather than in pairs. The result does not satisfy Mena who says 'I think B should go over first and D should go over last', even though she saw that C was last. Nicola begins to question the assumption Mena is making and this might have led Mena to reconsider it, either by the force of argument or evidence or both.

They are interrupted, however, by the excitement over the discovery of the 'magnetism' of the blocks. It is interesting that none of the group members questions the use of the term 'magnetic' in relation to the blocks. They may indeed consider the effect to be exactly the same as found with a magnet or they may be using the word metaphorically. In either case the influence of previous knowledge in this interpretation of their observations is clear. The magnetic power of the blocks is tested by seeing if one block will support another hanging beneath it. They find the blocks differ in their ability to do this. Neither the test nor the conclusion from it are very soundly based but there is no challenge, from the teacher or the group, to make them reconsider it. Thus the idea that the blocks were 'magnetic' remained with them and was later reported as a finding from their group work, although not recorded here.

The magnetism sequence is briefly interrupted when Lisa reminds the others that they are to look for other things that were different about the blocks. The colour of the wood is an obvious difference and Mena leaps immediately from the observation of difference to a relationship which is more of an inspired guess than a pattern based on evidence ('the lightest in colour is the lightest in weight'). Indeed it is *after* this statement that the weights of the blocks are estimated by 'feel'. Nicola goes a stage further to try to explain the relationship, 'you know it's like white is very cool and dark is very hot', again using previous knowledge, in this case of differences relating to colour.

In the final part of the extract the group 3 girls repeat in a more systematic way something that they had already done earlier (not covered by the transcript). They had held the blocks at the bottom of the bowl and noticed a difference in the rate at which they came up when released. They had a clear hypothesis about which block would reach the surface first and tested it by looking, not just for differences, but for whether these differences fitted their prediction. The pattern based on their ideas was indeed confirmed.

Common themes

The girls in the last group did indeed show the same kinds of approach to their enquiries as the other groups. Classroom observations in other contexts, too, suggest that such exchanges go on among children whenever they are truly co-operating and collaborating on a shared problem. Some of the recurring themes illustrated here are that:

- since the problem had been assigned to children and was not one that they had found for themselves, some time was needed for them to 'make it their own'
- there was an initial period of activity in which many predictions and explanations were aired during what seems superficial and non-quantitative exploration, followed by more focused, quantitative investigation
- the children were constantly importing knowledge from previous experience, some relevant and some not
- their explanations, so readily offered, which sometimes seemed like guesses, preceded the evidence of whether or not they fitted the observations
- they used many of the process skills (observation, prediction, measurement), but these were used erratically, rather than being combined in a systematic approach
- although they challenged some of each others' ideas, provoking them to look for evidence to support their ideas, there were still many ideas left unchallenged even though there was no evidence to support them.

In the sequences recorded here there was no teacher intervention and we don't know how this may have assisted or inhibited the children's investigations. We consider in a later chapter what kind of intervention might be appropriate, but it is worth noting here that, without it, the children did not use the results of their inquiries as much as they could have done to reflect on their initial ideas or to develop their understanding of floating. Nor was their approach to testing ideas as systematic as it might have been. None the less these observations enable us to see some significant features of how children go about solving problems and making sense of events and phenomena. They also provide a clue to how teachers can intervene so that children's thinking is developed as a result of their activities. This will be taken up in a later chapter once we have looked at the nature of the ideas that children bring to activities in a wider range of topics.

Summary

In this chapter we have looked in detail at how some groups of children investigated the different ways in which some blocks of wood floated in water. The close study of their talk showed how they pursued ideas from previous experience to try to make sense of what they observed and used various process skills in their investigations. It was also noted that, although their investigation became more systematic and quantitative as time went on, in the absence of teacher intervention, some ideas went unchallenged and untested.

Points for reflection

- There is no teacher intervention in the sequences described. What difference might the presence of the teacher have made?
- What kinds of intervention might have increased the educational value of the activities?
- What kinds of intervention might have had a negative influence on the children's activity?

Further reading

Transcripts of children's talk are included in:

Qualter, A. (1996) *Differentiated Primary Science*. Buckingham: Open University Press.
Ollerenshaw, C. and Ritchie, (1988) R. *Primary Science: Making it Work*. London: David Fulton.

4

Children's ideas

The goals of 5–12 science identified in Chapter 2 included ideas under eight broad headings. In Chapter 3, evidence from the close observation of children engaged in an activity with floating blocks of wood showed how children used ideas from previous experience to try to explain what they found. The role of these ideas in learning means that it is important to be aware of what ideas children may bring to their classroom experiences. It is the purpose of this chapter to present some examples of children's ideas across a range of topics relevant to the goals of learning in science. This is by no means a comprehensive, or even representative, coverage of what is known about children's ideas, but it provides evidence from which to draw out some general characteristics relevant to helping the development of ideas in the areas identified at the end of Chapter 2.

Even though each child's experiences within and outwith school must be unique in many respects, research shows that there is a remarkable similarity in the ideas they have to explain to themselves things in the world around them. Research in many different countries has produced findings similar to those reported here. Many more can be found in the reports of the research carried out by the Science Processes and Concepts Exploration (SPACE) project (SPACE Research Reports, 1990–98).

Some ideas in the main areas of understanding

Living things and the processes of life

Characteristics of living things

The idea that there is a group of living things called 'plants' and another called 'animals', basic to biology, is not a simple matter of definition. Osborne and Freyberg described some results of research by Bell (1981) in New Zealand which established that:

Children often have a much more restricted meaning for the word plant. In a sample of 29 children, she found 10-year-olds, 13-year-olds and 15-year-olds who considered a tree was not a plant.

'No, it was a plant when it was little, but when it grows up it wasn't, when it became a tree it wasn't.' (10-year-old)

Other children suggested that a plant was something which was cultivated, hence grass and dandelions were considered weeds and not plants by some 13- and 15-year-olds. Further, almost half the pupils interviewed considered that a carrot and a cabbage were not plants; they were vegetables. Over half those interviewed did not consider a seed to be plant material. Despite considerable exposure to science teaching many of the 15-year-olds held similarly restricted ideas to the 10-year-olds.

(Osborne and Freyberg, 1985, p. 7)

Following the individual interviews, Bell and colleagues carried out a survey of much larger samples of pupils. Some of their findings are given in Figure 4.1, which shows the percentages of pupils at various ages who considered a tree, a carrot, a seed and grass to be plants.

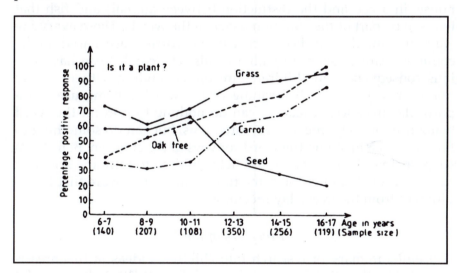

Figure 4.1 Children's ideas about plants
Source: Osborne and Freyberg (1985, p. 7)

In similar investigations of children's ideas about what are 'animals' it was found that:

Many of the pupils considered only the larger animals, such as those found on a farm, in a zoo, or in the home as pets, as animals. Reasons for categorising something as an animal, or not doing so, included the number of legs (animals are expected to have four), size (animals are bigger than insects), habitat (animals are found on land), coating (animals have fur), and noise production (animals make a noise).

(Osborne and Freyberg, 1985, p. 30)

It is clear that the everyday usage of words has a considerable effect, which is particularly strong in the case of the concept of 'animal'. Research carried out by Bell and Barker (1982) involving interviews and a survey of children from age 5 to 17 years showed that children's initial idea of what is an animal is restricted to large land mammals. For instance, a high proportion of their sample of 5-year-olds recognised a cow as an animal and the proportion rose to 100 per cent by the age of 7 years. However, creatures such as worms and spiders were not considered to be animals by three-quarters of the 9-year-olds and only a slightly lower proportion of 12-year-olds. Only a fifth of the sample of 5-year-olds considered a human being to be an animal and this proportion rose to just over a half for 9- and 12-year-olds.

Commenting on these findings Osborne (1985) makes the point that signs in shops such as 'No animals allowed' would reinforce a narrow view of the notion of animal. So would the label 'animal house' in a zoo and the distinction between animals and fish that tends to be part of the common usage of the words. These everyday ways of using the word conflict with the 'correct' use, based on the common features shared by all animals. The conflict can have serious consequences in children's misunderstanding if there is any uncertainty as to which meaning of the word is being used in a particular instance. A teacher can do nothing to prevent the word being used loosely in everyday situations, but can do something to find out what meaning the word conveys to the children. Bell (1981) suggests that the teacher should help children to form the scientific idea of 'animal' and at the same time make them aware that this is different from the everyday meaning.

Processes of life

A useful summary of research into children's ideas in this area is provided by the SPACE project Research Report (1992). In general it shows that children's ideas develop to make sense of their expanding knowledge of living things around and of their own bodies. For instance, young children become aware of the insides of their bodies, starting with the heart, as separate organs each with a single function. Later they come to perceive connecting channels between the organs which enable them to work together. In the SPACE research children were asked to draw on an outline of the human body what they thought was in their own bodies. It was found that children draw those organs or parts which are more easily sensed – the heart which beats, bones which can be felt and the brain because the capacity for self-conscious reflection and awareness has developed by this age. In general, organs such as kidneys, lungs, intestines which are not sensed, are not part of children's knowledge of the body.

(SPACE Research Report 1992, p. 31)

A further investigation by the SPACE team of children's ideas about the conditions that a plant needs to grow showed the impact of their everyday experience. Children of 6 or 7 years indicated that the plant needed water or soil or sun, with few mentioning all three. Older pupils tended to replace 'sun' by light and heat and the number of requirements mentioned increased with age. The role of the soil in helping plants to live was regarded as simply being for support; very few children indicated that it would provide 'food' or substances needed by the plant.

Interaction of living things and their environment

In preparation for some work on camouflage some 12-year-olds were asked for their ideas about why brown bears are found in mountains in America and white bears in the Arctic. Many of the written answers used the word 'camouflage' (deliberately not used in the question) as if it were an explanation, for example, as in Figure 4.2. Those who attempted more of an explanation gave this in

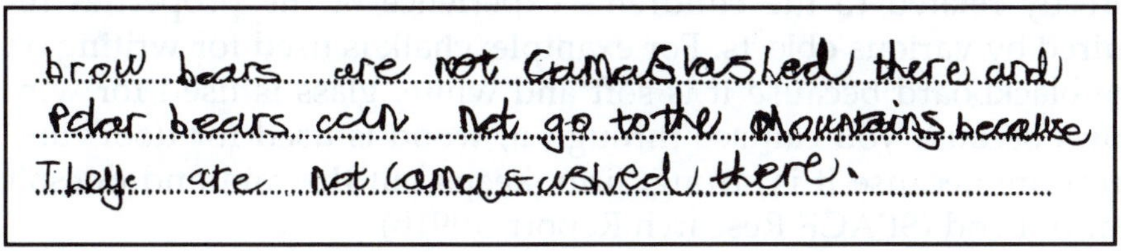
brow bears are not camaflasled there and
polar bears can not go to the mountains because
There are not camafaushed there.

Figure 4.2 A 12-year-old's answer to: 'Why do you think you don't find white bears in the mountains and brown bears in the arctic?'

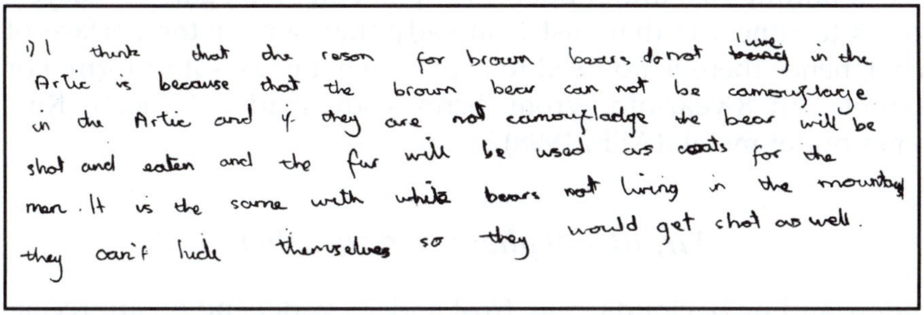
1) I think that the reson for brown bears do not live in the
Artic is because that the brown bear can not be camouflayge
in the Artic and if they are not camoufladge the bear will be
shot and eaten and the fur will be used as coats for the
man. It is the same with white bears not living in the mountay
they can't hide themselves so they would get shot as well.

Figure 4.3 An 11-year-old girl's answer

Figure 4.4 An 11-year-old boy's answer

terms of human activity, as in Figure 4.3. However, a few mentioned climate and some, as in Figure 4.4, the predator–prey relationship.

Other examples show that children used their own experience in explaining why some living things are found in certain places and not others. It is as if they regard the difference between things as given and the habitat is then 'chosen' by a creature to suit it.

Materials

The ideas children have about the use of materials for various purposes are at first circular: we use paper for writing on because paper is good for writing on. There seems to be no explanation needed in terms of properties of the material, just that it is chosen because it serves the purpose. Later the use of materials is recognised as being directly related to the children's experience of the properties required by various objects. For example: chalk is used for writing on the blackboard because it is soft and white; glass is used for windows because you can see through it; wood is used for doors and furniture because it is strong, firm, keeps out the rain and doesn't tear or bend (SPACE Research Report, 1991b).

In relation to changes in materials, too, there is a stage in which there seems to be no need for explanation. Children use their experience of finding rust under bubbles of paint on metal gates or bicycle frames to conclude that rust is already there under the surface of metal, hence there is no need to explain what causes it to form. For example, an 8-year-old wrote 'Screws are made of metal. Rust comes out of metal' (ASE, 1998).

Air, atmosphere and weather

Understanding of clouds, rain, frost and snow depend on appreciating that water can exist as vapour in the air. Without this, their ideas about clouds depend on some mechanism such as 'sucking up' water as in Figure 4.5. Here the 'reason' for rain is that 'the flowers need water'.

Young children do not see the need to explain why water dries up – 'it just goes by itself' (SPACE Research Report, 1990a). Later some recognise the effect of the sun, but give it a very active role, such as in Figure 4.6.

Figure 4.5   A young child's ideas about rain
Source: SPACE Research Report (1993, p. 67)

'The sun is hot and the water is cold and the water sticks to the sun and then it goes down'   (Age 7 years)

Figure 4.6   Evaporation according to a 7-year-old
Source: SPACE Research Report (1990a, p. 29)

Some children even included what looked like a drinking straw reaching from the sun to the water! In the views of some children the clouds have this active role, being permanent features ready to receive evaporated water:

> When the water evaporates it goes on a cloud and then the cloud goes in any place and later it will go out as rain. It will keep going until it is all gone and then it will go to another place with water and do the same. The cloud is like a magnet so the water does through the cracks and goes up, that is what I think.
>
> (SPACE Research Report, 1990a, p. 30)

The use of the word 'evaporates' here is ambiguous (it seems to cover both evaporation from the ground and condensation in the cloud). It is common for children to speak of 'water rising' and the clouds 'bursting' to give rain without mentioning the processes of evaporation and condensation. Attempts to help children understand the water cycle can cause confusion if they do not take into account the ideas the children may have about evaporation and about clouds.

Rocks, soil and materials from the Earth

Quite young children are aware that rocks are found under and above ground. Their ideas are influenced by what they see around then and they often restrict the use of the word 'rock' to pieces that are jagged, not smooth, large, rather than small and usually grey but sometimes coloured. Younger children attribute changes in rocks to human action, whilst older children are more likely to recognise erosion by wind and sea, or just 'ageing'.

Children interpret the word 'soil', as materials in which there are pieces of decayed plants and rock fragments, rather than seeing these as constituents. Soil is most commonly associated with growing plants, at first as a means of support and later as being the source of food and water. Clearly, understanding that water in soil dissolves material taken up by plants is necessary if they are to recognise the need to replenish these nutrients and the effects of drought and water erosion.

The Earth in space

Children's early ideas about the movement of the Sun and Moon derive from their perceptions of rapid movements of the positions of these bodies caused by the children's own movement from one place to another. If they stand in the shadow of a tree the sun appears to be behind the tree. If they move out of the shadow the Sun no longer appears to be behind the tree. The fact that they can see the Sun wherever they are gives them the idea that it follows them around. Older children can distinguish this apparent rapid and irregular movement from the regular patterns of movement day by day, although these will inevitably be interpreted as the Sun moving round the Earth.

In their drawings children represent the Moon and stars in conventional manner – a crescent moon and pointed stars, since they frequently see representations like this. They also see globes, drawings and even photographs from space, that show that the Earth is spherical and this experience is reflected in their drawings. However, there is evidence that they may not really be convinced that this is the case and some ask: why we do not fall off the surface of the globe? This question in itself indicates the children's views of what causes things to fall and what 'down' means in the context of space. Ideas about gravity have to be brought in to give a convincing answer to this dilemma, illustrating yet again the interconnections between different ideas needed to explain the phenomena around us (Vosniadou, 1997).

Forces and movement

The relationship of forces acting on an object to its movement is a difficult area for primary science because so often the accepted scientific view is counter-intuitive. For example, it is a matter of everyday experience that a moving object such as a ball rolling along the ground stops moving apparently 'by itself' without any agent to stop it. But this ignores the forces exerted at the contact with the ground and with the air. Many forces like these are 'hidden', including the important one of gravity, and are ignored by children in making sense of why things stop moving. Thus a ball thrown upwards into the air will be thought to have an upward force on it when it is moving up, zero when it reaches its highest point and a downward force when it is moving down.

Gravity is a universally experienced force and it is perhaps because it is always present that children do not take it into account. Things that are dropped fall downwards 'naturally'. The SPACE research showed that various kinds of activities designed to help children to see gravity as a force acting towards the Earth from all directions, resulted in a large shift in primary children's recognition of gravity as a force pulling things down, although few described the force as being towards the centre of the Earth.

Gunstone and Watts (1985) identified some 'intuitive rules' from their review of research into ideas about force:

- Children identify force with living things – there is some intention involved.
- Objects in constant motion need a constant force to keep them moving in the same way.
- An object that is not moving has no forces acting on it.
- A moving body has a force acting on it in the direction of motion.

These are all ideas which have certain logic in relation to limited everyday experience and are held by many secondary school pupils and not a few adults. Their apparent 'common sense' makes them difficult to change.

Floating is a phenomenon depending on the balance of forces acting on an object in water, but children often consider that other factors are involved, such as the speed of movement of the object and the depth of water. In addition, the concept of what is 'floating' is problematic. Some research in New Zealand (Biddulph and Osborne, 1984) explored what children understood floating to mean by using cards showing pictures of various objects in water, some floating and some not. The children ranged in age from 7 to 14 years and over 100 were interviewed individually. The results from the interviews were backed up by a survey of a larger number of children, which served to confirm the main findings and establish where there appeared to be a trend with age in the children's ideas.

When discussing the pictures showing objects floating with part above the water surface and part below (a person floating in a life-jacket for instance) the children's decision as to whether or not it was floating appeared to be influenced by how much of the object was above the water and how much below the surface. If a large proportion was above the surface there was general agreement that it was floating, but if only a small part was above the surface (as in the case of a bottle floating with only the neck above water) there were many (42 per cent in the survey) who said it was partly floating and partly sinking. A 9-year-old was reported as saying in an interview that: 'It's floating and not floating. The top is floating and the bottom's not.'

The inferred movement of an object also affected judgement as to whether or not it was floating. Half of the pupils thought that the yacht in Figure 4.7(a) was not floating, and several of the younger children also claimed that the speedboat in Figure 4.7(b) was not floating because it was moving. An 8-year-old said: 'It's going fast, and floating is staying still and floating around.' With objects totally

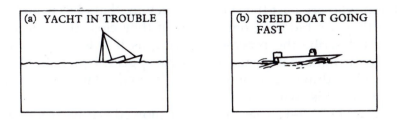

Figure 4.7   Floating: (a) yacht in trouble; (b) speedboat going fast
Source: Biddulph and Osborne (1984)

submerged (such as a person snorkelling) just under a half described them as not floating.

The children were also asked about a range of possible variables that might affect floating, such as the size of the object or the depth of water. The results show a definite trend with age. Only 10 per cent of the 8-year-olds thought that a whole candle would float at the same level as a short piece of the candle. This proportion was 30 per cent for 10-year-olds and 65 per cent for 12-year-olds. Even at the age of 12 years, however, a quarter of the children thought the full-length candle would float lower than the short piece. To investigate the effect of changing the depth of water the children were shown the picture in Figure 4.8 and asked to compare the level of floating of the launch in the deep and shallow water. Half of the 8-year-olds said it would float lower in the deeper water, but only about a fifth of 10- and 12-year-olds gave this answer. About two-thirds of the 10- and 12-year-olds said the level of floating was unaffected by the depth but only 40 per cent of the 8-year-olds said this was so.

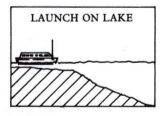

Figure 4.8   Floating launch on lake
Source: Biddulph and Osborne (1984)

Energy sources and uses

Light

Investigations of children's ideas about light have shown remarkable similarity in relation to the role of the eye in seeing things.

Children who are past the stage of believing that objects no longer exist if they are hidden from view or if they close their eyes, nevertheless describe the process of seeing as if it is their eyes that produce the light that makes the objects appear. Figure 4.9 shows a 10-year-old's drawing of how you see a bottle standing on a table when the light is switched on.

In a class of 26 9–11-year-olds, eight showed arrows from the eye to the bottle, four showed the light rays with arrows from the bottle to the eye and two had them going both ways, as in Figure 4.10. The remainder (12) showed no connection between the eye and the bottle. Their responses, however, leave one in no doubt that they have worked out their own explanation of experience, which is not the same as the explanation given by physics.

It is perhaps understandable that the eye is seen as an active agent rather than a receiver, for this fits the subjective experience of 'looking'. When we choose to look at something we do feel our eyes turn as if we are the active agent in the process, and indeed the arrow from receiver to object does represent the line of sight.

A variation on this idea is to regard the presence of light as somehow activating the eye, as described in Figure 4.11.

Figure 4.12 is typical of the responses from a class of younger children (7–9-year-olds). All but four of the 27 in the class showed light spreading to the eye and the bottle but nothing between bottle

Figure 4.9 The 'active eye'

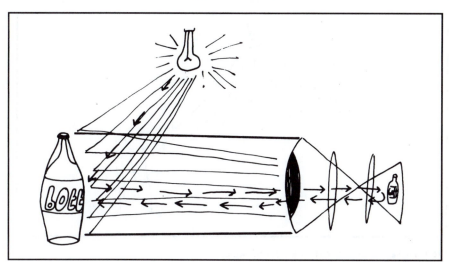

Figure 4.10 A 10-year-old's view of how the eye works

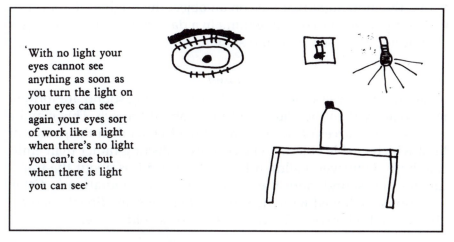

Figure 4.11 The eye as activated by light

and eye. The children's interpretation of the situation does not take into account the need for light to fall on the object and to be reflected by it, or to be given out by it, for it to be seen. Piaget showed in his early work that 9- and 10-year-olds did not connect the onset of darkness at night with the lack of sunlight. Instead they 'explained' darkness by describing it as night, something that comes because people get tired and need to sleep (Piaget, 1929). Thus the children's grasp of the relation between what is seen and the person seeing it depends on their linking up various ideas about daily experiences and noticing the patterns in them:

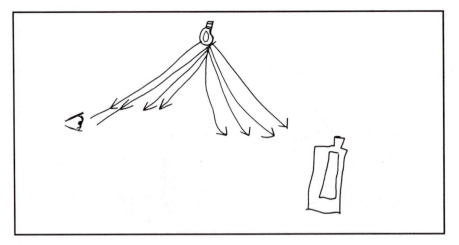

Figure 4.12   An 8-year-old's view of how we see

- that the sky goes dark when the sun disappears
- that the more light that falls on an object the brighter it appears
- that if you want to see something in a dark room you shine a light on it not into your eyes, and so on.

Sound

Ideas about the ear's role as a receiver in hearing sound are formed more readily than the equivalent ideas about the eye. This may be because the sources of sounds are more obvious than the source of light which enable objects to be seen by reflecting rather than emitting light. However, children have different ideas about the transmission of sound and the part played by 'vibrations'. Often vibrations are linked with the source when they are directly observable but not otherwise. For example, a 7-year-old wrote:

> I stretched a rubber band between my finger and thumb and plucked it with my other hand. I noticed it doesn't make very much noise, it vibrates and hurts my hand. I plucked a rubber band that was on a box. I noticed it makes a loud noise and it doesn't vibrate. I can play a tune.
>
> (SPACE Research Report, 1990d, p. 50)

There is also a distinction in many children's minds between sound and vibration. Describing how a 'string telephone' made with yoghurt pots and string works, a 10-year-old wrote: 'The voices went to the string and were then transfered into vibrations which went down the string and when it got to the other yoghart pot and were then transfered back into a voice' (unpublished SPACE research).

Electricity

Inquiries into children's ideas about simple electric circuits have shown that the representation of a single connection between battery and bulb, as in Figure 4.13(a), is persistent. It is even produced by pupils who have had experience that it does not work in practice (SPACE Research Report, 1991a). The representation in Figure 4.13(b) is arguably a more sophisticated view, but one which fails to recognise that there are two different connections to complete the circuit within the bulb. Figure 4.13(c) shows two different connections but ones which would not work.

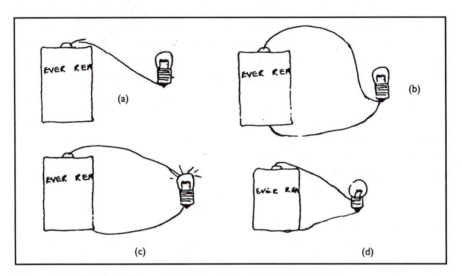

Figure 4.13   Children's ideas about connections in a simple circuit

The SPACE team reports a marked increase in the correct connections depicted following activities in which the children were asked first to discuss and draw how they would make connections, then to try out their plan. When they achieved success they were asked to compare what they did in practice with what they first thought.

General characteristics of children's ideas

These examples have not been presented as a formal review of research but as indicative of findings of many different researchers working in a variety of contexts. The fact that similar ideas are found from working with children of quite different backgrounds suggests that the ideas are the product of children's reasoning about things that are experienced everywhere – the weather, the variety of living things, the materials and so on. This view is supported by studying the ideas and noting that, once children see the need for an explanation of things, they base their ideas on their experiences of them.

It is easy to see how, from a child's point of view, their ideas make sense of their limited experiences. Indeed these ideas make more sense than the 'scientific' view, which is often counter-intuitive. The scientific view frequently makes use of ideas based on things that are not observable by children, such as water vapour, unseen forces, vibrations in air, etc. For example, the notion that moving things come to a stop if you stop pushing them suggests that it is 'natural' for movement to stop, whereas the scientific view is that there must be a force to stop the movement. Thus, not surprisingly, the children's ideas have several shortcomings when compared with the scientific view. It is useful to examine the reasons for these shortcomings since they give clues as to how to help children develop their ideas. These reasons include one or more of the following:

- Their experiences are necessarily limited and therefore the evidence is partial – so they may well consider rust to be within metals if they have only paid attention to it when it appears under paint or flaking chrome plate.
- Children pay attention to what they perceive through their senses rather than the logic which may suggest a different interpretation – so if the sun appears to move around and follow them, then they think it does move in this way.
- Younger children particularly focus on one feature as cause for a particular effect rather than the possibility of several factors – as in the conditions needed for living things to grow healthily.
- Although it may satisfy them, the reasoning they use may not stand comparison with scientific reasoning. For example, if they made genuine predictions based on their ideas, these ideas would be disproved. But instead they may 'predict' what they know to fit the idea.
- They may use words without a grasp of their meaning – we have seen that this can happen with 'floating', 'vibration' and 'evaporation', but many more examples could be cited.
- They may hold on to earlier ideas even though contrary evidence is available because they have no access to an alternative view that makes sense to them. In such cases they may adjust their idea to fit new evidence rather than give it up, as in the idea that 'light turns the eye on'.

Looking across research findings from children of different ages reveals that sometimes younger children have ideas which seem more 'correct' than those of older pupils. This is not backward progress but the result of earlier ideas becoming confused by the greater complexity of experience as they grow older. For example, a young child may well refer to all animals he or she knows as animals, but it is later, when introduced to the words 'insect', 'mammal', and so on, that there is confusion about what is an animal.

Implications for teaching

The clear evidence that children have worked out these ideas for themselves and that they make sense to them, within the confines of their limited experience and their limited ways of reasoning, means that the ideas cannot be ignored in teaching. To do so, research suggests, is likely to leave these ideas untouched with pupils learning 'the right' ideas by rote for the purposes of meeting the demands of school and examinations. The main implication for teaching is, then, that these ideas which seem rational to the pupils must be taken as the starting point.

The task of the teacher when setting out to introduce a topic that will help development of certain ideas is, first and foremost, to find out the existing ideas of the pupils about this topic. This can be done by including specific activities in the 'scene-setting' or by introducing activities that would be a normal part of starting a topic but are designed to reveal the pupils' ideas. Specific techniques are proposed in a later chapter (Chapter 9) but already some indications have been given about what this may mean in the evidence of children's ideas in this chapter. Many of the ideas were revealed through asking pupils to draw what they think is the reason for something happening, or to write about it, or, most often, to talk about it in structured small groups or a whole-class discussion.

The next step, having revealed the ideas, is to find an appropriate way of responding to them. There is no one method for this, but a set of strategies from which the most suitable for a particular situation can be chosen. The choice will depend upon diagnosing the possible reasons and acting appropriately. For example:

- if an idea is derived from a narrow range of evidence (as in the case of the rust within the body of the metal) then the strategy would be to provide more evidence
- if testing a prediction based on it could challenge an idea then the pupils should be helped to make such a prediction and to plan a 'fair' test of it. This is likely to involve helping pupils to develop their use of process skills since it is likely to be failure to apply

rigorous process skills that led to the pupils forming the idea in the first place

- if the use of words is suspect, then the pupils can be asked to give examples and non-examples of what they understand the word to mean
- if, as often happens, children have a 'locally correct' idea about a phenomenon in one situation but do not recognise that the same explanation holds in a different situation, they need to be helped to make links between the situations. For example, the evaporation of water from clothes blowing on a line may be explained in terms of water 'going into the air' while puddles on the ground may be thought to disappear only because the water seeps into the ground.

These strategies are discussed in more detail in Chapter 11. At this point it is worth underlining that children need a range of experiences to help them develop their ideas. Moreover the interconnections between one idea and another mean it is better to make small advances in several and return to each later than to try to press one forward at a time. It is rather like trying to raise a heavy platform on a number of supporting jacks: each one must be raised by a small amount at a time to maintain stability. This analogy is quite apt, for it reminds us that we should not be in too much of a hurry to force the development of children's ideas and skills. It is a slow process and important that there is a reasonable equilibrium between children's ideas and their experience. This gives them confidence that they can make sense of the world around and provides the motivation to do so. Then as experience expands, as it must do, they will strive to relate their ideas to new challenges and change them as found necessary.

Summary

This chapter has set out some evidence from research about children's ideas in a range of topics. These covered, albeit rather unevenly, the eight areas of understanding identified as goals of 5–12 science. Themes in the discussion led to certain characteristics of children's ideas being identified. These included shortcomings which appear to result from the children's necessarily limited experience, ways of reasoning and focus on what is directly observable. The recognition of the possible reasons for children's non-scientific ideas helps to suggest the kinds of further experience (to be considered in Chapter 11) that will help children's learning.

A further theme emerging is the importance of the way children think and reason about their experiences. They will develop scientific ideas only in so far as they develop scientific process skills. The relation between process skills and concept development is the matter to which we turn in the next chapter.

Points for reflection

- Since children's ideas make sense to them, why is it necessary to change them?
- Are children's ideas about things they can investigate directly more 'scientific' than ideas about things they can only observe or know about at second-hand?

Further reading

SPACE Research Reports: Title published are: (1990) *Evaporation and Condensation*; (1990) *Growth*; (1990) *Light*; (1990) *Sound*; (1991) *Electricity*; (1991) *Materials*; (1992) *Processes of Life*; (1996) *Earth in Space*; (1993) *Rocks, Soil and Weather*; (1998) *Forces*. Liverpool: Liverpool University Press.

Vosniadou, S. (1997) On the development of the understanding of abstract ideas. In K. Harnqvist and A. Burgen (eds), *Growing up with Science*. London: Jessica Kingsley.

5

Changing ideas

The examples of children's ideas given in Chapter 4 suggest that children derive these from experience, using both their direct experience of their environment and how they hear things being described by others. Our response, as adults, to these ideas is likely to be equivocal. On the one hand they seem strange to us but on the other hand we can see that they make a certain sense to the children and are not just a matter of imagination. So in this chapter we look at the questions of how children might have come by these ideas and, more importantly, how might their ideas be modified and developed and become 'bigger' and more scientific.

It is helpful to tackle these questions in reverse order, since there will already have been some change in the ideas that are held at any particular time. We start with a model of how ideas may change and then look at how ideas begin in children's early experience. The model of change draws attention to the role of process skills in learning, which is taken up in the latter part of the chapter.

A model of the development of ideas

A model is a mental framework for understanding a process and for taking action. A model of change in ideas should not only represent reality as far as possible but should be able to account for failure to change in certain circumstances as well as for the incidences of change. But any model is no more than a hypothesis. There is no certain knowledge of how children's ideas are formed or how change in them can be brought about. All that anyone can do is to study the evidence in children's behaviour, put forward a possible explanation for it and then see how well this is supported by further evidence.

This is what Piaget (1929) and Bruner, Goodnow and Austin (1966), and others who have produced theories about children's ideas, have done. They looked in detail at children sorting pebbles, swinging pendulums, solving problems involving physical principles, and so on, and hypothesised about what might be going on in children's minds to explain the outward behaviour they observed. Evidence of this kind is always open to various interpretations and sometimes the evidence itself is disputed. What children do with pebbles or with a pendulum depends on so many other things than their concepts and skills. It depends on, for example, on:

- whether they have seen the same or similar things before
- their interest in them or in other things competing for their attention
- how the things are presented to them and by whom
- whether they are in company or alone
- what they did immediately before
- how tired or alert they feel.

Any generalisation about changes in children's ideas must be interpreted as being an account of what is likely to be happening but not one which necessarily will hold in all situations and for all children.

When children encounter something new to them – as in the case of the wet blocks of wood sticking together in Chapter 3, p. 34 – they call upon previous experience in the attempt to find an explanation. There may be several ideas which could be used to try to explain the observations in a particular situation. Which of these existing ideas is 'activated' by being linked to the new experience will depend on the observation of similar features or properties (the ability of one block to hold another without apparent connection calling up the ideas of magnetism, for example). In other circumstances it may depend on words, which can readily form links. This is not always helpful, particularly when a metaphorical use of words is taken literally. The linking constitutes a hypothesis – which is that what worked or explained a previous similar situation must be working in the new one. In other words, an existing idea is used to explain the new experience.

Whether the idea is useful in explaining the new experience is then tested. First the reasoning that 'if it is this, then it follows that . . . ' results in a prediction. Then available evidence is used, or more is sought through investigation, to see if the prediction fits and the explanation can be said to work. The evidence is then interpreted in terms of the idea being tested.

The possible outcomes of the testing are that:

1 The linked idea is found to 'work' and emerges unchanged, but strengthened by the extension of its range.

2 It does not and cannot be made to work, in which case the only way to try to make sense of the new experience is to start again and link another existing idea to it.
3 The idea does not work but can be made to by some modification and so emerges as a modified idea.

In all three cases (and in the range of possible variations on these three), some change in ideas occurs. In (1) and (3) existing ideas are strengthened or modified and thereby become more widely applicable ('bigger'). In (2) the idea that fails to explain the current experience is not dismissed as useless for explaining other experiences but its applicability is limited and it may gain a more specific definition.

The parts of the process of learning through developing ideas are represented in diagrammatic form in Figure 5.1. It is important to note here that the outcome of events in the model is dependent not only on the available 'existing ideas' but on the way in which the processes are carried out. That is, it is affected by how the prediction is made, by what and how evidence is brought to bear, and on how the evidence is interpreted. Thus the process skills play a central role in the development of ideas. We return to this later in this chapter.

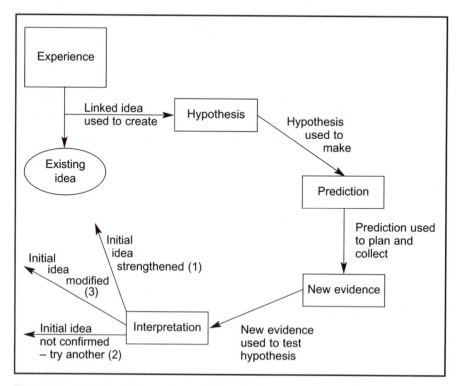

Figure 5.1   A model of learning through changing ideas

Testing the model

Ideas about floating

Before taking the model further let us see how it accounts for the events in some examples. There were several occasions in the group discussion on pp. 27–37 when children made predictions about what might or might not happen. After the girls tested to see which block 'went flat' last, Mena said, 'I think it shouldn't be that, it should be D'. Mena made a prediction, tested it and found it did not fit. Later, they pressed the wet blocks against the side of the bowl, above the water level and waited to see which would slip down first. Ann said, 'This one should come down first' based on some idea she had that the force holding them varied among the blocks.

There was also the prediction by Richard's group of the connection between the weight of the blocks and the level at which they floated. This was eventually tested by predicting the relative weights from the way the blocks floated and then weighing them to see if the order was the same. Quite separately, Mena's group, having put the blocks in order of weight, predicted the order in which they would rise to the surface if all the blocks were held down at the bottom and released together. They predicted correctly and concluded 'so it came out right, we know our facts are right'.

The hypothesis that the blocks which stuck together were magnetic was not used to make a prediction and was not tested. It remained an untested assumption, along with several others, for example, about the colour of the blocks being significant.

Ideas about keeping warm

Another example illustrates how different existing ideas and experiences determine the outcome of children's attempts to understand phenomena. A group of children of a wide age range were discussing the common experience that expanded polystyrene feels warm to the touch. They had a big block of the plastic which was going to form part of the props for a school play. There was general agreement at first that 'there is something hot inside'. The younger children apparently found this quite a reasonable explanation. Their experience, after all, of large warm objects such as hot-water bottles and radiators was that there was something inside that was hot and stayed hot for a considerable time. So their prediction was that the polystyrene block would stay warm, and it did.

The older children, however, brought to this problem the more complex idea that hot things generally cooled down if there was nothing to keep them hot. They knew that there was nothing but polystyrene right through the block and so predicted that if it was warm at one time then it should get cooler as time went on, and it did not. They even tried to make a piece cool down by putting it in a fridge and it obstinately refused to feel cold. It was quite a puzzle to them and they had to think of some altogether other way of explaining the warmth they felt. In the event they came to it through playing with some other pieces of polystyrene in the form of very small pellets. They ran their hands through the pellets and one said, 'It's like putting on warm gloves'. 'But gloves aren't warm, they just keep you warm', said another. 'That's what's happening with the blocks, it just keeps your hand warm, it isn't warm itself.' Here was a possible explanation (though expressed with a great deal of certainty, it was still a hypothesis) and an associated prediction. If the idea was right then the block would not be any warmer than anything else around. This could be checked with a thermometer, and it was.

Note that the 'new' idea was not new in the sense of being discovered from the observations, it was only new in that it had not been brought to bear on the problem before. In itself it was well known to the children that gloves and clothes keep them warm without having any heat source to do this. What they had to do to use this existing idea was, first, to recognise the possible connection, second, create a possible explanation (hypothesis) based on it, third, to use it in making a prediction and, fourth, to test the prediction.

In reality the thinking often happens in a flash and it is in no way being suggested that children consciously think through from one step to another. After all, we have seen that it is not possible to account in a rational way for how scientists arrive at new ideas. The steps are a convenient way of looking at what happens. In the polystyrene example the same processes led to different emerging ideas for the younger and older children: the younger finding their ideas confirmed and therefore not needing to change them and the older finding a conflict because the ideas they brought to it were different and did not fit the evidence.

The origin of ideas: old wives' tales or products of thinking?

We now return to the question of where the 'existing' ideas come from. Are children born with 'existing ideas'? If not, how does the process of developing ideas start?

Action and thought

The clearest guide seems to come from the work of Piaget, who did more than anyone else to show that children have their own ideas which make sense to them in terms of their own logic. Piaget also studied the behaviour of very young children. His ideas suggest that for young children (in what he called the sensorimotor period), actions take the place of thought. Children at this stage appear to 'know' the world through patterns of their own action. Gradually, these patterns of action are internalised and the child's world is no longer essentially centred on himself. These internalised actions later become the thoughts and thought processes. External experience can then be considered separately from internal ideas, but before this they are as one.

It seems likely then that the answer to whether it is ideas or experience which comes first is that it is neither. The young child's actions are all that exist and these gradually separate into what later are described as 'ideas' (internal) and 'experience' (external). Once distinguishable, the interaction of these may, according to the suggested model, bring about the development of ideas. In the course of this development they pass through a range of stages such as Piaget described.

The influence of children's ways of thinking

It is sometimes hard to believe that some of the more strange ideas of children come about through experience. An adult interpretation of experience often suggests something totally different from what children appear to believe. But this is because children's ideas are a product of the way they process experience as well as their existing ideas, and this does not always lead to what an adult would view as a logical outcome. The notion of ideas being formed from experience is not therefore contradicted by the fact that children's ideas seem very strange and illogical to adults.

'Ready-made' ideas

But do all ideas arise from experience? Can they be generated in other ways or even just accepted as ready-made ideas? It certainly seems that there are many ideas about that do not evolve through thinking and reasoning. We are all bombarded every day with ideas from the media, casual conversation and direct instruction – ideas which are not the product of our thinking. 'Nothing tastes better than butter' is not usually an idea developed from experience. So does it have the same status in making sense of experience as an idea which has been developed, as it were, from within? There are plenty of ideas around that would have a confusing influence on children's scientific understanding if they were taken seriously. For example, my mother 'taught' me that if the sun shone through the window on to the fire it would put the fire out, that maggots were made of cheese and developed spontaneously from it, that placing a loose-fitting lid on a pan of boiling water made it boil at a low temperature, that electricity travelled more easily if the wires are straightened out. In my science education I found that these ideas did not stand up to the test of experience (but my mother still believed them). Many similar examples can be found every day, where people are explaining things in terms of ideas which can very easily be shown not to fit experience.

These everyday examples are only some of the ready-made ideas to which children are exposed. Many of them have a more serious influence on children's lives than those just mentioned. For example, children are exposed every day to ideas about what is a healthy diet, about the attraction of 'junk' food, about the use of alcohol, the value or danger of becoming sun-tanned. The expression 'ready-made' is used to denote generalisations which have been created by someone else and not generated through the processes of applying, testing out and modifying existing ideas. Many of the potentially useful ideas presented to children in lessons at school come into this category. These presented ideas are intended to be better for explaining scientific events than children's own ideas, but they will not be immediately available for use in understanding events in the same way as the 'owned' ideas which are already part of the children's way of thinking.

In order for the presented ideas to become part of the web of existing ideas, they have to be tried out as alternatives to existing ideas and judged in terms of their value in making sense of experience. Unless, or until, this happens the presented ideas will not be used; the children will stick to ideas which arise from previous experience. There are implications here for the way in which new ideas are presented to children; they should come as additional ones to try out against their own and to be tested in the same way as their own. Any implication that they are necessarily correct and not subject to any testing will leave them outside the set of ideas which are understood as if they were the children's own.

The role of processes in the development of conceptual understanding

It was noted on p. 60 that the outcome of testing ideas depends on the processes of testing as well as on the nature of the ideas themselves. This may well explain why so many 'old wives' tales' stay alive and believed. Whether a prediction based on an idea is seen to fit the evidence depends on how the 'prediction' is made and tested. Consider, for example, the 'old wives' tale' that the sun shining on the fire will put it out. Here is how it might be incorporated into a person's own ideas:

Ready-made idea: The sun puts the fire out.
Prediction: If this is true, when the sun shines on the fire it will burn less brightly.
Test of prediction: When the sun shines on the fire the flames cannot be seen and it glows less brightly.
Result: The evidence is consistent with the idea; it works.

Here the 'prediction' is no more than a reiteration of what has already been observed. A true prediction requires new evidence to be used. For example:

Ready-made idea: The sun puts the fire out.
Prediction: If this is true, a fire on which the sun has shone will go out more quickly than one on which no sun has shone.
Test of prediction: The sun makes no difference to how quickly the fire goes out.
Result: The evidence is not consistent with the idea; it doesn't work.

The difference between these cases is central to the distinction between a scientific and an 'everyday' approach. A scientific approach involves a prediction which is a logical result of applying the idea and the test of it involves doing something to obtain relevant evidence. The 'everyday' approach does not extend the prediction beyond what is already known; a circular argument replaces a logical prediction. The test is therefore bound to be confirmatory, for no new evidence is sought. 'Everyday' ideas can be accepted because whether or not they 'work' is judged in an 'everyday' way.

These arguments can account for the acceptance by my mother and others of her generation that cheese maggots are spontaneously created from cheese, whereas I and others of my generation regard such an idea as strange and would not accept it as our own. My mother, having had no science education, would seek and notice only confirmatory evidence. She is not, of course, the only one to have strange ideas. Thurber's mother apparently thought herself surrounded by devices which had to be treated in particular and peculiar ways to prevent all kinds of disaster:

> The telephone she was comparatively at ease with, except, of course, during storms, when for some reason or other she always took the receiver off the hook and let it hang. She came naturally by her confused and groundless fears, for her own mother lived the latter years of her life in the horrible suspicion that the electricity was dripping invisibly all over the house. It leaked, she contended, out of empty sockets if the wall switch had been left on. She would go around screwing in bulbs, and if they lighted up she would hastily and fearfully turn off the wall switch and go back to her *Pearson's* or *Everybody's*, happy in the satisfaction that she had stopped not only a costly but dangerous leakage. Nothing could ever clear this up for her.
>
> (Thurber, 1945 p. 186)

In more serious vein the chance of acceptance of ready-made ideas handed to children at school must now be considered. There is no doubt that some scientific ideas seem as strange to pupils as 'old wives' tales' seem to teachers. 'What we're taught in science is often difficult to believe' is a remark from a thoughtful 12-year-old, really trying to make sense of some ready-made ideas handed out by her teacher. She found the teacher's ideas difficult to believe because she tested them out in an 'everyday' way, not in a scientific way, and they did not fit experience as well as 'everyday' ideas. Take the idea that air has water vapour in it. This idea was used by the teacher to 'explain' the formation of dew on the grass. But the girl already had an explanation for this in her own idea that the coldness of the grass created the water. Her own idea also fitted other experience: the coldness of a fridge created water drops on bottles and cans taken out of it. What she was unable to do was to test either her own or the ready-made idea in an adequate way. Although the teacher's idea did not make sense to her, she was not free to reject it; it remained as an idea which she knew about, and could recall if asked, but it was not her own idea.

Children are exposed all the time to ideas of others (their teachers, other children, parents) and those which come through the media. There is no way in which children can be cut off from these other ideas and be allowed to form their own, nor would this be desirable. They must have access to a range of ideas which may be different from their own and challenge their existing ideas. If they are to consider these alternatives rationally, and not simply recite the ones which are forced hardest on them, they must have the mental and other skills needed to test them adequately against experience.

We have focused here on how predictions are made as a basis for testing ideas. However, equally relevant points can be made about other process skills involved in the development of ideas as represented in the model (Figure 5.1). When evidence is collected, observations may be narrowly focused on the evidence which confirms initial ideas, ignoring contrary evidence. When investigations are conducted, significant variables may not be controlled. When data are interpreted they may be used selectively. In other words, *the way* in which the processes are carried out crucially influences the ideas which emerge.

It is important to note that when appropriate ideas do not emerge it may appear on the surface that similar things are happening – there are observations, predictions may be made, investigations may be carried out. But these may not be carried out in a way which we would call scientific. The process skills have to be used rigorously if useful ideas are to emerge. These are strong reasons for paying attention in children's learning experiences to developing their process skills, as we discuss in the next chapter.

Summary

This chapter has presented a hypothesis in the form of a model about how children's ideas change and develop. Its key features are that:

- children use existing ideas to try to explain to themselves new experience
- which existing ideas are linked to the new experience depends on several things, such as similarities in observable features or in words used in the two situations
- ideas are tested to see if they 'work' by making a prediction and gathering new evidence to see if it fits the prediction
- ideas are changed as a result of this process: if they fit the evidence or can be modified to do so, they become 'bigger', since they then explain a wider range of observations than before
- process skills play a determining role in conceptual understanding.

Evidence from the account of children learning in Chapter 3 has been used to test the model. An important implication for teaching is that ideas developed through children's thinking and reasoning make sense to them in the way that ready-made ideas from others do not.

Ways of thinking, of testing ideas, determine whether ideas are accepted and believed. But 'everyday' ways of thinking – which lack the rigour of science process skills – lead to 'everyday' ideas being believed and perpetuated. So it is central to the development of scientific ideas that children are helped to develop process skills and attitudes that enable them to gather and use evidence to test their ideas with scientific rigour.

Points for reflection

- How important is it to use scientific ideas in everyday life, or do 'everyday' ideas suffice (for example, believing that electricity runs better in wires that are straightened out, or that maggots are generated spontaneously)?
- Does the model of changing ideas help in understanding adult learning and learning in areas other than science?

Further reading

Brown, A. L., Campione, J. C., Metz, K. E. and Ash, D. B. (1997) The development of science learning abilities in children. In K. Harnqvist and A. Burgen (eds), *Growing up with Science*. London: Jessica Kingsley.

6

Children's learning experiences

In this chapter we pick up the theme of making decisions about children's learning experiences within the framework proposed in Chapter 1. It may be helpful, then, to begin with a résumé of where we have reached so far.

The framework in Chapter 1 indicated that decisions about learning experience follow from a view of learning and of the goals of science education. The goals were identified in terms of development of conceptual understanding, process skills, attitudes and values (Chapter 2). The view of learning has been developed from evidence of children's learning (exemplified in Chapter 3) in the course of which they use existing ideas to try to explain new experiences. The characteristics of the ideas they bring to bear in making sense of the scientific aspects of the world around them were presented and illustrated through examples in Chapter 4. The model described in Chapter 5 served to formalise the process of learning as one of changing ideas in the course of trying to explain newly encountered events. An important result of looking at learning in this way was to draw attention to the key role of process skills in the development of conceptual understanding.

This chapter now considers the consequences of this thinking for decisions about children's activities. Whilst children encounter activities as a whole, it is important for teachers to consider separately two aspects of activities: their content (or subject-matter) and the way in which the children encounter or interact with the content.

Content is closely related to development of ideas, for clearly activities with snails lead to ideas about living things, not about magnets. The relationship between the development of skills and the content is different; activities with both snails and magnets can develop skills of gathering evidence and interpreting it. The content must provide the interest and motivation for children to become involved in an activity that is going to challenge and develop ideas.

The way children engage with the content is the main determinant of opportunities for development of process skills and attitudes.

So in the first two parts of this chapter we consider decisions about these two aspects of activities separately, even though they are one as far as the children are concerned. In the third part of the chapter we bring together these two aspects of activities in looking at different kinds of investigation and, in the fourth part, we consider the experiences suitable for the early, middle and later stages of education 5–12.

Opportunities for developing ideas

The content of activities provides the opportunities for children to develop ideas in the eight areas identified as goals of science education. In order for their activities to be genuine learning opportunities, however, children must be able to engage with the content. There must be incentive for 'minds on' and, where possible, for 'hands on'. Three things about the content will help this engagement:

- the potential to lead to a satisfying degree of understanding
- that it is of interest to the children
- that it is of relevance to understanding things around them.

These are not as straightforward as they at first seem to be. 'Interest' and 'relevance' can be virtually meaningless unless we consider what they may mean in practice.

The potential for understanding

Bruner famously said that 'any subject can be taught effectively in some intellectually honest form to any child at any stage of development' (Bruner, 1960, p. 33). In stating this hypothesis he was drawing attention to the importance of taking into account 'the child's way of viewing things'. This is why we need to have in mind the strengths and limitations of children's ways of thinking when we consider what kinds of activities are really learning experiences on pp. 82–88. The ideas that satisfy young children are those that answer their questions about their immediate environment. These are conveniently called 'small' ideas because they explain small parts of experience rather applying across a whole range of experiences. For example, they answer questions about 'what these seeds need to grow' rather than about the needs of living things in general. As time goes on, steps have to be taken to link the small ideas into bigger ones but these will not be effective unless the small ideas have been put in place through earlier experiences. As we have said before, conceptual understanding cannot begin with the broad generalisations. The content has to be such that it can be understood in terms of appropriately small ideas.

Interesting to children

Interest is important for children to engage with and make an effort to understand what is happening in their activities and experience. However, interest is not intrinsic to these happenings; it depends on how they are encountered. The result of 'following children's interests' has often been to narrow children's range of experiences by seizing too early on things in which they have already shown interest instead of attempting to expand their interests. The readiness with which children are intrigued by new things, or new ways of looking at familiar things, shows that interest can be created. It is perfectly possible for children to become completely absorbed in activities that they did not themselves suggest, but this does not mean that their interest can be captured by any activity. The criterion of interest should be applied after there has been chance for children to encounter new phenomena. This makes the question of starting points for topics particularly important.

What makes an activity interesting? It is generally because there is something *puzzling* about it, something that we have an urge to settle in our own minds. If I have always wondered how they make plastic bottles without a seam showing, then I am interested to visit the factory where such bottles are made. If someone shows me a new material that I have never seen before ('Potty putty', for instance) then I am interested to touch it, play with it and perhaps investigate its properties in a more ordered way. Each person's puzzles are slightly different, of course, and so what interests me will not necessarily interest another. It will depend on their previous experience and whether the links between this and new experiences raise questions to be answered.

It is not just the new and unexpected that can puzzle children. The familiar has puzzles in it and these are often the most intriguing to them. Who would have thought that four blocks of wood floating in a tank of water would keep children busily investigating literally for hours? This is what happened to the children quoted in Chapter 3, and not just those children; the same activity invariably creates similar intense interest. There was nothing apparently new except that the materials were selected to make them puzzle about floating in a way that they may not have done before and offered the chance of working on this puzzle. So in seeking to create interest we should have in mind links with previous experience when presenting either novel phenomena or familiar ones in a new light.

Relevance to things around

The difficulty here is the complexity of real things and events. Whilst experience of things around can develop children's ideas of the range and diversity of materials, living and non-living, the degree to which children can understand something as familiar as why the wind blows in a certain direction is limited. So, on the one hand, relevance means using the environment to develop, for example, the idea of the variety of different living things on the shore, at the zoo, in the park, in the wood, according to the location of the school. On the other hand, some ideas are not so directly related to real life, for reality is not simple.

If children tackled real questions raised about their environment the complexity could be so confusing that the underlying basic ideas may not be apparent. A way of avoiding this would be to simplify the real situation and take it apart to study its component ideas separately. So, in the case of why the wind blows in a certain direction at a certain speed, we might look at how air moves upwards over a source of heat, and then at how it moves towards places where the pressure is reduced and so on. The danger here is of creating activities which the children may not be able to relate to what is happening in the world around and which they cannot combine in puzzling over the real problem. Science activities then become things that the children do in science lessons rather than a means of increasing their understanding of things around them. Fine, if the study of a swinging pendulum really does have some function in helping to understand things in the world around, but not if the link is theoretical and obvious only to the scientist.

There is no easy solution to this dilemma; in some cases the better course of action may be to accept the complexity of the problem and in others to break it down into simpler component problems. It may help in deciding which is better in a particular case to recall two points: first, that the children's ideas at any time need not be the ones that remain with them for ever; second, that they will form some ideas about the things around them even if we, as educators, consider them too complex. If we want children eventually to understand that wind is moving air and how its movement is created we can discuss and investigate the children's ideas about the wind so that they realise their ideas do not fit all the evidence and they will keep puzzling about it. Or we can ignore the children's ideas and attempt to create the 'right' ones about how air is made to move, through activities designed to illustrate relations, such as heat causing air to rise, and which 'work'. Experience at the secondary level, where the latter approach has been tried for years (and with children who might be more able to abstract the relevant ideas), suggests that it is not very successful. Many pupils do not see the point of the activities they do and are far from making a connection with the world around.

In practice there is often a compromise to be reached between the two courses of action. Once the children are investigating a relevant problem it may well be possible to separate out one aspect for study, to test out an idea or hypothesis. This does no harm, as the connection with the real problem is already established. For example, when some children were working on the problem of how to keep an ice cube from melting (without putting it in the freezer), they wondered whether the same materials they used to surround the ice to stop the 'cold' getting out would or would not keep heat getting out of a warm object. They ended up using food cans filled with hot water and covered by jackets of various materials. This is a fairly common activity, suggested in books both at primary and secondary levels, and can mean little to those undertaking it if it comes 'out of the blue'. For the children who came to it via the ice-cube problem, however, it had a great deal of meaning and marked a considerable advance in their ideas about heat and changes of temperature.

Opportunities for developing scientific process skills and attitudes

Clarifying meanings

The terms used to describe process skills vary. One reason for this is that any definition of separate skills and attitudes is a convenience rather than an attempt to describe reality. The skills and attitudes identified in Chapter 2 are components of the complex activity that we call inquiry, or investigation. It is important to look at the component parts so as to help children develop skill in all aspects of the development of understanding. Different people at different times identify the parts in different ways. Here the whole has been divided into seven skills and five attitudes, and we now look briefly at the meaning to be attached to each one.

Raising questions

In the context of science activities, our concern is with questions which can be answered through scientific inquiry. Although raising questions of all kinds is important to children's learning, in developing children's understanding in science we are concerned with one particular kind of question, the investigable kind. We are not intending to give the impression that this is the only kind of question worth asking.

Science addresses questions about what there is in the world and how it behaves. In answer to such questions assertions can be made which can be tested; for instance: 'Does wood float?' and 'Do you find trees on top of mountains?' Answers can be found by investigation or by consulting someone who has found out. These are science-related questions. The situation is very different, though, for questions such as: 'Is happiness the only real aim in life?' or 'What is knowledge?' These are philosophical questions and are not answered from observation or logical argument. Nor can science address questions of value or aesthetic judgement. It can tackle 'Which watch keeps better time?', but not 'Which watch is more attractive?' or 'Which is worth more money?'

Within the range of questions which science attempts to answer we are particularly concerned in the education of 5–12-year-olds with a small subset of questions. These are the questions to which children can find answers through their own activity. So raising questions in this context means asking questions which lead to inquiry (investigable questions) and recognising the kinds of questions that can be answered in this way.

Developing hypotheses

The process of hypothesising is attempting to explain observations or relationships, in terms of an idea. There were several example of hypotheses put forward by the children quoted in Chapter 3: 'It's the varnish . . . ', 'got more air . . . ', 'the heavier it is the lower it floats'. Hypothesising involves the notion of applying: an idea found to explain things in one context is applied in a new situation. If the new situation is almost the same as the previous one, it is a matter of recall rather than application. Hypothesising is a process that acknowledges that there may be more than one possible explanation. This is consistent with the view that scientific theories are tentative (p. 20).

Predicting

Predicting plays an important part in the model of learning described in Chapter 5 and for that reason alone it is necessary that its meaning is made clear. In particular it is important to distinguish predicting from hypothesising and from guessing.

Predicting often has a close relationship with hypothesising. Although a prediction may not seem to be based on a hypothesis, it invariably is so implicitly if not explicitly. For example, the prediction that 'this cup will be better than that one for keeping coffee hot because it is thicker' includes the hypothesis that thick cups retain heat better than thin ones. The prediction as to which will be best then follows from it, even though it preceded the hypothesis.

A prediction can also be made as a result of finding a pattern in how one variable changes with another. In this case the pattern is an hypothesised connection between the two. For example, a child finds that a clockwork toy goes 1 m 20 cm when the key is turned round three times, 1 m 50 cm for four turns and 2 m 20 cm for six turns. On the basis of these results the child predicts how far the car will go with two, five, seven turns. Even though it might not be explicitly stated, the prediction is made on the basis of the hypothesis that 'the more turns the further the toy goes'.

Neither hypotheses nor predictions are the same as guesses. As we have seen, they both have a rational basis in an idea or in observations and a guess does not have this property. Guessing is exemplified in the actions of a teacher with a group of reception children while cutting open fruits of various kinds to see what was inside. There was one of each kind of fruit and before the grapefruit was cut, the children were asked to 'guess' how many pips there would be in it. Their answers were random guesses, for even if they had used existing knowledge of grapefruit to suggest a number of the right order, there was no way of estimating how many would be in that particular fruit. This was not a prediction, it was indeed a guess and the teacher was using it to add excitement to the activity and to focus attention on the presence of the pips.

Gathering evidence: planning

Children use evidence in building their understanding through inquiry and investigation. The evidence may come from direct experience with materials, but also at second-hand by consulting books, the media, experts, discussion with other children and, of course, their teacher. Gathering evidence from interaction with materials has two related parts: finding or setting up situations so that relevant observations can be made, then making the observations.

Setting up situations involves making decisions about what, when and how observations or measurements are to be made, and what materials and equipment to use. These decisions are not necessarily made before action takes place. For young children, planning and performing an investigation are interwoven; they may plan no further than the first step and from the result of this think what to do next. Older children can be helped to plan things before setting out in an investigation, but they will often need to make changes in the light of unanticipated events.

Gathering evidence: observing

Observation means using all the senses to gather information, but it is more than merely 'taking in'. Observations are directed by preconceptions and expectations, that is, the tendency to see what we are looking for, whilst missing other things that may be right under our noses. Observations are quantified through measurement, sometimes by directly comparing one thing with another or, where appropriate, comparing with standard units of measurement.

Interpreting evidence and drawing conclusions

An investigation usually involves collection of various observations or findings of different kinds. Interpreting these findings means using them to answer the question that the investigation or inquiry was designed to address. According to the type of inquiry, this may mean:

- putting together various pieces of information so that something can be said about the whole that is different from recounting each separate piece of information
- finding a trend or pattern in a set of observations or measurements
- relating the result of testing a prediction to the idea on which the prediction was based.

Communicating and reflecting

Communicating and reflecting are put together since it is through attempting to make things understandable to others that we are caused to examine them for ourselves. Communication is two-way.

It involves, on the one hand, using speech, writing, drawing or an artefact to share things with others and, on the other hand, listening to or looking at information or argument from others or other sources. Effective communication means being clear and systematic in presenting information and using forms of communication appropriate both to the type of information and those who are to receive it. It requires knowledge of conventions of communicating information in various forms, such as through graphs, tables and symbols on charts. It also includes communicating with oneself through keeping notes and records.

Curiosity

A child with curiosity wants to know, to try new experience, to explore, to find out about things around him or her. It is obvious that this is an attitude that will help learning of all kinds and especially learning by inquiry. Curiosity often shows in the form of questioning, but asking questions is not the only sign of curiosity nor the only manifestation to be encouraged. Young children and those with a limited attention span may get no further than asking the superficial question that expresses interest before they turn to another topic. Questioning brings satisfaction if it helps them to share their pleasure and excitement with others. This is part of a natural course of development and to discourage it by disapproval will risk a decline in curiosity.

On the other hand, the satisfaction that comes from expressing curiosity will help children reach a more mature stage where interest is sustained for longer and questions are more thoughtful. There may be fewer questions, indeed curiosity can be expressed in other ways, but there will be more interest in finding the answers, for the questions will be designed to help relate what is already known to the new experience. Then curiosity appears not so much as a flow of questions but as wanting to know. This desire to find out stimulates effort to find out, perhaps by investigation, perhaps by using a library or making a special visit. The questions need not have been asked of anyone else, the motivation comes of having asked them of oneself. When children have reached this stage, putting new experiences in their way is more likely to lead to learning through their own effort.

Respect for evidence

Developing understanding in science is essentially a process of gathering and using evidence to test or develop ideas. Although a theory may have its beginning in an imaginative guess, it has no status until it has been shown to fit evidence or make sense of what is known. Thus the use of evidence is central to scientific activity; this is true at school level as much as at the level of the work of scientists, so attitudes towards it are of great importance in science education.

Children talking among themselves have a keen sense that an unsupported statement is not necessarily to be believed. 'How do you know that's true?' and 'Prove it' feature in their private arguments in one form or another. (There is an example in Chapter 3, p. 27, where Cheryl challenges with: 'How do you know it's the varnish when we haven't even looked at it?') Even young children can respect evidence in this sense but it takes rather more maturity to extend this respect to situations where new evidence conflicts with the current ideas or there are different ideas to explain it. A desire to obtain and use evidence to decide between ideas is a sign of a further development of this attitude.

Flexibility

Flexibility of mind bears a similar relation to the product of scientific activity as respect for evidence does to the process. The concepts that we form to help our understanding of the world around change as experience adds more evidence to develop or contradict them. Sometimes it is a gradual refinement, as when the idea of energy develops from being related to what people can do, to being associated with moving things, to being possessed by things which can move other things and existing in a variety of forms. In other cases there has to be a sudden change, as in conceiving of light as behaving both as wave motion and as particles. The changes are most rapid in children's early years since their limited experience means that their first ideas are often quite different from what they need to understand wider experience later. Unless there is flexibility, each experience that conflicts with existing ideas would cause confusion and create a rival idea instead of modification and growth of an existing one. Flexibility is needed to adapt existing frameworks to fit increased experience.

Young children manage this adaptation quite readily though they may not realise how much their ideas have changed. As children become older and their ideas closer to those of adults they change less often. There is a danger that flexibility of mind may decrease and the idea creep in that at last they now have the 'right' ideas. This is disastrous to continued scientific development. Instead the aim should be for flexibility to mature and extend to the recognition that ideas are tentative.

Critical reflection

In the context of science activities this means looking back over what has been done, deliberately to see if procedures could have been improved or ideas better applied. It is an attitude that is related to respect for evidence and flexibility but relates to making a more conscious effort to consider alternatives to what has been done. In practice it may be manifest in self-critical comments, in repeating part of an investigation or even starting again in another way. On the other hand, there may be no critical comment to make; the recognition of having taken a useful course of action is also evidence of having reviewed what has been done. In any event the attitude shows in reflecting on what has been done, using it as something to learn from; pausing instead of dashing off without a second thought to another activity.

The value of developing this attitude is clearly that it increases the potential learning, of the processes and ideas of science, from each activity. It is an important attitude for learning from experience and avoiding repetition of mistakes.

Sensitivity in investigating the environment

In science education children are encouraged to investigate and explore their environment to understand it and to develop skills for further understanding. Unless investigation and exploration are governed by an attitude of respect for the environment and a willingness to care appropriately for the living things in it, such activities could result in unnecessary interference or even unpleasant harm. So it is important that growth in skills of inquiry and concepts should be accompanied by a development of sensitivity towards living things and responsibility towards the environment.

Young children soon pick up the signs that certain living things have to be treated differently from non-living things. The analogy is with themselves and their own need for food, rest, etc. Keeping ants, snails, a wormery, etc. in the classroom is certain to help children appreciate these as interesting creatures with fascinating and complex behaviour patterns. Such animals can be brought into the classroom for a while to be studied and then carefully replaced in their natural environment. Helping their teacher do this is a significant step towards adopting such caring behaviour themselves.

The mature form of this attitude shows in responsible behaviour to the city environment as much as to the countryside environment, to animals of all kinds as much as to pets. This requires commitment, and a degree of understanding, not reached by many children in the primary years. In the meantime it is necessary to ensure that children are willing to obey simple rules designed to prevent thoughtless harm to the environment. At first rules will have to be imposed by the teacher and discussed with the children so that they appreciate that there are reasons behind them. Later the children can be involved in deciding the rules and procedures as part of the preparation for a visit, a field trip, or starting a school garden patch.

Types of investigation

The purpose of children's science activities is to develop their understanding and for this, as we have argued in Chapter 5, they need to use and develop process skills. Inquiry that involves investigation of materials gives opportunity for all the process skills to be used to some degree, but the way in which an investigation is set up and carried out depends on the kind of question to be answered. Different questions require different approaches. For example, the notion of the 'fair test' has been widely used, but it is not helpful to think of all investigations as being of this kind. Fair testing is appropriate where it is possible to separate the things that can vary and to change one variable independently of the others so that the effect of changing it can be judged in an 'all things being equal' way. These kinds of investigation are important because they encourage children to develop understanding of the need to make fair comparisons.

However, not all scientific problems are of the kind where the variables can be separated. Often changing one condition inevitably affects another. For example, if you deprive a potted plant of water you inevitably also deprive it of the minerals dissolved in the water and may well raise its temperature since it will not be cooled by the evaporation of water from the soil. There are also questions that cannot be investigated experimentally because the variables are not susceptible to experimental control in classroom activities. Questions such as: 'Does the Moon's phase affect the weather?' 'Are the trees whose leaves open early in the spring the first ones to drop their leaves in the autumn?' In these cases there is no control over the independent variable (the Moon or the opening of leaves on the trees) and the investigation has to be devised so that the information is gathered from situations which arise naturally rather than those which are created experimentally.

Different types of investigation have been identified during the course of the AKSIS (Association for Science Education and King's College Investigations in Schools) project. The project's work with teachers of children across the age range 8–14 produced the following six types (with examples of questions provided by the project):

1 Fair testing
    What affects the rate at which sugar dissolves?
    What makes a difference to the time it takes for a paper spinner to fall?
    Which is the strongest paper bag?
2 Classifying and identifying
    What is this chemical?
    How can we group these invertebrates?
3 Pattern-seeking
    Do dandelions in the shade have longer leaves than those in the light?
    Where do we find most snails?
    Do people with longer legs jump higher?
4 Exploring
    How does frog-spawn develop over time?
    What happens when different liquids are added together?
5 Investigating models
    How does cooling take place through insulating materials?
    Does the mass of a substance increase, or decrease, during combustion?
6 Making things or developing systems
    Can you find a way to design a pressure pad switch for a burglar alarm?
    How could you make a weighing machine out of elastic bands?

The last of these is technological in nature and the fifth more appropriate in the secondary school than the primary. The first four are most relevant for 5–12-year-olds and illustrate how different types of investigation are needed to answer different questions. Within this age range, however, there are considerable differences in children's capacity for the various kinds of investigation.

We now look at some characteristics of children in the lower, middle and upper parts of this age range that have relevance for the kinds of activities that likely to provide real opportunities for learning. These are, of course, broad generalisations and provide a rough guide; there will always be individual children whose development varies from this pattern.

Activities at different stages

We consider here the characteristics relevant to learning of children at three stages: early, middle and later stages within the 5–12 age range. These are characteristics, or 'ways of viewing things', which have been described by researchers and confirmed by teachers' experience. The implications for activities that provide genuine opportunities for learning are discussed for each stage.

Learning opportunities at the early stage (5–7 years)

The relevant characteristics of children's ways of thinking at this stage are:

- The need to carry out actions to see their result rather than 'think through' them. Whereas, for instance, older children could work out that if they increase their size of stride they will take fewer strides to cross the room, the 5- or 6-year-old will have to get up and do it, with small strides and then with longer ones.
- Looking at things from only one point of view, their own. They may not realise that a different point of view makes things look different unless they physically move to the other position. Even then they may not realise that it is a different view of the same thing.
- Focusing on one aspect of an object or situation at a time. For example, the youngest children identified either sun or water or air as needed to keep plants alive, but not a combination of these, as did older children (Chapter 4, p. 43).
- The idea that the cause of a particular effect rests in the presence of some feature or object. So the drum makes a sound 'because it is very loud', the candle burns 'because someone lit it', the washing dries 'because of the Sun'. So-called explanations are often tautologous and merely express an observation in a different way: 'the car went because of the wheels'.
- Identifying only parts of a sequence of events. They are likely to remember the first and last stages in the sequence, but not the ones in between. For example, a 6-year-old, after watching sand run through a timer, was reported as being able to draw the timer and its contents at the beginning and end, but not in between. Given five drawings of the timer as the sand was running out he could not arrange them in sequence (Match and Mismatch, 1977).

These points have clear consequences for the sorts of activities the children will be able to learn from. The children's limitations are obvious. It will be no use expecting them to see patterns in events until they have begun to connect events in a sequence. The notion of a cause being related to an effect is still developing, so the idea of separating two or more variables to test the effect of each separately is still a long way off. Their limited experience will mean that their ideas tend to be based on a few very specific instances, selectively observed, having little explanatory power as far as new experience is concerned.

Equally clear are the indications for the kinds of experience that are appropriate at this age. Action and thinking are closely related to each other, reflecting their even closer identification at an earlier, pre-school, stage. Thus infants need to be able to act on things, to explore, manipulate, describe, sort and group them. Firsthand experience and exploration of objects in their immediate environment is the chief aim of teaching science to infants. The content of the activities is therefore found in what is around the children and suitable topics start from everyday events. Common topics, encompassing activities across the curriculum involving science, include cooking, shopping, travelling, pets, holidays, Christmas and other religious festivals, toys, the park/shore/street, etc.

We shall deal with the teacher's role in planning and implementing activities in Chapter 7. Our concern here is with the overall nature of activities and their goals. Starting from the familiar the content should gradually introduce new experiences to the children (making a periscope with mirrors, for example). Though the main emphasis in terms of process skills used will be on observation, raising questions and discussion, there should be a gradually increasing demand in the use of these and development of other skills. When the children have had plenty of experience of acting on things and using the skills they already have with success, they will become able to replace some action by thought. They are then on the way to rational thinking and the development of higher levels of process skills.

Appropriate activities

The children's activities should therefore include plenty of:

- looking, handling, using other senses on material collected and displayed in the classroom
- watching, standing and staring at things in their natural state in the immediate neighbourhood
- collecting things and sorting them

continued overleaf

- trying things out
- making things, particularly models, that in some way 'work'
- taking things apart and reconstructing them
- talking about what they have observed and sometimes recording it in pictures and models and in words when they can
- discussing their ideas and trying to think of explanations for things they have noticed.

The most relevant types of investigation are 'classifying and identifying' and 'exploring'.

Learning opportunities for the middle stage (8–10 years)

On the assumption that children have had the kinds of experience indicated in the infant-school years, they will reach the lower-junior stage having already made some advances in their thinking. A major advance is the ability to use thought instead of action, to think things through, in certain circumstances. The ability to do this develops gradually from the age of 8 or 9. It is limited at first, restricted to those actions with which children are very familiar and which necessarily involve the real concrete objects they have been exploring. The main characteristics of children's thinking at these ages follow from the limited ability to carry out actions in thought. The advances over the previous thinking are that:

- they begin to see a simple process as a whole, relating the individual parts to each other so that a process of change can be grasped and events put in sequence
- they can think through a simple process in reverse, e.g. they can imagine a ball of plasticine that has been squashed out flat being rolled up into a ball again, which brings awareness of the conservation of some physical quantities during changes in which there appears to be an increase or decrease
- they may realise that two effects may need to be taken into account in deciding the result of an action, not just one (for instance, that heat *and* moving air help wet things to dry more quickly); there is some progress towards being able to envisage things from another's point of view, as long as this point of view is one that they have experienced for themselves at some time
- they can relate a physical cause to its effect and are less likely than before to say that, for instance, the leaves fall to the ground because the tree wants to get rid of them.

The limitations are that:

- these kinds of thinking are carried out only on the familiar; they are no substitute for action and firsthand experience when new things are encountered
- thought about whether changes have really happened or are only apparent depends on how strong the visual impression is; thus apparent changes in volume of the same amount of liquid in different containers (which can confuse adults, after all) are less easily challenged by thought alone than changes where reasoning can more easily contradict perception
- the quantities that can be manipulated in the mind are those that can be seen and easily represented mentally, such as length and area; mass, weight and temperature are less easily grasped
- as might be expected, the complexity of a problem or situation influences the ability of children to approach it using rational thinking; they may be able to investigate the effect of one variable but if there are two operating together it is unlikely that their effects can be separated.

The implications for children's activities are that they should expand in two main ways. The range of content should be increased beyond the immediately familiar. The way in which the children interact with this new content might well be similar to their activity in the earlier phase, mainly finding out by observing, discussing, questioning and recording. Their experience of the variety of living things, for example, may be increased, through visits, books and films. Their knowledge of different materials may be extended by making and handling collections of plastics, rocks, various kinds of wood, metal, fabric and building materials. Their awareness of the way different things work may be expanded by investigating simple machines and mechanisms.

The second type of expansion in activities is a change in the way of finding out more about the already familiar things around them. The children can be helped to realise that some of the questions they ask can be answered by doing more than just observing things closely. They can see what happens when they do something to make a change and do this in such a way that they are sure that the effect they find is the effect of their action and not of something else. The idea of 'fairness' that is involved here is an important step towards investigation in a controlled manner. They also begin to make fair comparisons between things: to find out which toy car goes furthest, which paper towel soaks up water best, which paper dart is the best flyer, etc.

Appropriate activities

Again, the provision of activities should be such that opportunity is given for children to use the skills and ideas they have already developed and to extend them. Giving them more of the kinds of activities they learned from as infants is not sufficient; there has to be more challenge in the form of:

- a wider range of objects and events to observe and to relate to their existing experience
- tasks that require close observation of detail and sequence of events
- investigations of the effect on some object or system of changing a variable systematically, keeping other things the same
- tasks that require a search for patterns or relations in observations
- problems that demand fair comparisons between objects or materials
- encouragement to try to explain how things work; expectation that they find answers to their own questions by systematic and controlled investigation rather than just 'do something and see what happens'.

Thus 'fair testing' joins 'exploring' and 'classifying and identifying' as the appropriate types of investigation.

Learning opportunities for the later stage (10–12 years)

The progression in children's thinking in these years is towards both more widely applicable ideas and more structured and rigorous thinking. The children become able to deal with more complex phenomena and can entertain the idea that more than one variable may be influencing a particular outcome. This has a significant impact on the activities that the children can tackle at this time. Investigations can be carried out in a more controlled manner than before. Children respond to the need for measurement in their investigations, the need for accuracy in observation and precision in the use of words and in recording.

So the strengths of the thinking of children at this stage are that:

- they can begin to handle problems which involve more than one variable
- they can use a wider range of logical relations and so mentally manipulate more things
- they show less tendency to jump to conclusions and a greater appreciation that ideas should be checked against evidence
- they can use measurement and recording as part of a more systematic and accurate approach to problems
- they can think through possible steps in an investigation and produce a plan of necessary actions.

However, the limitations of the thinking are still considerable:

- The ability to separate and manipulate variables is confined to simple cases where the variables are obvious and can be physically separated.
- The things that can be manipulated mentally are restricted to those that have a concrete reality for the child. The reality can be conveyed through books, pictures, television as well as firsthand perception of distant things such as the Sun, the Moon and stars.

As long as these limitations are kept in mind there is a great deal that children of these ages are capable of doing to help their growing understanding of the world around them. They will not be able to think in terms of abstractions and theories. Their focus will be on how things behave rather than on why they behave as they do. Their conclusions will be limited and they should not be encouraged to generalise prematurely. 'All the kinds of wood I have tried float' is a more suitable, and accurate, conclusion than 'all wood floats'.

Appropriate activities

A very wide range of activities is now available for these children and the main challenge in providing learning opportunities is to make sure that the full range of kinds of learning are covered. Investigations must extend beyond the 'fair-testing' type and should include all the types identified on p. 81. In more detail, the range of activities should include:

- problems that can be tackled by detailed observation carried out for a recognised purpose and involving the use of instruments to extend the senses, such as magnifiers and a microscope, where appropriate and available
- discussions in which children raise questions about phenomena or objects in the surroundings, suggest how the answers to various types of question could be found and so begin to realise that science can answer only certain types of question
- production of plans for investigations before they are carried out
- discussion of how problems have been tackled in practice, how to tackle new ones, how observations and results of investigations might be interpreted, how to report work to others
- the creation and testing of possible explanations of phenomena
- extension of knowledge through use of books or other sources of information
- extended investigations that involve using all process skills and a range of different resources.

The emphasis that there was in the earlier stages on *doing* gradually gives way in the later years to a more equal emphasis on doing, planning, discussing and recording.

Measurement plays an increasingly important part in investigations as these begin to demand that more accurate observation and careful distinctions are made than previously. Measurement has to be refined and the use of new techniques and instruments introduced and practised. Repetition of measurements and regard to accuracy should become part of a more careful quantitative approach by the end of the primary years.

Progress in the skills and attitudes may well depend on children being allowed to try their skills in gradually more demanding and complex problems. So it is understood that the list of activities above indicates what the children should be doing for themselves, through their own thinking, rather than by following instructions for actions devised by others. It is through trying, and sometimes failing, that, at this point as before, development takes place. A child who tackles a problem requiring the separation of variables, but who fails to keep other variables constant while varying one, will get results that do not make much sense. In the discussion of what he or she did he or she may realise the mistake and take a step towards a new way of thinking about such problems. Without being allowed to make the mistake the child may well not have learned so much. However, whilst a certain amount of learning by mistakes is a good thing it is important that children do not keep repeating mistakes that could be avoided by review, reflection and planning.

Summary

This chapter has discussed aspects of classroom activities that have to be taken into account if they are to be genuine *learning experiences*. In relation to the selection of content, the main points that have been made are that:

- it has to engage the children, be interesting and seems to them to be relevant and to provide a satisfying degree of understanding
- finding activities with these characteristics is not unproblematic, since the interest created by real-life situations has to be set against the complexity of real life and the advantages of providing simple experiences that enable basic ideas to be developed.

In relation to the process skills and attitudes needed for learning with understanding, the chapter has attempted to:

- outline the nature of what is behind the labels for these skills and attitudes
- identify types of investigations that provide opportunities for children to develop understanding through using process skills.

Putting these things together, suggestions have been made for the kinds of activities that are likely to be appropriate for children at different ages and stages, by:

- considering the strengths and limitations of children's thinking at the early stage (5–7 years), the middle stage (8–10 years) and the later stage (10–12 years)
- proposing appropriate kinds of activities that provide for progress in understanding through inquiry.

Points for reflection

- Is it appropriate to emphasise the use of certain process skills more than others at certain stages or to attempt to develop all at all stages?
- To what extent can any content be made appropriate at any stage as long as children's ways of thinking are taken into account?

Further reading

Anne Goldsworthy, Rod Watson and Valerie Wood-Robinson discuss some of the AKSIS project findings in their (1998) Sometimes it's not fair! *Primary Science Review*, **53**, pp. 15–17.

7

The teacher's role: overview

The framework for decisions in Chapter 1 identified roles for the children, for the resources and for assessment as well as for the teacher, in implementing learning. However, all roles depend on being set up and managed by the teacher and, indeed, all the remaining chapters in this book are about different aspects of how the teacher mediates children's learning.

This chapter attempts to look in the round at what the teacher needs to do, before details of various aspects of the role are considered in subsequent chapters. Figure 7.1 represents the interactions of teacher and child as being set within the context of the teacher's planning and organisation of activities for the class. These activities in turn are dependent upon the provision of resources, equipment and, most importantly, an environment that supports learning. We begin the discussion from the outer layer and work inwards.

Setting up the learning environment

The physical environment: classroom or science room?

Whether science activities are carried out in the regular classroom or in a special science room is a matter for the school policy rather than the individual teacher. There are obvious pros and cons of each arrangement. The advantages of a special room are likely to be access to water and other services, good storage, ease of sharing equipment and resources between classes, and convenient working surfaces and space. On the other hand, using a special room means that science has to be timetabled and this may restrict time for extended investigations and the integration of science with other subjects. If their science is conducted away from the classroom, children do not have unlimited access to any investigations they

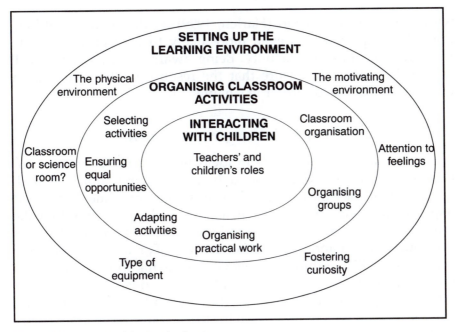

Figure 7.1 Aspects of the teacher's role

may have set up and to displays of material for observing at odd moments. Further, there is a hidden message in moving from the familiarity of the regular classroom to do science in another place; it makes science separate from other work. However, the balance between the advantages and disadvantages depends on particular circumstances and the extent to which the disadvantages of either type of organisation can be minimised.

Type of equipment

Familiarity is also a factor to be borne in mind in relation to equipment. Equipment needs to be robust and simple rather than delicate and complex. Traditionally, pre-secondary science has used 'everyday' utensils and materials rather than laboratory equipment and chemicals, and there are some advantages in this. In making decisions about equipment it is useful to heed the warnings from research into secondary science, that shows that complex equipment can obscure what is to be learned from a practical activity rather than helping to reveal it. When involved in using such equipment the children's attention is absorbed by the minutiae of how to use it rather than the phenomena they should be noticing. They are indeed busily engaged on their tasks but with procedures and not with trying to understand (Harlen, 1999). With younger children, unfamiliar equipment is even more likely to present a barrier to learning from practical activity. Being aware of these factors will enable the teacher to ensure that the resources take their role in learning as discussed further in Chapter 14.

The motivating environment

A view of learning as change in ideas brings with it the need for children (and other learners too) to be willing to relinquish or modify ideas that they may have held firmly for some time. When this happens they will need to use the changed ideas not only to make sense of new experience, but to rethink earlier experience that was previously understood in a different way. For example, at some stage most children think that heavy things sink in water and light ones float regardless of size. When they investigate the floating of different objects more systematically they find this is not the case and the idea of 'weight in relation to size' is found to be more useful in fitting the evidence. They will then need to review earlier reasons they used to explain why things did or did not float.

It is important for children to be able to say, 'I used to think that it was just the weight, but now I know the size matters as well', or, 'I used to think that when you put salt in water it disappeared but now I know it is still there'. The emotional environment has to support this kind of rethinking, and to avoid making children cling to ideas for fear of being thought wrong or silly. In a group activity children are often influenced by each other's ideas and the teacher has to ensure that differences of view are expressed and, indeed, are valued. Unless children feel free to express their ideas the teacher will not know what they are and so cannot be sure that these are taken into account and tested. So it is important to pay attention to children's feelings as well as to their ideas.

Recognising children's feelings

Children sense the classroom climate through their teacher's behaviour and respond in their own behaviour. Teachers who are polite in dealing with children are likely to be successful in encouraging children to be polite to each other. Aspects of teachers' behaviour that children value and comment upon when asked about why they like a teacher include: showing patience; explaining things clearly; being strict at times so that children can get on with their work, but always being kind, friendly and fair. Ways in which teachers can encourage the kind of atmosphere supportive of learning are, for example:

- finding out about the children's attitudes and feelings through discussion and conversation them but, importantly, listening to them
- showing real interest in what they feel as well as what they think
- using knowledge of their attitudes and feelings to set realistic expectations; not expecting more co-operation or responsibility than is appropriate to their maturity
- providing a classroom organisation which supports responsibility and enables them to achieve their best (e.g. by enabling children to have access to and look after materials; giving enough time for them to finish their work)
- encouraging effort and socially desirable behaviours, not just achievement
- setting an example by being patient, sympathetic, encouraging and fair.

Fostering curiosity

An environment that lays the foundation for continued learning and the development of scientific literacy should not only accept but also motivate change in ideas and ways of thinking. We need to create a desire to learn, to understand things around, and to make this enjoyable. Fostering curiosity and the persistence and creativity to satisfy it are essential for lifelong learning (Jenkins, 1997). This is most important at the beginning of formal learning, for if children do not enjoy science when they first encounter it as part of their school education, they are unlikely to recover interest in it later. Indeed, research shows a positive relationship between achievement in science of 10-year-olds and 14-year-olds (Keeves, 1995).

Enjoyment in learning comes from understanding at the level that satisfies curiosity at a particular time. Understanding is 'a continuous function of a person's knowledge' (White and Gunstone, 1992). It is not a dichotomy (not a matter of 'we either understand or we don't') nor a linear process (gradual advance from not understanding to understanding). Understanding grows as ideas become 'bigger', linking more phenomena, and thus being more powerful in explaining things. However, it clearly has to keep pace with experience and younger children are satisfied with 'smaller' ideas until their experience extends. We should not try to explain things that children have no knowledge of nor try to give ideas that they are unable to use. It is essential to safeguard children's enjoyment in understanding. These points are useful to have in mind as we turn to the next layer of Figure 7.1, the matter of the selection of organisation of classroom activities.

Classroom activities

Selecting activities

The last decade has seen an enormous proliferation in the amount of advice available on the content of activities for 5–12 science. In England and Wales, the Qualifications and Curriculum Authority (QCA) has published a scheme of work for Key Stages 1 and 2 (children aged 5 to 11) which converts the National Curriculum programme of study into 37 units of work (DfEE, 1998). There are six units for each of the first five years of the primary school and seven for the final year (including three short units which revise earlier topics in preparation for the national tests at the end of the primary school). Each unit sets out learning objectives, teaching activities and learning outcomes. The scheme does not have to be followed, but it exemplifies how the content of the National Curriculum can be organised into a school programme and reflects what many schools were devising for themselves.

Ensuring learning opportunities for all children

While all children vary in their response to science activities, these variations are overlaid by differences which are related to gender, cultural background and learning difficulties. Thus the selection of learning activities must include consideration of these factors if the activities are to provide equal opportunities for learning. Where discrimination against particular pupils exists it is generally unconscious. In a busy classroom it is not necessarily seen as a problem that certain children seem reluctant to take part in practical work or that ideas are rarely offered by certain groups. Thus the first task is to become aware of what is happening. Thereafter, conscious steps can be taken to prevent discrimination and to monitor the effectiveness of the steps taken.

Although they arise for different reasons, the situations that result in discrimination (albeit unconscious) reduce the participation of pupils in direct handling and investigation of objects in the world around them. In the case of girls, participation may be increased by including a balance of topics of interest to girls and boys and, where possible, ones which are gender-neutral. But this may not be sufficient if boys tend to dominate practical work whatever the topic. Where teacher intervention does not succeed in preventing boys from 'elbowing-out' the girls from the action, it may be useful to have single-sex groups for practical work. Some teachers have also found that having small group discussions at the reporting stage provides girls with opportunity for reflection and restructuring their ideas which they shy away from in whole-class discussions.

To provide learning opportunities for children from all cultural backgrounds, activities should be designed to include materials and events of relevance to all their homes and customs. Children of Asian ethnic origin may also need encouragement to express their ideas and to ask questions, if by tradition they expect school to provide information from an authority. A gradual approach is necessary, enabling them to see other children expressing ideas and to realise the role this has in the activities. Also, work in small groups may help children to voice their ideas and so begin to engage in activities which develop them.

Children with learning difficulties are likely to need to spend longer in handling and playing with materials and in observing events more than once. Often, because of the extra time needed for most things, the reality is that they have less time for these important experiences which are basic to science. Thus the main aim will be to enable the children to spend more time in direct experience of concrete materials. It will also be important for these children to use the full range of techniques for expressing their ideas – talking, drawing, building models, pointing and showing – so that children with writing or other communication difficulties are not disadvantaged when it comes to contributing ideas. Some may discuss or show their ideas more willingly in a one-to-one situation, while others may be more responsive in small groups.

Bringing these suggestions together shows that most apply to all children, but special attention needs to be given to those in the groups discussed, who may benefit particularly from:

- the inclusion of materials and events which are familiar and of interest to them
- ensuring that they have plenty of time to spend in direct contact with objects and materials to be investigated
- establishing a classroom climate which values and responds to all ideas expressed by children
- encouraging a wide range of ways of expressing and sharing ideas

- providing opportunities for children to work and discuss in small groups where there is a supportive rather than a competitive atmosphere.

Having taken some action it is important to keep it under review. School policies should make explicit reference to ensuring equal opportunities and their implementation should be reviewed. Monitoring equal oportunities is likely to be part of the subject leader's role (see Chapter 15). There are several publications from the ASE (1997a, 1997b and 1997c) which provide help in drawing up and implementing policies for ensuring equal opportunities for all children.

Adapting activities

There are many published programmes which suggest activities to cover the curriculum. Teachers can, therefore, find ready-made schemes of work or ones that can be adapted and there is no need to add to these here.

What these materials do not, and cannot, do is to guide every detail of what to do to organise, introduce and bring children to engage with the content in a way that leads to understanding. For this, they have to use process skills effectively so that evidence is found and used in a scientific way. Bringing this about can be helped by forward planning, but it is equally dependent on the decision that a teacher makes on the spot whilst the work is in progress.

We first consider how planning can try to ensure that children use process skills, that is, that they 'think' through what they do and not just 'do' by following instructions. Take an activity such as the one presented on a work card in Figure 7.2.

What makes ice cubes melt?
Find out where ice cubes melt most quickly.

1. Take three ice cubes that are all the same size as each other.
2. Put one by the window inside the classroom.
3. Put one outside.
4. Put the third in a refrigerator.
5. See how long each one takes to melt.
6. Explain why they take different times to melt in the different places.

Figure 7.2 Work card activity

This activity, aimed at 9-year-olds, clearly aims to lead children to the idea that it is the temperature of the place where the ice cube is that decides how quickly it melts. Let us leave aside for the moment the inadequacy of this explanation to account for the children's everyday experience of where ice melts. The activity gives instructions that the children could readily have thought out for themselves if there had been some discussion of possible reasons for ice melting and how they might test these out. Had the children decided where to put the ice cubes and that they needed to use ice cubes that were all the same size to be 'fair', then they would have had some ownership of, and a great deal more interest in, the investigation. It would have tested *their* ideas.

The activity has another flaw, however, by focusing on the temperature of the surroundings rather than other possible ideas about how ice might be made to melt or, more challengingly, prevented from melting. Children have ideas from their everyday experience about these things; they have seen ice not melting even in warm places (when surrounded by insulating material, in 'cool boxes' for example). It is much more useful for their understanding of everyday experience, as well as for the development of 'big' ideas about change of state of matter, if they test their ideas about what is needed to melt ice or prevent it melting.

In one classroom where this was discussed, one child thought that putting ice in a plastic bag would prevent it melting, whilst another considered that wrapping it in newspaper would be best. Designing the test to be fair was important to them in order to see which prediction was better. It also made them try to explain their findings and they did this in terms of how quickly heat needed to melt the ice could reach it through the material. In their discussion they went on to speculate that a freezer must be taking heat away from water when it turns it into ice. The whole activity was a genuine learning experience, in contrast with the limited experience of the activity on the card.

The point here is not that the activity in Figure 7.2 was presented on a card, since a teacher could have set up just the same activity by oral instruction, but that it was prescriptive and did not engage the children in developing their ideas or their investigative skills. In planning, therefore, teachers should screen activities by asking questions such as:

- What opportunities are there for the ideas that the children bring to this activity to be revealed?
- What opportunities are there for the children to decide what to do to test these and other ideas?

Unless there are good answers to these questions, the time spent on the activity may not be well spent. We will consider the teacher's role in helping the children to reveal and test their ideas in more detail in Chapters 9 and 11.

Before leaving the nature of activities to turn to their organisation, it is worth recalling that not all investigations are of the 'fair testing' kind. Ideas can be tested through other types of investigation such as pattern seeking and exploring. In addition, direct experience of materials in the environment serves the further purpose of extending children's experience of living and non-living things. It is important for the teachers to be clear about the purpose in a particular instance and, where appropriate, to share this with the children. For the purpose to be achieved there must be time to report findings, discuss the meaning of what has been observed or found and to reflect on the experience. In other words the organisation has to ensure that activities will be 'minds on' as well as 'hands on'.

Classroom organisation

The organisation of practical work is often seen as the most difficult part of teaching science. This concern gives rise to the impression that practical activity is everything there is in science education and obscures the balance between practical activity and whole-class discussion, group discussion, individual work in consulting books or other resources, or recording their work.

In general practical activities should be preceded by whole-class discussion to introduce a topic, gather children's initial ideas and explain arrangements for the practical work. After the practical work there should be further whole-class discussion so that children can share experiences and reflect on what they have done and learned. At other times during investigations, the teacher may initiate discussions with each group separately rather than bring the whole class together. The discussion the teacher has with groups has an essential part to play in preparation for a useful whole-class discussion later. By taking part in the discussion of each group, and by listening, the teacher can pick up the points of interest and concern, the ideas and the problems, that can usefully be shared between groups. Bringing out these points when the whole class gets together for discussion is then likely to lead to exchanges between pupils which are of interest and benefit to all of them. This helps to avoid the whole-class 'discussion' being of interest only to a few at any time and more a question and answer session between teacher and individuals in turn than a genuine discussion.

Ways of organising practical work

So practical work will not be the only type of activity that needs to be planned and organised. But when it is taking place, the main options for organisation are:

- whole-class working in groups on the same activity at the same time
- whole-class working in groups at the same time but on different activities (possibly related to a common theme or not)
- groups working on science activities at different times whilst other children are engaged on different subjects
- demonstration to the whole class (perhaps with help from some children while others watch).

There are advantages and disadvantages of each of these, which vary according to the type of activity and the age of the children. In making decisions in particular cases, however, it is useful to keep in mind some overall guiding principles.

First is the importance of discussion, perhaps during practical work but certainly when it is completed. It is in this that children can reflect on their ideas and on how they have carried out the activity. Without this, the practical work may be just an enjoyable experience but not serve the learning purpose intended. So an important consideration will be how the organisation chosen makes this possible. On this point, a teacher of 6-year-olds wrote:

> I have tried a number of ways of organizing practical science in the classroom – with varying success. For many activities the class is split into groups. One possibility would be to have one group of 4 to 6 children doing some practical science while the rest of the class is involved in other things. I find that this does not work well. Children are often very stimulated by practical science and discuss their observations excitedly with their co-workers. I certainly do not want to discourage this enthusiasm and the exchange of ideas, but the noise can be distracting for another child involved in a piece of creative writing! Another disadvantage of small group work is that the time for teacher/group interaction is limited, particularly for the important initial discussion and the discussion of results at the end of the session.
>
> A second possibility is to have all the class doing practical science, but to keep the group system and give each group its own set of experiments. This can work well, particularly if the separate investigations are all different aspects of a single theme – group results can be pooled, and discussed by the class at the end of the session.

> (Glover, 1985, p. 27)

A second overall consideration is the amount of time that the teacher can give to the science activities, to observing how the children are tackling the work as well as making interventions. If non-science activities are going on at the same time as science, the teacher's attention has to be divided not only to different groups but also to different subjects. Following the themes of all the work in these circumstances can impose an impossible overload.

A third concern is the potential for differentiation in activities to suit the development of individual children. There is little point in finding out about children's existing ideas and skills if there is no opportunity to use the information in deciding learning experiences that are best suited to certain children at a particular time.

A fourth consideration is the matter of safety and the availability of equipment. If the materials or equipment the children have to use are only sufficient for one or two groups at a time, then having all groups working simultaneously will not be possible. The group working will have to be staggered, some groups working on their science activities while others are involved in other activities. But the whole-class discussions can still be held, being planned to take place when all the groups have completed a particular phase of the group work. Staggering group work may also be necessary if the use of the equipment requires careful supervision for reasons of safety or for the teaching of a particular skill. However, if there are no good reasons for staggering, then having all the groups working together on activities related to the topic has many advantages.

A fifth point, again bearing on the importance of reflecting and not just 'doing', is the value of children being interested in the findings of other groups and being able to hear what others have done while the work is fresh in everyone's mind. This is likely to be the case if the groups are working on activities, related to a common problem or topic, but which are not exactly the same. A great deal more learning with understanding is then likely than if each group works on its own topic and has no shared experience to talk about with others.

Finally, it is important to note that the value of firsthand experience to young children should not mean that we dismiss the occasional demonstration by the teacher. This is appropriate if there is any danger or difficulty in using equipment, but more often it will serve the purpose of providing an experience that provokes curiosity and motivates children. A demonstration will also make it possible for the teacher to ensure that children focus on the relevant aspects of a phenomenon. As we noted on p. 91, in their own practical work, the manipulation of equipment can sometimes be the focus of attention and relevant observations go unnoticed. However, this is definitely *not* a reason for demonstrating what children have to do before the children simply repeat it.

Organising groups

When children work in groups, questions arise about the size and composition of the groups. On the matter of size the ideal is not necessarily realistic. Groups of four might be ideal from the point of view of fostering genuine collaborative working, when children work together on a common enterprise. However, this may mean a greater number of groups than the teacher can comfortably handle, given that the more groups there are the less time he or she can spend observing or interacting with each one. So groups of five or six are often necessary and roles within the group have to be carefully monitored to ensure that some children do not become mere onlookers.

Groups formed for other purposes, such as reading and mathematics often decide the composition of groups for practical work in science. Perhaps it is fortunate that teachers find that children's ability in science does not generally reflect ability in these other subjects, for there is convincing evidence that children make better progress in science when working with those whose ideas differ from theirs. Children with different ideas can be of particular help to each other, not in the same way as in a teacher–pupil relationship, but simply by extending the range of ideas available to a group. This has been confirmed by research in which the progress of pupils in groups formed in different ways was assessed. One set of groups was formed of children whose ideas about the activity varied widely (the differing groups) and the other set was formed of children whose ideas were similar. The results were quite clear cut:

> Looking at the change from the pre-tests to those post-tests that were administered several weeks after the group tasks, it is clear that on five of the six comparisons the children from the differing groups progressed more than the children from the similar groups. Moreover, when the differing groups contained children whose level of understanding varied, the more advanced children progressed as much as the less. This being the case, we felt our results provide reasonably consistent evidence for the task being more effective with differing groups.
>
> (Howe, 1990, p. 27)

An important feature of these results is that the differences showed later rather than at the time or immediately after the activities. From this the researchers concluded that 'interaction when concepts differ is a catalyst for development and not the locus of it' (Howe, 1990, p. 27). Thus there are good reasons for avoiding grouping by science achievement in terms of helping progress. This adds to the case for mixed groups, which can also be seen to be strong on grounds of motivation and equity (Harlen and Malcolm, 1999).

Interacting with children: teachers' and children's roles

This is at the centre of Figure 7.1, for it will be the most important factor in children's learning. Establishing a supportive learning environment and selecting, adapting and organising practical activities are important conditions for learning, but they will not be sufficient on their own. Somehow the teacher has to help the children to engage in thinking about the things they are observing and investigating. The nature of fruitful interactions in different circumstances and at different stages of children's investigations will be discussed in more detail in coming chapters. Here we give an overview and a framework so that the whole can be kept in mind as separate parts are considered. In what follows, the roles of teacher and children are identified in various phases of an investigation, illustrated by a classroom example. The focus is on the interaction and not matters of equipment and class organisation at this point.

The teacher's role begins before the children are involved. For each topic there is a planning phase in which decisions have to be made.

Planning phase

- How to introduce the topic; what links can be made with previous experience.
- What kinds of question to ask.
- The main ideas, skills and attitudes that can be developed through the topic.
- How to find out about the children's ideas.
- What ideas children are likely to hold about the subject.
- What help these children are likely to need.
- What groups to focus on for assessing skills and attitudes (this refers to planning for formative assessment, explained on p. 133)

A teacher of a class of 9–10-year-old children was introducing activities within an overall topic about clothing. The teacher planned that the children should discuss and investigate the selection of different fabrics and materials for different purposes. He had in mind that the children should undertake some investigations of different fabrics, so he provided a collection of suitable pieces of fabric, etc. to which the children contributed. He wanted the investigations to advance the children's ideas and therefore to be based on their initial ideas and questions. It would have been easy to ask the children to find out, for example 'Which is the most water-proof material? Which is the most wind-proof?' etc. and to start the children's investigations from these questions. These are perfectly good questions for children to investigate and likely to be among those the children ended up investigating, but he wanted to hold back his questions to find out what the children would ask and what ideas they had.

When the lesson begins, the teacher's role and the children's role go hand in hand.

Exploratory phase	
Teacher's role	Children's role
• Provide experiences which encourage exploration of the scientific aspects of the topic. • Use open, person-centred questioning to elicit children's present understanding and ways of explaining things. • Engage children in suggesting how they would test their ideas.	• Engage in exploration of materials/events/ objects relating to topic. • Give ideas to explain observations. • Suggest how ideas can be tested.

The first part of the work was an exploratory phase of looking at the range of materials. In groups, the children were given samples of the materials, some hand-lenses and some very open instructions:

• put the pieces of material into groups according to what they would be used for
• explain what was the same about the items in each group
• explain how the groups differed from each other.

This task required children to use the ideas the teacher wanted them to develop in making their observations, it encouraged them to look closely at the materials and to think about the differences they found. It was not a long activity but gave the teacher time to visit each group to listen in to what the children were saying about the materials. Many of their statements at this stage contained hypotheses and predictions.

Deciding and planning the investigation phase	
Teacher's role	Children's role
• Collect ideas from children and decide together which one(s) are to be investigated. • Ask children for their ideas of how to go about their investigation, how to make sure it will give a fair result, how they will judge the result. • Help children to plan details and to make a start.	• Make suggestions for how to tackle the investigation. • Decide how to make the investigation fair. • Plan the details either at the start or as they go along.

There was then a whole-class discussion, pooling ideas from different groups. Two groups were both interested in investigating one of the ideas emerging from the initial exploration, that natural materials are harder wearing than manufactured ones. Others followed up ideas about warmth and thickness and others did indeed investigate what makes some materials more water-proof than others. Although having different foci, the investigations of all the groups were relevant to developing the idea that the uses of materials are related to their properties.

Investigation phase	
Teacher's role	Children's role

• Observe how children are
  – planning
  – collecting evidence
  – recording
• Interpret observations with process skill and attitude goals in mind.
• Ask questions which require explanations in terms of understanding of the ideas involved in the investigation.
• Interpret answers with appropriate conceptual understanding goals in mind.
	• Carry out the investigation, making observations and measurements.
	• Record their results in suitable ways.
	• Interpret their results.
	• Attempt to explain their results.

In the investigation phase the teacher used information about the children's ideas to set them going on investigations which addressed these ideas. The investigations provided opportunities to help the children develop their process skills, in order to carry out systematic and 'fair' tests through which they would arrive at findings useful in developing their ideas. So during the investigation the teacher needed to gather information about the children's process skills and to use this to give them any help they may have needed in thinking through how to collect evidence and make a record of it. At the stage where results had been obtained, the teacher needed information about how the children were interpreting what they had found out and whether their initial ideas had been changed.

The teacher encouraged the children to make notes of what they found as they went along and then use these to prepare a report from each group to the whole class. This gave the teacher further information about how the children interpreted their findings and about their communication skills. Sharing the group reports also gave the teacher the opportunity to ask questions which challenged children to explain some findings – possible reasons for one fabric being more hard-wearing than others. He asked them to apply their ideas to other materials to find out the extent to which the children's ideas were becoming more widely applicable. He also asked them to reflect on which parts of their work they had enjoyed most, which would they do differently if they could start again and what they now felt they could do better than before.

Reporting and reflecting phase	
Teacher's role	Children's role
• Hold discussions with children on the interpretation of results: what they mean in terms of the purpose of the investigation; whether and how their initial ideas have changed. • Ask questions which require application of the ideas emerging. • Ask children to review what they have learned and how they could improve their investigation. • Engage children in some assessment of their own work and of what they have learned.	• Make a report of their work. • Compare what they found with what they thought they would find. • Reflect upon and use ideas in other contexts to give oral or written answers. • Take part in assessing their work.

The teacher's role does not end at the end of the classroom work. There is the important task of reviewing, recording and reflecting and using the experience in future planning. Reviewing involves recalling the observations made, particularly of the group which was the 'target' for gathering information about skills, and reviewing the children's notes and reports.

Reviewing and recording phase

- Reflect upon and record where pupils are in ideas and skills and what help they need to make further progress.
- Use this information either to plan further work to follow up the investigation, or in planning work at a later date.

Summary

This chapter has attempted an overview of many aspects of the teacher's role that are necessary for enabling 5–12-year-olds to learn science with understanding. Teachers' decisions that affect this learning are taken at three levels:

1 Setting up the learning environment. Two main aspects were considered: the physical environment, where it was suggested that science should be taught with, through and surrounded by familiar things; and the motivating environment, which supports and encourages children in changing their ideas and fosters their curiosity so that they continue to learn.
2 Organising the classroom activities. Again there were two main aspects: selecting activities and adapting them so that they give opportunity for children to work things out for themselves; and classroom organisation and the organisation of children in groups for practical work to maximise opportunities for children to share ideas and learn through discussion.
3 Interacting with children. The roles of teacher and children at various points throughout a practical investigation have been proposed and illustrated.

Aspects of these roles are considered further in the coming chapters as we look at the part that assessment takes in children's learning and at what teachers can do to help their development of scientific ideas, process skills and attitudes.

Points for reflection

- How might the advantages of organising practical work so that all children are involved at the same time vary according to the age of the children, size of the class and other circumstances?

- The interaction with children was illustrated using an example of a 'fair-testing' investigation. What difference, if any, might there be in the roles of the teacher and children if the investigation were one of the other types identified in Chapter 6 (p. 81)?

Further reading

Classroom observations of two primary teachers are included in the article by Kenneth Tobin and Patrick Garnett reproduced in their (1993) *Teaching, Learning and Assessment in Science Education*, (D. Edwards, E. Scanlon and R. West (eds). London: Paul Chapman Publishing and the Open University.

The practices of two teachers are also described by Jonathan Osborne and Shirley Simon in (1996) Primary science: past, and future directions, *Studies in Science Education*, **27**, 99–147.

Matters relating to equal opportunities are well covered by Michael Reiss in his (1998), Science for all, in the *Association for Science Education Guide to Primary Science*. Cheltenham: Stanley Thornes.

8

Assessing for learning

Gathering and using evidence about children's ideas, skills and attitudes is at the heart of the interaction between teacher and children
that advances learning. This chapter sets out a rationale for this
process, which is identified as assessment for learning, or formative
assessment. Describing something that is so much a part of teaching
as assessment needs some justification and this is given in the first
section, on the meaning of assessment. Various different purposes
for assessment are then discussed and formative assessment is distinguished from assessment for summarising learning and for evaluating teaching and schools. The chapter ends by drawing attention
to research evidence on assessment and classroom learning that
shows that formative assessment has a considerable potential for
raising standards of achievement.

Meaning of assessment

Any activity that is called assessment involves:

- collecting evidence in a planned and systematic way
- interpreting the evidence to produce a judgement
- communicating and using the judgement.

The ways in which these things are done have to serve the purpose
of the assessment and thus will vary according to the purpose. Some
of the ways in which these things can be done are now briefly
indicated.

Collecting evidence

The range here extends from observation by the teacher during the
usual interactions between teacher and children, to the reading of
written tests or examination papers. Observation, which includes

watching and listening, can be structured so that children are observed responding to particular tasks or questions. Some evidence will be in the form of a permanent record that can be studied after the event in which it was produced but, if there is no permanent record, then it is necessary to gather the information by observation at the time. However, even where there are drawings, writing or other products to be assessed, information about when and how these were produced is important in the assessment. This applies particularly to young children, whose products may need to be discussed at the time and annotated by the teacher if they are to convey meaning later.

Making a judgement

In making a judgement the evidence is compared with some standard or criterion. In educational assessment the three ways of doing this are:

- comparing with the standard of others of the same age and/or experience (norm-referenced)
- comparing with criteria for certain levels of performance (criterion-referenced)
- comparing with the individual's previous performance (child-referenced or ipsative).

In the first of these the outcome of a child's assessment will depend on how other children perform as well as on his or her own performance. In formal standardised tests the 'norm' is a certain mark derived from testing a representative sample of children and finding the average. In a less formal way a teacher may apply standards derived from experience of other pupils in deciding what is the expected level of performance.

When criterion-referencing is used, the assessment is in terms of how the child's performance matches criteria describing certain kinds of performance. This judgement does not depend on how other pupils perform, although the choice of criteria is likely to be influenced by what it is reasonable to expect of pupils of comparable age and experience.

Ipsative or child-referenced assessment judges a child's performance against what he or she has done previously and may result in a teacher appearing to use different standards for different children. One child who completes a certain piece of work may receive praise because it represents an improved performance while from another pupil this same work would have received a less favourable reaction if the teacher judges it to be of lower quality than the child is capable of producing. This is appropriate when assessment serves a formative purpose but not for other purposes.

Communicating and using the judgement

There are several points to be considered here: feedback to the child; use by the teacher and ways of communicating to others. The form of feedback to children about their work has an important impact on their self-esteem and research has shown that the use of judgemental comments, marks or grades is best avoided (see p. 120). The use by teachers is to help classroom decisions about the ways of helping children's progress and this may not require formal records. However, for communication with others it is important that information is conveyed in the amount of detail that can be used and that the basis of judgements in terms of levels, grades or standards is made clear. These matters are taken further in Chapter 13.

Purposes of assessment

The three main purposes of assessment relevant to children aged 5–12 are:

- *Formative assessment* (assessment *for* learning). This is assessment which is embedded in the approach to teaching and learning described in this book. Teachers need to know children's existing ideas and skills at any particular time and to base interventions on this knowledge. Both finding out and using evidence about existing learning are integral to formative assessment.
- *Summative assessment* (assessment *of* learning). This provides a summary of the achievements of individual children at particular times. It is the basis of reports to parents, other teachers and the children themselves on what has been learned at these times.
- *School evaluation and target-setting* (assessment of learning of groups of children). This provides information about the average performance of classes or whole-year groups as indicators of the effectiveness of teachers or of a school as a whole. This information may be collected and used by the school staff or by authorities outside the school.

In addition to these three, there are two more general purposes of assessment which will not be discussed here. These are selection or certification, which is a particular application of summative assessment, and national monitoring, where information is collected to monitor overall standards of achievement across the educational system of a country, region or state. The Assessment of Performance Unit, which monitored achievement in England, Wales and Northern Ireland between 1980 and 1985, the still operating Assessment of Achievement Programme in Scotland and the National Assessment of Educational Progress in the USA, are examples of assessment programmes for national monitoring. Only a sample of children is assessed and each child takes only one or two of a large number of tests. So the results are only meaningful when brought together across the whole sample and no results for individual children are given.

In this chapter we are concerned with assessment for learning, but the meaning of this is best clarified by comparing and contrasting its characteristics with those of the two other purposes that have an impact on teaching and learning for the 5–12 age group. This discussion makes reference to the reliability and validity of assessment.

Reliability and validity

Reliability is the term used to express the degree of accuracy of the result of assessment, i.e. if the assessment were to be repeated, the extent to which the second result would agree with the first. The reliability of assessment of a child's skill in writing is likely to be less than the reliability of a test of addition and subtraction sums, mainly because it is far easier to mark the latter consistently.

Validity refers to the extent to which what is assessed really reflects the behaviour it was intended to assess. For example, a multiple-choice test of knowledge about materials that conduct electricity would not give a valid assessment of understanding of a simple electric circuit, although it would be an assessment of quite high reliability.

Reliability and validity are not independent qualities of assessment. Attempts to increase reliability tend to restrict the range of evidence that can be used and hence reduce validity. Similarly, attempting to increase validity often means extending the range of the assessment to learning outcomes such as attitudes and values, which do not lend themselves to reliable assessment.

Formative assessment

Assessment for learning is essentially carried out by teachers as part of teaching. This means that it is ongoing and a regular part of the teacher's role. However, the fact of being carried out regularly does not necessarily mean that assessment serves a formative purpose. Regular tests are not always formative in function; it depends on how the results are used and who uses them. So it seems best to describe the types of assessment in terms of function rather than occurrence.

Formative assessment includes diagnostic assessment. The term 'formative' is preferred, however, since 'diagnostic' carries the connotation of concern with difficulties and errors, whereas formative assessment is relevant at all times. It helps the teacher to decide the appropriate next steps in learning both for those who succeeded in the earlier steps and those who encountered difficulty.

So formative assessment involves identification of where children are in their learning to inform the action to take. There is an equal emphasis on *using* the information as on finding what has and has not been achieved. Children have a role in assessment for this purpose since it is, after all, the children who do the learning. No one else can really change their ideas or develop their skills. Thus the more they are involved in knowing what they should be trying to do, the more likely it is that their motivation and effort are enlisted in advancing their learning. This means teachers sharing short-term goals with children as well as enabling them to judge the quality of their own work. Ways of doing this are suggested in Chapter 9.

The parts of the process involved in formative assessment are represented in Figure 8.1. This figure attempts to show how

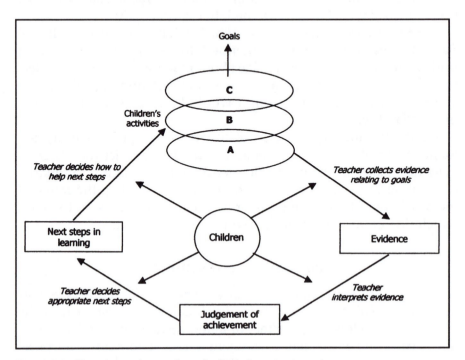

Figure 8.1   The roles and procedures for formative assessment

collecting evidence during children's activities leads to judgements about appropriate next steps and to helping children take these steps in further activities.

Collecting and interpreting evidence

Starting from activity A, the teacher plans the collection of evidence about the children's ideas, skills and attitudes, using various strategies, and involves children in this process. The teacher then interprets the evidence, taking account not only of the goals but the experiences and past achievement of the children. Thus the judgement of an individual child's work is not based purely on the goals achievable through the activity but on such things as the recent progress and the effort of the child. This means it is child-referenced (ipsative) as well as criterion-referenced. There is a role for the child here, too, since he or she will know whether the work was done carefully to the best of his or her ability, or could have and should have been given more thought and care. The discussion of how the work should be judged will be part of the process of communicating a view of the quality that is expected.

Deciding next steps

The discussion of where expectations were and were not met often indicates the next steps that need to be taken. How to help children take them is a more difficult matter that requires knowledge of the course of development towards goals and of ways of promoting development. Because we are concerned here with reacting to and using information that emerges as activities take place, it may not be possible to anticipate how to take the next steps. It is important, therefore, for the teacher to have knowledge of a range of strategies for advancing children's ideas and skills and to know how to select from these at an appropriate time. Chapters 10 and 11 consider such strategies which are, of course, at the heart of teaching and learning.

A cycle of events

The outcome of the process is the next learning experience, activity B, which takes children further towards achievement of the goals. The process then continues in a cycle, leading to activity C, and so on. This is a theoretical model of the process and some points need to be made about what happens in reality:

- Activities B and C may not necessarily follow immediately; they may take place some time later, when the topic is revisited or when similar types of investigation are encountered.
- Although described as a series of steps, in practice the processes within a cycle often run together and are more of a whole.
- Because information is gathered frequently as part of teaching it is not necessary to try to cover all aspects at any one time. In one 'cycle' the focus might be on children's reports of their work; on another, their ability to raise questions and to plan ways of answering them, or on linking up experiences to develop ideas relevant to the content of the activities.
- Another way of focusing during group work is to plan to focus the formative assessment on one group, whilst not neglecting the other groups (see pp. 133–134).

Formative assessment in action

Some of these points are evident in this example which occurred in a class of 8-year-olds:

> Julie's group had been collecting seeds of many different kinds. Julie added a sticky bud with the scales removed to the collection. She told the teacher that the things inside were seeds. When the teacher asked her what she thought was surrounding the little 'seeds' she said they were leaves that would grow into horse-chestnut leaves. She was convinced, however, that the things inside were the seeds of the tree. The teacher recalled the 'conkers' that they had collected some months earlier and how some of them had sprouted. But although Julie seemed to appreciate that conkers would grow into trees, they did not seem to fall into her idea of seeds. The teacher asked Julie how she would be able to collect the 'seeds' that she had identified. She said they would show when the sticky buds opened. So more twigs were gathered and Julie and other children observed the buds regularly as they opened. Later they continued observation of the opening of buds on the tree from which the twigs had been taken and noted that the 'seeds' turned into flowers and the new small conkers began to form. These various activities extended Julie's idea of the life cycle of plants as well as her notion of the variety of forms that seeds can take. At the same time all the children learned that trees had flowers, which they had not recognised before.

Here evidence was gathered by observing, listening and questioning during the seed collection (activity A). To interpret the evidence, the teacher clarified whether Julie knew that the twig and conker were related to the same type of tree. It appeared that the problem was not this, but Julie's narrow conception of seeds as small and spherical. The next step was to help Julie to recognise a wider range of things that were seeds. She first tried to make a link with earlier experience, by reminding Julie of the sprouting conkers. However, although the link to earlier experience was made, Julie persisted with her idea. The teacher then helped Julie to test her idea in a way that she found convincing, leading to further activities (activities B and C) that advanced her understanding of seeds and life cycles.

Essentials of formative assessment

Formative assessment can be more structured and formal than this. It can take the form of asking questions or setting special tasks that are designed to reveal the extent of development of particular ideas and skills. What makes the assessment formative is the *use* that is made of the information. This is the chief difference between assessment for formative and summative purposes. Before turning to consider the characteristics of summative assessment, we first bring together the important points about formative assessment.

Characteristics of assessment for formative purposes are that:

- it is an integral part of teaching for understanding. It is not optional; it cannot be taken away without changing the whole nature of the teaching and learning
- it relates to progression in learning but takes individual progress and effort into account; that is, it is both criterion-referenced and child-referenced
- it leads to action that supports further learning
- it can be used in all learning contexts
- it provides information about all learning outcomes
- it involves children in assessing their performance and deciding their next steps
- it uses methods that protect validity rather than reliability.

The last point often raises objections on the ground that an assessment that is not reliable cannot be said to be valid. But it is matter of degree and emphasis. No assessment can be 100 per cent reliable and, as noted above, the interconnection between the two means that emphasising one infringes the other. There are two reasons why the requirement for reliability in formative assessment can be less stringent than for assessment for other purposes. First, the information is both gathered and used by the teacher, so he or she knows the basis on which it was produced. Second, the cyclical nature of the process means that repeated observations are made that will soon reveal any errors in judgement that may have been made.

Summative assessment

Assessment that serves a summative purpose indicates individual children's achievement at a certain time. It summarises learning at that time and is used to give this information to others, mainly parents, other teachers, and the children. Assessment for this purpose may take place frequently, as in a regular weekly test (more usual in mathematics or language learning than in science), or more commonly at the end of each term or year. As just indicated, an important difference between summative and formative assessment lies not so much in the way of gathering evidence as in the use made of it. The process is not cyclical and the information does not have an immediate impact on future learning experiences, although it may do so in the longer term. Further, since the end point is to be a summary, in a readily communicable form, the degree of detail about each aspect of achievement is necessarily limited. These and other differences are evident from comparing Figure 8.1 with Figure 8.2.

The differences arise from the purposes of these two types of assessment. Formative assessment is both generated and used by the same people – teachers themselves, with child involvement where possible. This is not the case with summative assessment. Those receiving reports summarising achievement need to be

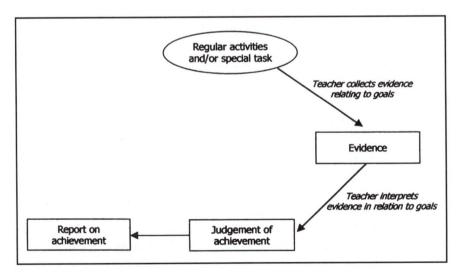

Figure 8.2   The roles and procedures for summative assessment

assured that the information is reliable so that, if necessary, children can be fairly compared with each other. This means that the basis for making the judgement of evidence has to be the same. Child-referencing is not appropriate and the judgement has to be in terms of criteria related to the goals. (It could also be norm-referenced, but this gives much less direct information about what has been achieved.)

The need for reliable judgement in summative assessment also reduces the involvement of children in the process. Although some involvement is beneficial, for the same reasons as given in the case of formative assessment, ultimately the judgement must be reliable and it is the teacher's responsibility to ensure fairness in judgements for all the children. This is particularly important if the assessment is to be used by other teachers or schools for selection or grouping by achievement.

Using evidence from formative assessment in summative assessment

As Figure 8.2 suggests, the evidence used in summative assessment can come from a review of what has been achieved over the period being reported on, or from a special task or test given at the end of this period. Or it can be a combination of the two. In some procedures teachers' ongoing assessment is used to indicate achievement and this is then confirmed by a test. In others, there is a combination of teachers' assessment and testing, with a certain weighting given to each part. Generally, when teachers' judgements are used there is some procedure for moderation, or quality assurance, built in.

The particular combination of evidence from different sources will govern the extent to which the full range of goals can be covered by the assessment. Testing will only be able to cover a limited range, whilst teachers' assessment will have all the richness of the evidence used for formative assessment. If the formative assessment is used, an important distinction has to be made here between the *evidence* and *judgement*. The judgements made in formative assessment take account of individual progress as well as the intended goals, and so are not comparable between children. So if evidence gathered and used in formative assessment is also used for summative assessment, it has to be reviewed and judged in terms of progress towards the goals only. (The relationship between formative and summative judgements is discussed further in Chapter 13.)

Essentials of summative assessment

To summarise, the characteristics of summative assessment are that:

- it takes place at certain intervals when achievement is to be reported
- it relates to progression in learning judged against publicly available criteria
- it gives results for different children that are based on the same criteria and so can be compared and combined if required
- it requires methods that are as reliable as possible without endangering validity
- it involves some quality assurance procedures.

Using assessment for school evaluation and target-setting

Using assessment of children's achievement for this purpose is controversial, but nevertheless widespread. It involves summarising information about pupil assessment to form an average score, level or standard for groups of children. Average pupil performance is a product not just of the school, but of out-of-school influences, such as the social and educational home background of the pupils. One approach to allowing for this is to take into account pupils' achievement on entering school and calculating a measure of 'value-added' by the school, but this requires a measure of earlier achievement and leads to more testing. Currently many schemes for 'baseline' assessment (of children at or near to entry to formal primary school) have been created. These are claimed to serve a double purpose, of providing information about the strengths and needs of new entrants to school and of constituting a baseline from which to measure the improvement in achievement at a later stage of schooling.

The ways in which evidence about children's achievement is gathered for school evaluation is influenced by the use made of the information produced. If it is for internal use within the school, there is less pressure to rely on tests and more willingness to use the richer information available from teachers' judgements than if the assessment data are to be used by outsiders. If information is used to make comparisons between schools on the basis of pupil performance then there will be a demand for 'visible' reliability, resulting in a move towards formal testing rather than the use of teachers' judgements.

The greater the impact on status, reputation and support for the school, the more attention is given to reliability and hence the dependence on test data rather than teachers' judgements. Thus the process is usually as represented in Figure 8.3.

Points to note about assessment based on tests for this purpose are that:

- the teacher's role is confined to administering a test and either marking it according to a set scheme or sending the children's test papers away for external marking
- although marking may be a burden, at least it provides the teacher with information about where the children did and did not succeed. If the papers are externally marked, the teacher does not have the benefit of this feedback
- children have no part in this assessment and it is separate from their normal activities. The emphasis in fairness is such that formal test conditions are likely to be imposed, often creating anxiety in some children
- since the amount of time for which it is reasonable to test children is limited, the information is bound to be only a small sample of what the children can do, and the more easily assessed parts of it.

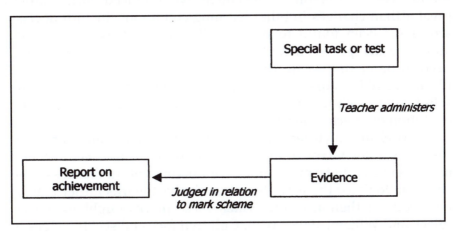

Figure 8.3 The roles and procedures for assessment used for school evaluation

Recently the use of assessment data for target-setting for schools has been presented as a means to improve schools' effectiveness. Its more immediate impact, however, is to focus attention on children's achievement in the tests that are used to set targets and to measure whether targets have been met. Similarly, when test results are used to compare school with school, high priority is inevitably given to ensuring good performance in the test. The dangers of this have often been pointed out. Teaching to the test, particularly tests that only assess knowledge and not skills (as in the case of the standard achievement tests in science for 11-year-olds in England and Wales) distorts children's learning experiences. It also emphasises the summative role of assessment and deflects attention from the important formative role.

It is appropriate, then, to end this chapter by returning to assessment for learning. There is strong evidence of its effect on learning, providing that certain essential features are included in its implementation.

The case for improved formative assessment

An extensive review of research on classroom assessment published in 1998 by Black and Wiliam (1998a, 1998b) concluded that 'formative assessment is an essential feature of classroom work and the development of it can raise standards' (Black and Wiliam 1998a, p. 19). This emerged from studies where various steps had been taken to strengthen formative assessment, and which had explored the conditions under which the greatest effects were found. The effects on achievement were indeed large, much greater than changes in other learning conditions, including class size, have been found to produce. The research was clear, too, about the changes to current practice in classroom assessment that need to be made to gain the benefits which are there to be had. Black and Wiliam discuss these changes under three headings: the self-esteem of children; self-assessment by the children; and the evolution of effective teaching.

The way in which teachers feed back their judgements to children was a key factor in relation to children's self-esteem. Where judgements are in terms of grades or ranking within the class, then children 'look for the ways to obtain the best marks rather than at the needs of their learning which these marks ought to reflect' (Black and Wiliam, 1998a, p. 9). Children focus on seeking clues to the 'right' answer and the easiest way to get the best marks. Meanwhile those who get low marks or ranking feel discouraged and may take these judgements as indicating a limit to their ability and give up trying to improve. To avoid these negative effects, feedback should be given about how the work could be improved, with no judgemental grade, or mark. Even giving praise is less effective than a constructive comment about the work, because when praise is given, children do not attend to any other comments that are made.

The research evidence gave strong support for children being involved in self-assessment. This should involve children knowing what the desired goals of particular activities are, of being able to recognise where they are in relation to these goals and knowing how to take further steps towards achieving them. There is not a great deal of good practice in these matters but Black and Wiliam (1998a, p. 10) claim that: 'When pupils do acquire such an overview, they then become more committed and more effective as learners: their own assessments become an object of discussion with their teachers and with one another, and this promotes even further that reflection on one's own ideas that is essential to good learning.' Some aspects of practice that were identified as effective in improving formative assessment were: including formative assessment in planning; teachers' questioning; and dialogue between children and teacher that encourages thoughtful responses, explores understanding and gives all children the chance to express their ideas.

Summary

This chapter has defined assessment as a process in which evidence about achievement is collected systematically, judged and communicated for various purposes. Three purposes of assessment have been discussed and compared: formative, summative and evaluative. The procedures for formative assessment have been given most attention and set out in terms of a cycle of procedures involving collecting, interpreting and using evidence about children's learning to help progress towards achievement of goals. The wholeness of the process has been emphasised, so that this can be kept in mind as we consider separate parts of it in the next chapters.

Finally, reference was made to research evidence that indicates the potential for improving children's achievement through enhancing formative assessment. This has also helped to identify the key features of providing feedback in a way that preserves children's self-esteem, involving children in self-assessment and teacher interventions that promote children's thinking and reflection.

Points for reflection

- How can teachers use assessment to inform teaching and learning yet avoid making the children feel that they are being assessed all the time?
- Can giving positive, non-judgmental, feedback to children on their work be reconciled with the award of 'stars' or other signs of approval?

Further reading

The pamphlet Beyond the Black Box (1998, available from the School of Education, King's College, University of London) summarises the outcomes of the extensive review of research by P. Black and D. Wiliam (1998) entitled 'Assessment and classroom learning', in *Assessment in Education*, **5** (1).

A further pamphlet, Assessment for Learning (1999, available from the School of Education, University of Cambridge) suggests action needed to increase the quality of formative assessment in practice.

9

Gathering evidence about children's learning

This chapter is concerned with how to carry out the first stage in the cycle of formative assessment: ways of gathering the evidence, which is then interpreted to form a judgement about where children are in relation to goals of learning. We will deal with the procedures for interpreting the evidence in Chapter 10. Here we first consider the various methods teachers can use for gathering evidence about children's ideas, process skills and attitudes. Most of these methods could be used for both formative and summative assessment, since the distinction between these purposes of assessment, as suggested in the last chapter, depends not on how evidence is gathered, but on how it is interpreted and used. The exceptions are some tasks and tests that are designed to sum up achievement and have greater value for assessment with a summative role than for formative assessment. These are discussed in Chapter 13.

The second section of the chapter emphasises the importance of planning to gather evidence for assessment as part of lesson planning, and suggests an approach to this planning. Finally, we look at ways of involving children in their own assessment.

Gathering evidence about children's ideas

Although there is some overlap between methods that can be used to gain access to children's ideas, on the one hand, and their skills and attitudes on the other, there are sufficient differences to make it worthwhile to consider each separately. We begin with children's ideas. Methods used here are mainly:

1 Listening to the words children use.
2 Questioning and discussing.
3 Studying non-written products.
4 Asking for drawings and writing.
5 Using concept maps.

Listening

Paying attention to the words children use when talking whilst they are working in groups gives evidence of how they are representing things to themselves. For example, words such as 'melt', 'dissolve', 'disappear' might be heard in activities on the solubility of substances and the way in which they are used indicates the meaning they have for the children. The teacher in the example at the end of Chapter 7 heard the fabrics being variously described as 'manufactured', 'natural', 'see-through', 'strong'. The children's meaning for words such as these needs clarifying and the teacher might well do this by questioning later rather than interrupt the flow of activity at the time.

Questioning and discussing

Certain types of teachers' question are more effective than others in revealing evidence of children's ideas. The most effective forms of question for this purpose are open and person-centred questions.

Open questions invite an extended response, as opposed to closed ones, to which there is a short or one-word answer. This means that questions to which the only answers are 'yes' or 'no' are unlikely to be useful. A question such as 'what difference do you think it will make if the water is stirred?' is preferable to 'Will the salt dissolve more quickly if the water is stirred?'

Person-centred questions are phrased to ask directly for the children's ideas, not the 'right' answer. So, a question such as 'Why do you think the cress grows better in this soil' is preferable to 'Why does the cress grow better in this soil?'

So the teacher's questions in the fabrics investigation (p. 103) would be:

- What is it about these materials that made you decide that they are manufactured?
- What do you think this was before it was made into this piece of cloth?

These kinds of questions are also very relevant in the discussion after practical work to help children reflect more consciously on the meaning of what they have found. They also help to reveal the extent to which ideas have been changed:

- Why did you think that one would be most wind-proof?
- What do you think it is about materials that make them water-proof?

Studying non-written products

There are often products or artefacts at several stages of children's activity and all have the potential to indicate children's ideas. For example, the way a bridge is constructed to support something, the shape of a boat moulded from plasticine, or the way in which fabrics were put together in piles in the fabric-sorting activity. These things alone may not provide very reliable evidence, but they alert the teacher to discuss with the children their reasons for doing things in certain ways and these reveal their ideas.

Children's drawing and writing

Children's drawing, which may not at first seem to give particularly rich information about their ideas, can be made to do so if they are asked to draw not just what they see, but what they think is happening or what makes something work. The drawing in Figure 4.6 (on p. 45) might well have shown just the container of water with the level going down had the children been asked to 'draw what happened', but instead the request was 'draw what you think made the water go down'. Framing a drawing task in a way that requires children to express their ideas makes a very great difference to the value of the drawing to both pupil and teacher. Figure 9.1 shows a considerable insight into a child's ideas about the needs of living things through asking for a drawing of 'where you think would be the best place for a snail to live'.

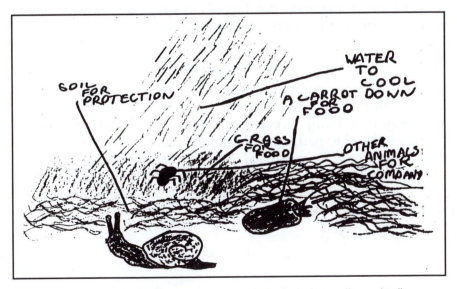

Figure 9.1   A young child's drawing (teacher annotated) of what snails need to live
Source: Unpublished SPACE research

For young children expressing ideas through drawings, with labels, may not be easy, of course, but it is then useful for the teacher to discuss the drawing with the child and to annotate it as a result of asking questions (as was done in Figure 9.1).

In the same way, children's writing may be made more productive for revealing children's ideas if the task requires ideas to be expressed. The same request which led to the drawing in Figure 9.1 led another child to produce the piece of writing in Figure 9.2.

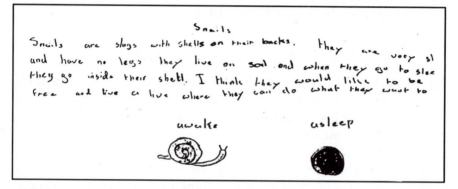

Figure 9.2 Ideas about snails and what they do

Accounts of investigations also reveal information about ideas, providing the children are encouraged to reflect upon and not just report their findings. All too often, however, the account describes events somewhat uncritically. The account in Figure 9.3 by an 11-year-old, whilst it shows some understanding of insulation, makes no comment on the apparent rise in temperature during cooling of one of the cups.

Concept maps

Concept mapping has various meanings. In this context it is concerned with making links between concepts. As such it is a very direct way of gaining access to children's ideas, but needs to be carefully tailored to particular children to ensure that they are familiar with the words that are used. The approach is to represent relationships between words by means of arrows, thus 'ice' and 'water' are two words that can be linked to form a proposition which expresses the relationship between them:

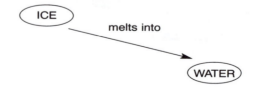

The arrow indicates the direction of the relationship; reversing it would mean 'water melts into ice' which does not make sense. When several concepts are linked together, the relationships form a web or map. The process is very easy even for the youngest children to grasp and the product gives some insight into the way they

<u>Water Experiment</u>

Donald, Sharon and I did an experiment to see which material could keep water hottest.

We had four polystyrene cups and filled them with hot water. We put a different material over each one. We put polystyrene over one, polythene over another, cotton wool on another, and aluminium over the last.

We left it for five minutes and checked the temperature with a thermometer.

The foil was 50°, so were the polythene and the polystyrene, but the cotton wool was only 40°C.

After another five minutes the cotton wool was the same, but the other three had fallen.

We left them a further five minutes to get a final result.

Aluminium foil came out at 41°C, the cotton wool had risen to 43°C and the polystyrene and the polythene were equal at 45°C.

This shows that the polythene and polystyrene are best.

I think polystyrene was best as it started off at 50°C and fell by only two or three degrees at a time.

I think the polystyrene being best could of had something to do with the cups also being made from polystyrene.

Insulation is good because it saves energy. If something isn't heated, it needs heated more often, but if something is insulated, heat can not escape so easily.

Figure 9.3 An 11-year-old's account of an investigation of insulation

associate things together or see cause and effect. In some cases it helps to have the words written on cards so that they can be moved around. Arrows, also on cards, can be laid between words the children want to join. It is important for the linking words to be written, either by the child, or by the teacher on behalf of the child, because it is the nature of the link that gives the clue to the way the child is making sense of the things.

The map in Figure 9.4 was drawn by a 6-year-old, Lennie. After some activities about heat, the teacher listed words which they had been using and then asked the children to draw arrows to link them together and write 'joining words' on the arrows. From reading Lennie's map it would appear that he has useful ideas about the effects of heat but sees a thermometer as measuring both heat and temperature and has not distinguished between these two. Although this is to be expected from a child of this age, to be sure of the interpretation it would be necessary to talk through his map

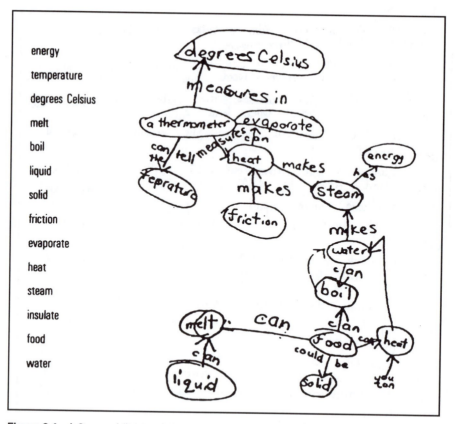

Figure 9.4 A 6-year-old's concept map
Source: Harlen *et al.* (1990, p. 13.7)

with him. As with drawings, the value of the product is greater if it is a basis for discussion between teacher and child.

Informal research reported by Atkinson and Bannister (1998) compared the information about their ideas from children's annotated drawings with that from concept maps. The study confirmed that concept mapping can be useful even with very young children. It also suggested that, in general, the older and more able children can express more ideas through concepts maps and the younger and less able express more ideas through annotated drawings.

Gathering evidence about process skills

Process skills and attitudes show in what children think and do. In some cases the products of this thought and action are useful indicators of the skills that have been used. In other cases, particularly for young children, it is necessary to observe the action as it takes place. But what is observed may not be easy to interpret without asking about, for example, why things were done in certain ways. Thus gathering evidence about process skills and attitudes is likely to require a combination of:

1 Observing children's actions.
2 Questioning and discussing.
3 Studying written work designed to reveal the use of process skills and attitudes.

Observing children's actions

Observing all the individual children in a whole class is a formidable task and is indeed an impossible one to accomplish at any one time. It becomes possible through planning and focusing. *Planning,* as suggested later, should be used to ensure that evidence is collected about different groups of children at different times. In any single activity one group is the target for detailed observation, whilst the teacher interacts as normal with all groups. Planning is taken up later in the next section of this chapter.

Focusing involves having a mental checklist of what to look for. Such a checklist could be derived from the list of process skills and attitudes which are the goals of learning science. It might take the form of questions such as:

• Does the child raise questions?
• Does the child attempt to explain things (develop hypotheses)?

- Does the child make predictions?
- . . . and so on.

This would require a considerable amount of interpretation by the teacher for each question. It would certainly be difficult to give a decided 'yes' or 'no' to these questions. What does 'making predictions' mean in terms of what the children might be doing? Does it mean the same for children at, say, the age of 7 as for children at the age of 11? Further, different meaning given to words such as 'hypotheses' might mean that evidence of different kinds might be collected by different teachers.

Having more detailed statements for each item, although making the list very long, can help by:

- making it a little more certain that we all mean the same thing when we say a child is able to do something (although there can never be certainty about this, here or in other contexts)
- giving more specific help about what to look for as evidence of skills being used
- indicating different points in the development of skills.

An example of an expanded list designed to serve these purposes is given in Harlen and Jelly (1997). The list for 'interpreting' is as follows:

Do the children:
- discuss what they find in relation to their initial questions?
- compare their findings with their earlier predictions?
- notice associations between changes in one variable and another?
- identify patterns or trends in their results?
- check any patterns or trends against all the evidence?
- draw conclusions which summarise and are consistent with the evidence?
- recognise that any conclusions may have to be changed in the light of new evidence?

(Harlen and Jelly, 1997, p. 56–7)

These statements describe a range of behaviours that are encompassed within the meaning of interpreting and drawing conclusions. Those near the beginning of this list describe behaviours that are likely to be developed earlier than those later in the list. Having read this list, an observer will have in mind a range of more specific things to look for than will be the case with only the title 'interpreting' as a focus. Moreover, by gathering evidence to answer these questions it will probably be found that at some point in working down the list, the 'yeses' turn into 'nos'. The evidence is thus being used to decide the point in development of the process skill.

A full list of questions relating to all the skills and attitude goals, based on this approach, is given on pp. 147–152 in Chapter 10 since they have an important role in interpreting evidence as well as in focusing observations.

Teachers who have used this approach in various ways find a preference for studying the questions before and after observing children, but *not* using them as a list to refer to during lessons. Using the questions beforehand focuses observation on significant aspects of children's activities. During the classroom work, all that a teacher can reasonably do is to make a mental note, and in some cases a note on paper, of relevant evidence. After the lesson the list is used to decide where there was evidence of the various aspects being shown. Of course, there is not necessarily evidence in every investigation of all aspects; the evidence has to be accumulated over several different kinds of activity. Becoming familiar with this approach takes time and experience shows that it is helpful to begin by selecting only a couple of process skills as a start and gradually extending the list as the items become internalised.

Such lists should be an aid not a burden. The detail is needed since it enables the teacher to identify the help which children may need in developing their process skills. For summarising achievement (summative assessment) this amount of detail is not needed but the questions serve as indicators of the type of evidence that enables more general criteria to be used for that purpose (see p. 200).

Questioning and discussing

The observation of children's actions does not always indicate their thinking and it may often be necessary to ask for some explanation. It would be inappropriate constantly to interrupt practical work to ask 'why are you doing it that way?' for the answer often emerges in what children do subsequently in any case. But occasionally it helps to clarify the intention behind an action when going over the activity after it has been completed. For example, when some children were dropping balls on to different surfaces to see if the surface made any difference to the rebound, the teacher noticed that the balls were held at the same height each time. Later he asked the child 'How did you decide where to hold your hand when you dropped the balls?' The answer came back in terms of convenience in relation to the height of the table; there had been no deliberate decision to control this variable, as might well have been assumed.

Children's written work

The records and reports that children write will add to the information obtained by observation. However, rarely do the reports of primary children indicate the detail that is needed to judge the extent to which various skills have been used. For example, in the investigation of materials described earlier, p. 103, one group of girls took eight pieces of different kinds of material and compared them by rubbing them against the ground. The teacher observed that they chose the same piece of ground to test all the materials and they counted the number of rubs it took to make a hole. They kept to the same procedures and the same person rubbing. This method took a considerable time, however, and Michelle suggested it would be quicker if they put a stone inside the material. So they wrapped each sample round a stone and started again. Their results were entered in a table drawn up for them by the teacher. Figure 9.5 shows the results recorded by Michelle's group.

At first the children used the results in Figure 9.5 to conclude that 'natural material is better than man-made' but later, after discussing their results with their teacher, they wrote:

> 'We don't know what's the best Material because when we done our second test Natural got the most points And man-made got the least points. But man-made material got the most point's with our first test so we think Man-made and Natural have strong points.'

The written work alone gives no information about the extent to which they attempted to control variables or how they came to their first conclusion. The discussion with the teacher caused them to have second thoughts about this. Through the discussion the teacher was able to judge their use of evidence in arriving at conclusions and, with the data from observation, collected a good deal of information which enabled him to see where these girls needed more experience.

Planning for assessment as part of teaching

Gathering information when the appropriate opportunity is there – and thus avoiding having to set up special tasks – means planning the assessment as part of the lesson planning. The plan should take account of the *frequency of opportunities* for assessing different aspects and the potential for using the information:

- Opportunities for children to use process skills and attitudes arise frequently.

Natural	Rubs	Manmade	Rubs
felt (wool)	20	cotton + polyester	108
rubber	210	Viscose	57
cotton	67	Satin	20
linen	15	nylon	2

rubber was the strogest material it took 210 rubs. Nylon was the weakest material it took two rubs rubber took 208 rubs more than nylon

Figure 9.5 One group's results from the fabric activity

- Opportunities to develop specific ideas occur only when relevant content is being investigated and so arise less frequently.

Planning to assess process skills and attitudes

Most science activities should involve children in thinking and doing, and thus provide the teacher with opportunities to assess and children to help to develop process skills. All activities should involve children in thinking and using most of the process skills. If this is not the case then there is a need for serious evaluation of the learning opportunities being provided. But assuming that there are *frequent opportunities*, this means that it is not necessary to assess all children at a particular time. As we have seen, observation is a key to assessing skills, supplemented by discussion and studying written work. It is better to observe a small number of children thoroughly throughout an activity so as to achieve a detailed picture of their skills than to attempt to cover a larger number more superficially.

It may take two or three months to complete the observation of all children in the class, and it will mean that different children are assessed when carrying out different activities. This is not a problem in the context of formative assessment, for two main reasons. First, since no comparison is being made between children then, providing the activities give opportunity for the skills to be used, one activity context is as good as another. If the purpose were to assign a grade or label to the children then the variation in content of the activities would be a source of error in the results, but when observations can be repeated and the purpose is to help the children's learning, it is not a problem. Second, the skills we are concerned with are ones which are assumed to be generally applicable and so, again, it is the case that one context is as valid as another, given that they provide similar opportunity for skills to be used. This is not to deny that the context influences the use of skills, however. With this in mind it should be emphasised that no single activity is sufficient to give a reliable assessment. Observations should be made during various activities over a period of time.

Focusing on a small target group at one time does not mean that other children are neglected. The children will be unaware of when they are targets, for the teacher interacts with all children in the normal way. When interacting with the targets, he or she will observe, question and probe with the indicators in mind and interpret this evidence after the event.

Planning to assess children's ideas

When it comes to assessing children's ideas, the opportunities are far *less frequent*. Ideas are linked to the subject-matter and particular ideas will tend to be expressed in activities relating to the appropriate subject-matter. Thus the opportunities to assess ideas have to be taken when they occur. This means assessing as many pupils as are working on that subject-matter at any one time. Fortunately it is far more feasible to use the products of children's work for assessing ideas than it is for assessing process skills. Children's reports, other writing and drawing and other products can be collected and studied after the event. This is not to deny the importance of the context, which should be noted, and the added value that comes if the work can be discussed with the pupils.

Groups or individuals?

In referring to a group of children here there is some ambiguity about whether the evidence is gathered about the group as a whole or about individual children. Teachers generally have no difficulty in identifying the separate contributions of children even when they are combining their ideas and skills in a group enterprise. But, we might question whether, *for the purpose of informing teaching*, it is always necessary to assess individual pupils. If the information is used to make decisions about the activities and help to be given to children as *a group*, then assessment of the group is all that is needed for this purpose. For group work, differences between children are not a disadvantage, since, as reported on p. 101, there is convincing evidence that in heterogeneous groups all pupils benefit when they are encouraged to share ideas and skills. Thus a group assessment may be considered to be all that is necessary where the activity is genuinely collaborative and ideas are pooled. Evidence of the achievements of individuals can be found from the products of their work and discussion of these products.

Involving children in formative self-assessment

One of the factors associated with good practice in assessment, as revealed from the review of research by Black and Wiliam, mentioned on p. 120, is the involvement of children in self-assessment. This should not come as a surprise since it was recognised by Her Majesty's Inspectorate (HMI) in an early study of the implementation of the requirements of the Education Reform Act, that effective practice included 'the involvement of pupils in both setting their learning objectives and assessing their achievements' (DES, 1991, p. 10).

The evidence and arguments in favour of self-assessment have only strengthened in recent years. The most compelling is probably the effect of achievement that Black and Wiliam revealed, as reported in Chapter 8. The particular value for low-achieving children (within the context of benefit for all children), and thus the promise of reducing the range of achievement in an age group, is worth reinforcing. The theoretical arguments as to why this works all point to the importance of the active involvement of the learner if any learning is to take place. If children know what they should be trying to achieve, then the teaching is more likely to be effective in producing this learning. Teachers themselves plan with both long-term and short-term objectives in mind, so why do they not share these with the children? The answer may be related to the following points:

- The view of teaching and learning held by the teacher: as we have argued in Chapter 1, this has a profound effect on classroom decisions. If the view of teaching and learning is that these are matters of transmission and reception, the child's role is a passive one. But if learning is regarded as an active process, that is in the control of the learner rather than the teacher, the learner needs to know how to direct his or her effort.
- The difficulty of communicating learning objectives particularly to young children in ways that they are likely to understand.
- Self-assessment requires ability to stand back and reflect on learning (meta-cognitive skills) and young children may not be able to do this in the same way as can be expected of older learners.

The first of these points suggests that sharing goals and self-assessment have to become part of the role that the teacher encourages children to take in their learning. If it goes no further than, say, children marking their own tests of arithmetic or spelling, then they may gain the impression that all that is important is learning by rote and getting the answers right. The other two points indicate that ways have to be found of communicating goals and standards of quality of work that are suitable for the 5–12 age range. These things cannot be communicated directly and an approach through concrete examples has been found effective, illustrated in these ideas from practice.

Discussing 'best work'

One teacher described an approach which can be used with children from about the age of 8. It begins with the children selecting their 'best' work to put into a folder or bag. Part of the time for 'bagging' should be set aside for the teacher to talk to each child about why certain pieces of work have been selected. During this discussion the way in which the children are judging the quality of their work will become clear. These are accepted without comment, whether or not they reflect the teacher's view of good work. They may have messages for the teacher. For example, if work seems to be selected only on the basis of being 'tidy' and not in terms of content, then perhaps this aspect is being overemphasised.

At first the discussion served to clarify the criteria the children use. 'Tell me what you particularly liked about this piece of work?' Gradually it will be possible to suggest criteria without dictating what the children should be selecting. This can be done through comments on the work. 'That was a very good way of showing your results, I could see at a glance which was best.' 'I'm glad you think that was your best investigation because although you didn't get the result you expected, you did it very carefully and made sure that the result was fair.'

Discussing the purpose of activities

Another example is the teacher who regularly discusses with the children the purpose of their activities, so that they know where to focus their attention. She sometimes does this in general terms with the whole class at the start, reinforcing it in discussion with groups later and identifying more specific targets to suit individual children. Sometime she does not give her ideas at the start about what is to be learned, but waits for the children to begin their exploration and then ask them what they could find out. The discussion goes beyond the details of the activities and extends to 'what will you be learning if you do that?' The fact that this comes from the children means that it has been put in words that they understand.

Using examples

Communication of the quality, or standard, of work that is to be aimed for is difficult at any level. Teachers find it helpful to have standards exemplified by children's work, and in a similar way, these are also helpful to children. Indeed there is no reason why some of the examples produced for teachers in publications such as *Exemplification of Standards, Science at Key Stages 1 and 2, levels 1 to 5* (SCAA, 1995) and Performance Standards: National Standards (New Standards, 1997) should not be shared with children, to show what other children have done. This can avoid problems that might arise by discussing examples taken from the work of classmates. Sometimes it is useful not to have a 'model' example but to discuss shortcomings as well as the more positive aspects of a piece of work. A collection of pieces of work could be created for this purpose but it is best if the authors of the work cannot be identified. Teacher from different schools can often agree to exchange examples of work for this purpose.

Demonstrating what has been learned

Children can be challenged to show what they have learned. One teacher set the children to make a practical test to give to each other to test their knowledge of simple circuits. The tasks were far harder than the teacher would have given. All the children, those setting and responding to the tasks, not only enjoyed this challenge but extended their learning in the process.

Feedback on children's work

Involving children in self-assessment for formative purposes means that they need to know how to improve their work. Feedback from the teacher is an important vehicle for this. However, as noted on p. 120, its effectiveness depends on the form of the feedback. Judgemental comments are seized upon by children and focus attention on how well they have done rather than on what they now need to do. One teacher noticed a considerable change in her children's motivation once she avoided giving any indication of judgement in her written comments on their work. She keeps all judgemental comments in her own records and feeds back to the children suggestions as to what to do next or questions that help them link what they found to other experiences. The children's work then becomes a medium for genuine communication between teacher and pupil.

For example, Andrea's account of dropping balls of plasticine of different weights (in Figure 9.6) seemed to leave some ambiguity in

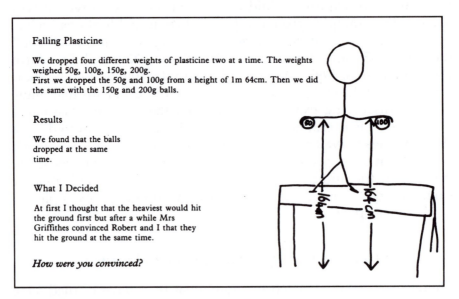

Figure 9.6   Andrea's report with teacher's question

Alarms
For our first experiment we made an ordinary switch. We needed a thin piece of balsa wood, six crocodile clips with plastic covered wire, a bulb, a bulb holder and a battery.
We nailed two paper fasteners through the copper strips and through the wood.

Then we connected the wire

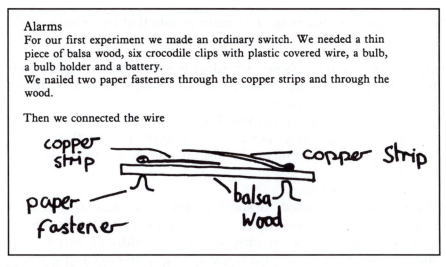

Figure 9.7 Andrea's account of how she made a switch

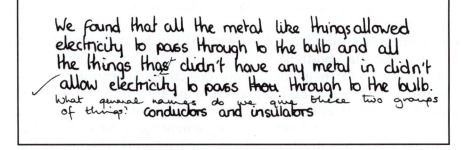

Figure 9.8 Question and answer on Andrea's work

the mind of her teacher. The question 'How were you convinced?' was written to remind both of them to clear this up.

In other parts of Andrea's work there are several examples of the teacher's question being answered in writing. At the end of the piece about the switch in Figure 9.7 the teacher wrote 'Connected it to what?' Before writing anything else in her notebook, Andrea answered this question.

Later Andrea tested several materials in a simple circuit. The final section of her report is shown in Figure 9.8, including the teacher's question and Andrea's answer.

Summary

This chapter has discussed methods that can be used for the first stage of the formative assessment cycle, gathering evidence of children's progress in learning. The main points that have been made are:

- Opportunities to assess specific ideas have, of course, to be taken when topics involving those ideas are being studied. Methods that can be used include:
    - paying attention to the words children use
    - questioning, using open and person-centred questions
    - studying the products of children's work: artefacts, writing, drawings
    - concept mapping.
- Process skills are used to some extent in all activities and so opportunities for assessment are more frequent, but teachers have to rely more heavily on observation of children's actions, although information can also come from questioning and discussing, and from written work.
- In order to ensure that information is gathered and used when opportunities arise, it has to be planned as part of lesson planning.
- In some cases the focus of assessment can be the group rather than individual children.
- Involving children in identifying objectives of learning, in assessing their own progress and knowing how to move forward are important to effective formative assessment. Reasons for this have been given and ways of implementing it have been discussed under five headings: discussing best work, discussing the purpose of activities, using examples, demonstrating what has been learned, feedback on children's work.

Points for reflection

- Are some methods of gathering evidence more suitable than others for gathering evidence about children's ideas in particular areas, for example, in relation to rocks and soil, energy, living things?
- If evidence about process skills is gathered by observing different groups at different times, this means that they will be working on different activities. How important is this and how might it affect the use that can be made of the evidence?

Further reading

SCRE (1995) *Taking a Closer Look at Science*, Edinburgh: Scottish Council for Research in Education (SCRE), provides examples of children's work with comments on aspects that signify achievements and indicate likely next steps.

National Research Council (1996) *National Science Education Standards.* Washington: NRC.

The ACER (Australian Council for Educational Research) published an Assessment Resource Kit (ARK) which includes M. Forster and G. Masters (1997) *Assessment Methods*, Camberwell, Victoria, ACER, giving ideas that are useful for assessment in all areas of the curriculum.

10

Interpreting evidence for formative assessment

The evidence gathered by the methods suggested in the last chapter will remain as a collection of disconnected events and products until it is interpreted in some way. Both formative and summative assessment require the teacher to interpret and make a judgement of the evidence in order to use it in teaching or to report on children's progress. It is not particularly helpful to know that a child has done this, but not that, or that this child knows more about something than that child unless we know how these things are related to the goals of learning. More informative, both for the teacher and the recipient of any report, is to be able to see where each child is in the course of progression towards certain ideas, skills and attitudes.

In this chapter we look at how judgements of evidence are made for formative assessment. As noted in Chapter 8, judgements in formative assessment are made by comparing evidence with indicators of progress towards goals, but also take account of realistic expectations for a particular child. That is, these judgements are partly criterion-referenced and partly child-referenced. Moreover, since the purpose of the assessment is to help learning, the more detail there is to guide next steps, the better. By contrast, summative assessment requires evidence to be judged in relation to the same criteria for all children and to be less detailed. These differences mean that it is best to consider interpretation for these two purposes separately and the discussion in relation to summative assessment is taken up in Chapter 13.

Interpretation in order to decide next steps means that the course of development has to have been identified. Issues involved in doing this and examples of maps of progression are discussed. The final part of this chapter provides a series of 'indicators of development' and suggested procedures for using them to identify where children have reached in progress towards the goals of learning science and to point to next steps.

Progression in learning

Development, experience or teaching?

The important point to keep in mind is that formative assessment is carried out to decide the next step in learning. This statement embodies the view that learning is progressive and that there is a typical and identifiable progression in development of skills and ideas. Not everyone agrees that this is the case.

Progression in process skills

Skills and attitudes are always applied in relation to some content which influences their deployment. It is not difficult to show, by considering extreme cases, that the influence could be quite large. For example, an 11-year-old who is able to find and use patterns in data concerning the girth of trees and their height might not be able to pick out patterns in the chemical properties of elements that explain their arrangement in groups. It would be unreasonable to judge the 11-year-old's pattern-finding ability in the latter context, but quite reasonable to do so for a 17-year-old studying chemistry.

Because of this context dependency, some people argue that skills do not develop, and that children become progressively more able to deploy them in relation to more complex content and a wider range of situations. However, evidence supporting the notion of development of process skills has come from research and from classroom experience where children are using skills with familiar content. For example, the APU findings gave evidence of how children's competence in using inquiry skills develops. There is undoubtedly a need for more systematic study to determine more reliably the course of progression in skills. Meanwhile the questions offered in the second part of this chapter for helping to focus and to interpret observations of children's process skills make use of the evidence and experience currently available.

Progression in ideas

In the case of children's ideas, the question of progression is again controversial, but for different reasons. The question of whether, say, concepts concerning living things develop earlier or later than those about magnets or circuits, is futile. This will depend entirely on when and how these topics are encountered. Arranging them in a curriculum sequence is a matter of convention and convenience rather than of developmental considerations. Recalling Bruner's comment (Chapter 6, p. 70), all that is necessary to teach anything at any stage is to present the topic through activities that take account of children's ways of thinking. But, development of ideas within a topic depends on more than the order in which they are taught. For example, ideas about sound are typically developed within the 5–12 age range in this sequence:

- Sounds are heard through our ears.
- Sounds are produced by vibrating objects.
- Pitch and loudness depend on the way that the source vibrates.
- Sound can travel through different materials and through some better than others.
- Sound transfers energy and can be changed into other forms of energy.

The order of acquiring the first three of these ideas might well be a result of teaching in a particular sequence. Sequences that seem logical to adults are built into curriculum materials, and they ensure that there is some rationale for the order in which topics are encountered and thus for deciding appropriate next steps at a particular point. These sequences are no less useful for formative assessment within a topic on account of being the result of teaching rather than some underlying cognitive development. However, the fourth idea, the notion of sound travelling through different materials, brings together a number of ideas from difference experiences. The fifth one, 'sound as energy', is an even bigger idea that requires ideas about energy to be linked with earlier ideas about sound. Thus there is an overall sequence here in the degree of abstraction and breadth of application of the idea.

Similarly, looking across the various concepts discussed in Chapter 4, the development can be seen as one of creating bigger, more encompassing ideas that explain a wide range of related phenomena from the earlier, smaller, ideas that explain only a few particular instances. It is this overall development that we should be seeking to describe and assist through formative assessment

Mapping development

In order to find out where children are in development of ideas, skills and attitudes, and to use this information to identify next steps, we need to have mapped this development. The evidence required to do this comes from a combination of:

- the experience of classroom teachers and subject specialists
- research into children's learning
- information about achievements of children at different ages and stages obtained by survey and monitoring programmes.

There is never enough firm information from these sources, however, and the course of development that is mapped out is tentative and always subject to refinement in the light of new evidence. The products have been described in various ways; an Australian project calls them 'progress maps' (Masters and Forster, 1996). Figure 10.1 is an example of a progress map of increasing achievement in number.

In Figure 10.1 there is no indication of levels or stages or relating to age; just a description of how increasing competence with number is likely to develop. Masters and Forster cite as other examples of progress maps, the sequence of level of attainment in the National Curriculum, in the US National Assessment of Educational Progress

Increasing achivement in Number

Represents common fractions on a number line.
Uses place value to compare and order numbers.

Completely solves division problems by interpreting remainders.

Divides a whole number by a 1-digit number.
Subtracts one 3-digit number from another involving regrouping.
Recognises equivalent fractions. Continues number patterns.
Places whole numbers in order.
Subtracts one 3-digit number from another.
Partly solves division problems by interpreting remainders.

Multiplies by a 1-digit number.
Interprets whole numbers written in words and uses a calculator to add whole numbers.

Represents word problems as number sentences.
Uses a calculator to subtract whole numbers.
Continues whole number patterns involving addition.
Adds 3-digit whole numbers. Multiplies small whole numbers.
Subtracts small whole numbers.

Adds 2-digit whole numbers.

Figure 10.1 Example of a progress map for number
Source: Masters and Forster (1969)

(NAEP), the Benchmarks of the AAAS, the Australian Curriculum Profiles and similar profiles produced in Canada and Hong Kong (Masters and Forster, 1996). These authors emphasise that a progress map is:

- not a description of a path that all children will follow (it describes typical progress but no two students learning exactly the same way)
- not a prescription for a learning sequence (it indicates the kinds of learning activities, but not a specific sequence)
- not based on the assumption that a child will demonstrate all skills and understanding below their estimated level of achievement (but probably most from below and some from above)
- not based on a single theory of learning (but on the combination of sources of evidence suggested above)
- not a description of a purely 'natural' sequence of development (it is the result of the curriculum conventions as well as general mental development). (Adapted from Masters and Forster, 1996, p. 11).

These are points that it is important to keep in mind as we consider the following lists of 'indicators of development' which have been created to map development in the process skills, attitudes and areas of understanding identified as goals of science 5–12.

Indicators of development

The lists that follow on pages 147 to 155 attempt to map the development in the process skills, attitudes and eight areas of understanding in terms of what children can do. Under each heading, the items are arranged in a sequence that reflects typical progression. The sequences have been created from currently available information, but there is no guarantee that this will fit every child. Indeed the points made above about progress maps should be kept in mind.

In all the lists, the earlier statements indicate ideas or skills that are likely to be developed before those later in the lists. In the case of areas of understanding, the importance of children being able to use ideas, rather than just know the words, is conveyed in the leading question: 'can the children use these ideas?'

Although the range of the statement has been carefully chosen to be appropriate to the ages 5–12, no attempt has been made to identify where children of a certain age or stage within this range ought to have reached. *This is not necessary for formative assessment, where all that is needed is to see where children are in making progress* and where the next steps ought to take them. In Chapter 13 we will consider how evidence collected by the teacher and used for formative assessment might be reviewed and judged against standards or levels for summative purposes.

Using indicators of development

In Chapter 9 it was noted that the list of questions for process skills and attitudes have two roles in formative assessment: helping to focus observation on significant aspects of behaviour and helping to interpret observations after evidence has been collected. Their role in interpreting evidence is in fact wider than helping to interpret evidence gathered by observation, and extends to making judgements about evidence of all kinds. The same applies in the case of assessing children's ideas. The questions can be used to interpret the full range of different kinds of evidence of their understanding that can be found from children's talk, artefacts, writing and drawings. Evidence from all these sources can be used to decide:

- which of the questions in the lists of process skills and attitudes can be answered by 'yes'
- which of the ideas in the relevant lists of ideas children have shown that they can use.

Finding where the positive answers to the questions turn into negative ones – or more realistically, where it becomes difficult to say yes or no – locates the child's development within the map. Furthermore, and importantly, this process indicates the next step, which is to consolidate the skills and ideas around the area where 'yes' turns into 'no'. This pointer to where progress is to be made is the whole purpose of formative assessment.

Examples of indicators of development of process skills

Raising questions

Do the children:

1 Readily ask a variety of questions which include investigable and non-investigable ones?
2 Participate effectively in discussing how their questions can be answered?

3 Recognise a difference between an investigable question and one which cannot be answered by investigation?
4 Suggest how answers to questions of various kinds can be found?
5 Generally, in science, ask questions which are potentially investigable?
6 Help in turning their own questions into a form that can be tested?

Hypothesising

Do the children:

1 Attempt to give an explanation which is consistent with evidence, even if only in terms of the presence of certain features or circumstances?
2 Attempt to explain things in terms of a relevant idea from previous experience even if they go no further than naming it?
3 Suggest a mechanism for how something is brought about, even if it would be difficult to check?
4 Show awareness that there may be more than one explanation which fits the evidence?
5 Give explanations which suggest how an observed effect or situation is brought about and which could be checked?
6 Show awareness that all explanations are tentative and never proved beyond doubt?

Predicting

Do the children:

1 Attempt to make a prediction relating to a problem even if it is based on preconceived ideas?
2 Make some use of evidence from experience in making a prediction?
3 Make reasonable predictions based on a possible explanation (hypothesis) without necessarily being able to make the justification explicit?
4 Explain how a prediction that is made relates to a pattern in observations?
5 Use patterns in information or observations to make justified interpolations or extrapolations?
6 Justify a prediction in terms of a pattern in the evidence or an idea that might explain it?

Gathering evidence: planning

Do the children:

1 Start with a useful general approach even if details are lacking or need further thought?
2 Identify the variable that has to be changed and the things which should be kept the same for a fair test?
3 Identify what to look for or measure to obtain a result in an investigation?
4 Succeed in planning a fair test using a given framework of questions?
5 Compare their actual procedures after the event with what was planned?
6 Spontaneously structure their plans so that independent, dependent and controlled variables are identified and steps taken to ensure that the results obtained are as accurate as they can reasonably be?

Gathering evidence: observing

Do the children:

1 Succeed in identifying obvious differences and similarities between objects and materials?
2 Make use of several senses in exploring objects or materials?
3 Identify differences of detail between objects or materials?
4 Identify points of similarity between objects where differences are more obvious than similarities?
5 Use their senses appropriately and extend the range of sight using a hand lens or microscope as necessary?
6 Distinguish from many observations those which are relevant to the problem in hand?

Interpreting evidence and drawing conclusions

Do the children:

1 Discuss what they find in relation to their initial questions?
2 Compare their findings with their earlier predictions?
3 Notice associations between changes in one variable and another?
4 Identify patterns or trends in their observations or measurements?
5 Draw conclusions which summarise and are consistent with all the evidence that has been collected?

6 Recognise that any conclusions are tentative and may have to be changed in the light of new evidence?

Communicating and reflecting

Do the children:

1 Talk freely about their activities and the ideas they have, with or without making a written record?
2 Listen to others' ideas and look at their results?
3 Use drawings, writing, models, paintings to present their ideas and findings?
4 Use tables, graphs and charts when these are suggested to record and organise results?
5 Regularly and spontaneously use information books to check or supplement their investigations?
6 Choose a form for recording or presenting results which is both considered and justified in relation to the type of information and the audience?

Examples of indicators of development of scientific attitudes

Curiosity

Do the children:

1 Give some attention to new things but are easily distracted and ask few questions?
2 Show interest in new things through asking factual questions, 'what' rather than 'why' or 'how'?
3 Explore things and ask questions about them in response to invitations to do so?
4 Examine things carefully and ask questions about 'how' and 'why' as well as 'what'?
5 Explore and investigate things around to answer their own questions?
6 Spontaneously seek information from books or other sources to satisfy their own curiosity?

Respect for evidence

Do the children:

1 Attempt to justify conclusions in terms of evidence even if the interpretation is influenced by preconceived ideas?

2 Realise when the evidence does not fit a conclusion based on expectations, although they may challenge the evidence rather than the conclusion?

3 Check parts of the evidence which do not fit an overall pattern or conclusions?

4 Accept only interpretations or conclusions for which there is supporting evidence?

5 Show a desire to collect further evidence to check conclusions before accepting them?

6 Recognise that no conclusion is so firm that it cannot be challenged by further evidence?

Flexibility in ways of thinking

Do the children:

1 Readily change what they say they think, though this may be due to a desire to please or conform rather than the force of argument or evidence?

2 Modify ideas enough to incorporate new evidence or arguments but resist relinquishing them?

3 Show willingness to consider alternative ideas which may fit the evidence, even if they prefer their own in the end?

4 Relinquish or change ideas after considering evidence?

5 Spontaneously seek other ideas which may fit the evidence rather than accepting the first which seems to fit?

6 Recognise that ideas can be changed by thinking and reflecting about different ways of making sense of the same evidence?

Critical reflection

Do the children:

1 Recount what they have done after an investigation and justify rather than criticise it?

2 Consider some alternative procedures which could be used without necessarily realising their advantages and disadvantages?

3 Discuss ways in which what they have done could have been improved even if only in detail?

4 Consider, when encouraged, the pros and cons of alternative ways of approaching a problem to the one they have used or plan to use?

5 Initiate the review of a completed investigation to identify how procedures could have been improved?

6 Spontaneously review and improve procedures at the planning stage and in the course of an investigation as well as after completion?

Sensitivity in investigating the environment

Do the children:

1 Take part, with supervision, in caring for living things?
2 Look after living things responsibly with minimum supervision?
3 On visits outside school recognise and observe a code of behaviour which protects the environment from litter, damage and disturbance?
4 Minimise the impact of investigation in the environment, e.g. by replacing disturbed stones, returning animals caught for study in the classroom?
5 Take responsibility for ensuring that living things are cared for in the classroom and for protecting the environment outside from damage and pollution caused by their own action?
6 Help to ensure that the actions of others as well as their own do not neglect living things or damage the non-living environment?

Examples of indicators of development of understanding

Living things and processes of life

Can the children use these ideas?

1 That there are different kinds of living things called plants and different kinds called animals, including human beings.
2 That living things produce their own kind.
3 That the basic life processes are common to all plants and animals.
4 That human beings need certain conditions to promote good human health and body maintenance.
5 That different kinds of plants and animals are able to live and find food in very different places.
6 That there are organs within the bodies of mammals arranged in systems which carry out major life processes.
7 That animals and plants depend on each other in various ways.

Interaction of living things and their environment

Can the children use these ideas?

1 That changes occur in living things in response to daily and seasonal changes in the environment.

2 That living things are suited to their environment in various ways.
3 That competition for life-supporting resources determines which living things survive where.
4 That some waste products from human activities are biodegradable and others are not, and some materials can be recycled.
5 That human activities can produce changes to the Earth's surface and atmosphere that can have long-term effects.
6 That human activity can interfere in the balance between resources and the plants and animals depending on them.

Materials

Can the children use these ideas?

1 That materials differ in properties and can be grouped according to their properties.
2 That materials are used for different purposes according to their properties.
3 That materials can be changed by heating (e.g. melting) and interaction with each other (e.g. dissolving).
4 That their properties (including solid, liquid or gas) can be explained by their composition and structure.
5 That new materials can be formed from chemical reaction of other materials.

Air, atmosphere and weather

Can the children use these ideas?

1 That the weather affects the lives of human beings and other living things.
2 That there are patterns in the weather related to seasonal changes.
3 That there is air all around us and wind is moving air.
4 That there is invisible water vapour in the air which condenses when the air is cooled and becomes visible as drops of water.
5 That certain conditions promote evaporation and condensation of water.
6 That the weather is the result of factors relating to temperature and the amount of water vapour in the air.

Rocks, soil and materials from the Earth

Can the children use these ideas?

1 That soil is a mixture of materials derived from rocks and living things.

2 That there is a wide variety of shapes and sizes of rock.
3 That changes in rocks can be caused by erosion and weathering.
4 That human activity can influence the fertility of soil.
5 That rocks are composed of different combinations of minerals, some of which contain ores from which metals can be extracted.
6 That there are constant changes to the Earth's surface, some caused by erosion and some by eruption of volcanoes and earthquakes.
7 That rocks have been formed over very long periods of time in different ways involving sedimentation and the effects of heat and pressure.

The Earth in space

Can the children use these ideas?

1 That the Sun, Moon and Earth are three-dimensional bodies that move relative to one another.
2 That there are regular changes in the appearance of the moon that repeat about every four weeks.
3 That the movement of the Sun during the day and stars at night can be explained by the Earth rotating once a day.
4 That the stars are like the Sun but very very far away.
5 That the Earth is one of several planets circling round the Sun that make up the solar system.
6 That seasonal changes can be explained by a simple model of the solar system in which the Earth rotates round the Sun and spins about an inclined axis and the Moon rotates round the Earth.

Forces and movement

Can the children use these ideas?

1 That to make anything move or stop moving there has to be something pushing, pulling or twisting it.
2 That speed is a way of saying how far something moves in a certain time.
3 That how quickly an object will start moving depends on the amount of force acting on it and the faster it is moving the more force is needed to stop it.
4 That it takes more force to start or stop a heavy object than a lighter one.
5 That things fall because of a force acting on everything on the Earth pulling towards the Earth (gravity).

6 That when several forces act on an object their effect is combined.
7 That when an object is not moving the forces acting on it cancel each other and there must be a force acting against gravity to stop it falling (as in floating).

Energy sources and use

Can the children use these ideas?

1 That light, sound and heat can be detected through our senses.
2 That light, sound, heat and electricity are produced in different ways.
3 That energy enables things to work and the more energy the more can be done.
4 That energy comes in various forms and can be changed from one form to another.
5 That energy can be stored and transferred to and from moving things.
6 That we need energy to survive and can obtain it in various ways.
7 That some energy sources are renewable but fuels from the earth are not and are being used up.

Summary

This chapter has described the process of turning evidence from children's performance into judgements of their achievement that help to indicate next steps.

The main points have been:

- For formative purposes, where the aim is to identify next steps in learning, detailed information is required relating to particular skills, attitudes and ideas.
- Maps of progress, or indicators of development, can be identified that are useful for these formative purposes.
- The mapping of development cannot be exact, for it is determined by the combined effect of experience, maturation and teaching.
- With these caveats, indicators can be used to interpret evidence of achievement to show where children can be helped to operate at a more advanced level.

Examples of indicators of development for the process skills, attitudes and areas of understanding identified as goals of learning science 5–12 have been set out.

Points for reflection

- Progress maps (and sets of indicators) can be created for subskills of those set out here and for specific ideas. What are the pros and cons of having more detailed maps and indicators? How helpful might it be for the maps and indicators to be at a less detailed level?
- If no evidence relevant to some indicators can be found, how might this be interpreted?

Further reading

Two titles in the ARK materials (see end of Chapter 9) are relevant here:

Masters, G. and Forster, M. (1996) *Progress Maps*. Camberwell, Victoria, Australian Council for Research in Education.

Masters, G. and Forster, M. (1996a) *Developmental Assessment*. Camberwell, Victoria, Australian Council for Research in Education.

11

Helping the development of scientific ideas

Chapter 10 looked at how evidence collected for formative assessment can be interpreted to identify the next steps in learning. In this
chapter and the next we look at the teacher's role in helping children
to take these next steps. This is at the heart of teaching and learning.
It goes without saying that the whole purpose of developing curriculum materials, planning activities, providing equipment and other
resources, and so on, is to enable children to develop the ideas, skills
and attitudes that help them understand the scientific aspects of the
world around them. The question of what kinds of interactions
between teacher and children support this development are, therefore, central. There has been a shift in the perception of the teacher's
role in science activities for 5–12-year-olds in the last decade, partly
in response to research into learning in general, and learning in
science in particular. The direction of the move has been away from
the teacher as provider of activities and passive facilitator towards
the teacher as a more active facilitator who intervenes to ensure
thinking as well as doing.

Developing understanding of ideas, which is the focus of this
chapter, has to involve the development and use of process skills
and is influenced by attitudes. So the development of these skills
and attitudes have themselves to be the focus of teaching, which is
the subject of Chapter 12. In practice developments of skills and
ideas go on at the same time and it is only for clarity and convenience that we are treating them separately here.

It was noted in Chapter 8 that knowing how to help children take
forward their ideas depends on particular circumstances and on
what the ideas are. It is not often possible to prescribe in advance
specific actions that will be effective. Therefore a teacher may have
to decide this on the spot, drawing on a 'tool box' of strategies. For
developing children's ideas, these strategies fall under three broad
headings:

1 Helping children to test their ideas. This includes extending children's experience and linking together specific ideas to make bigger ones
2 Providing access to alternative ideas. These will come from a range of sources, including other children and the teacher; taking them on board may involve 'scaffolding'
3 Communicating and reflecting. This involves discussion and the role of language in the development of shared understandings.

We will consider what each of these means in practice and give some examples of their applications in particular situations.

Helping children to test their ideas

Extending children's experience

Children's experience is clearly more limited than that of adults and a major role of science for younger children is to extend that experience so that they have more to draw upon in testing out and developing their ideas. For example, it is reasonable to hold the hypothesis that rust may originate inside the body of a metal if a child has only ever seen the exposed surfaces of metal objects. An 8-year-old girl interpreted her observations that the part of a nail that had been in water for a week went rusty as shown in Figure 11.1. Cutting through a rusted nail may be all that is needed to enable the girl to see that the evidence does not support this idea and noticing that the rust is only on the outside might lead her to another idea.

The teacher's role includes providing gradually extended experience as a matter of routine. This can be through classroom displays, which are added to as a topic proceeds: through posters and photographs mounted on the walls, information books at the right level,

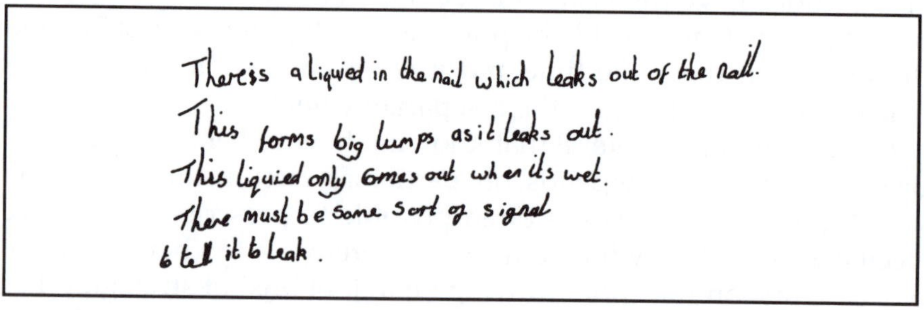

There is a liquied in the nail which leaks out of the nail.
This forms big lumps as it leaks out.
This liquied only comes out when its wet.
There must be some sort of signal
to tel it to leak.

Figure 11.1 An 8-year-old's writing about rust
Source: ASE (1998)

for reference in the book corner; through visits, visitors and full use of the school buildings as resources for observation and activity; through film, CD-ROMs and other information technologies.

Against this background of regularly varied experience, teachers have to introduce specific information and activities in response to particular ideas, such as in the case of the rusting nails. In another example, after some children expressed the belief that plants do not grow during the day but only at night, their teacher introduced 'fast-growing plants' into the classroom. These plants grow so quickly that a measurable difference can be detected during a school day, so the children's idea could be tested. There was the further value that, because their life cycle takes only a few weeks, the change from buds to flowers and the setting of seeds can be experienced in a time-scale that has an impact on children's understanding of cycles of growth and reproduction.

Using existing experience

Extending children's experience helps them test their ideas, but sometimes they do not use information that is already available to them. If we think about how children arrive at their ideas, it is often the case that they have taken account only of certain evidence and ignored anything that is contradictory, or that they have not compared like with like. For example, as mentioned on p. 50, the idea that the eye is the active agent in seeing by sending out beams to what is seen is only tenable in relation to a limited range of experiences. It will not easily explain how the brightness and colour of things can be changed in different lighting conditions. Or, the idea that wooden blocks can be magnetic would hardly stand up to testing a prediction that, if magnetic, they should be able to attract metal materials that magnets attract.

An important part of a teacher's role in science is to set up the expectation that all ideas have to be tested, not just the children's but any the teacher proposes or those found in books. If this becomes routine, then there will be no implied criticism in asking children to 'find a way to see if your idea works'. Once accepted, the teacher can help children to express their ideas in a way which can be tested and to gather and interpret evidence in a systematic way that ensures that they are properly tested. In other words, the focus is then on the way in which they use process skills and attitudes, as discussed in Chapter 12.

Not all tests of children's ideas will be of the kind suggested in books of scientific activities, and the teacher should be prepared to be as imaginative as the children in devising ways to address unexpected ideas. For example, children who suggested that mice drinking water from their tank left out at night (to explore ideas about evaporation) were responsible for the lowering of the level of the water, decided to test this idea by leaving some cheese beside the tank. Evidence of nibbling of the cheese, they said, would be a test of their idea about the participation of the mice. Untouched cheese, but continued loss of water, forced them to consider an alternative explanation.

Linking specific ideas to make bigger ones

Development of ideas has been described in terms of moving from small ideas that explain specific events to 'bigger' ones that can be used to explain a wide range of experiences. The change in thinking required is not just in the number of events that can be understood. There is a qualitative change in ideas. In science, the aim is to arrive at ideas that are context-independent; for example, an idea of what makes things float that can be used for all objects and all liquids, regardless of when or where. To move from realising why a particular object floats to the bigger idea of floating is a difficult transition, and if it is taken too far too quickly children will lose the link with their own ideas.

So it is important that ideas are expanded in step with children's experience and do not run ahead of this. For example, the teacher whose class proposed that thirsty mice were responsible for water disappearing from the tank introduced the notion of water evaporating, after the children's own ideas had failed the test. She did this by turning the children's thinking to water disappearing from clothes hung out to dry, asking the children to think about the similarities between the two events and about whether the same thing could be happening to the water in the tank. Further experimenting with similar dishes of water covered and uncovered provided evidence for the children to see that this was a possible explanation – although only after the demise of the hypothesis about mice, since this, too, would have explained the difference!

As a result of testing the idea drawn from other experience, the children developed an idea of what was happening to the water that was just a little broader than their initial one. The development of the bigger idea of evaporation would depend on children having more experience and ideas about, for example, water vapour in the air.

Providing access to alternative ideas

When no alternative that makes sense to the child is available, there is reluctance to give up existing ideas, even when these are shown to be inadequate. They deal with the conflict of idea and evidence by making a small adjustment to their idea in order to reconcile the conflict. So, for example, the child who held a view that we see things because of light coming from our eyes, was able to explain why we cannot see in the dark (evidence that conflicts with this idea) by adapting his idea to include light 'switching on the eye' (Figure 4.11 p. 51).

So how can children be made aware of alternative scientific ideas? It is not a simple matter of telling or explaining. It is all too easy to destroy children's confidence in their own thinking and reasoning if their ideas are swept aside by premature presentation of the 'right' ones. The best way of avoiding this is to ensure that more scientific ideas are introduced, not as being 'correct' but as alternatives worth considering, *and* that these are tested in terms of the evidence available so that everyone can judge the extent to which they 'work' in practice.

Ideas from other children

Discussion with other children is an important source of alternative ideas. These are not necessarily scientific, but becoming aware that there are other views different from their own helps to make children open to consider alternatives. As children progress in ways of thinking and experience they can be encouraged to seek alternatives, by argument and information from secondary sources and not only from what they can experience directly.

When children hear ideas from other children they are less likely to accept them without question than if the ideas come from the teacher or other 'authority'. And when their own ideas are challenged by others, they have to bring arguments or evidence that will convince others. Arranging for these things to happen requires planning and some structure.

> A class of 10-year-olds had been investigating 'the best way of keeping a cup of soup warm'. A fairly 'standard' activity that had involved children suggesting materials to use and then, in groups, carrying out investigations with containers of warm water. Groups had investigated the different materials that they had suggested. At the end of the practical work, the teacher arranged for them to combine their findings by reporting in a whole-class discussion. So they identified several materials that were good for retaining heat and others that were not so good.

It could have been left there – as often is the case – but there was more understanding to be built from this activity. The teacher asked the children to think about why some materials were better than others – what did some materials do that others did not? These were quite challenging questions, so the children were asked to consider them in their groups for ten minutes and come back together to report their ideas. This produced some quite contradictory ideas, for example:

- that the materials that were best for keeping things warm were warm themselves
- that the ones that were best were colder than the others.

In discussion it was found that the group who came up with the first of these ideas had compared how the materials felt before they were wrapped round the container. The other group had felt the outside of the materials when they were wrapped round the containers and noticed that they were cooler than others. The discussion led them to check each other's findings and was significant in leading all the children to the idea that when the water stayed warm, the heat was not getting away through the sides.

The teacher challenged them to predict which material would be best for keeping cold things cold. Not all the children were able to apply their ideas successfully in answering this, but they were all able, later, to test their ideas. These activities took the children beyond the knowledge that materials vary in the extent to which they allow heat to pass through them and towards some more widely applicable ideas about heat transfer.

Ideas introduced by the teacher: scaffolding

Teachers are often unclear about how, when or whether to introduce the scientific view of things. There is often fear that the children will not understand and will be more confused, or that they will not be able to explain it in ways that the children can understand. Consequently children may be left with their own 'everyday' way of thinking when in fact they could be trying out ideas that expand their understanding. 'Scaffolding' is a term used to describe the introduction of ideas at a time and in a way that helps children to advance their ideas towards the scientific view.

The theory behind scaffolding derives from the views of the psychologist Vygotsky (1962) who suggested that, for any learner, there is an area just beyond current understanding (where a person is in conscious control of ideas and knows that he or she is using them) where more advanced ideas can be used with help. Vygotsky called this area the 'zone of proximal development'. It is, in essence, what we have called the 'next step' that the child can be expected to take, identified by the cycle of formative assessment.

The teacher's role in scaffolding is to support children in using an idea that they have not yet made 'their own'. For example, Figure 11.2 shows what a teacher of 7- and 8-year-olds did to help the children to develop their understanding of light being reflected, using a football. The children did not make this link for themselves but were able to learn from it. They transferred the idea to a mirror, using the hole in unifix cubes to fix their line of sight (Figure 11.3).

Examples of scaffolding are readily found in helping skills such as knitting, weaving, playing tennis and even using a word processing package on a computer. The learner first needs to be shown how to do things, then later may need to be reminded of what to do, and at all times needs encouragement, until eventually the actions are carried out without external help. Similarly, help with understanding can be given by suggesting ways of thinking about phenomena:

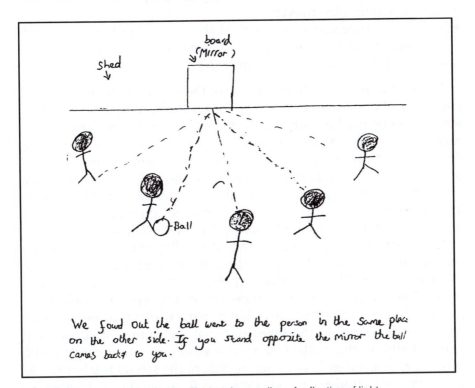

We found out the ball went to the person in the same place on the other side. If you stand opposite the mirror the ball comes back to you.

Figure 11.2   Using analogy to scaffold understanding of reflection of light
Source: ASE (1998)

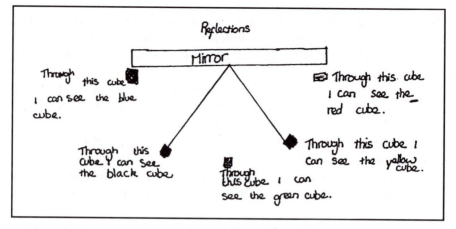

Figure 11.3   Applying the idea of bouncing to the reflection of light
Source: ASE (1998)

- About gravity – 'Suppose the Earth is trying to pull everything on it towards itself . . . what would happen to something that you let go?'
- About forces and movement – 'Suppose something was moving across a surface that was very, very slippery . . . when do you think it would stop moving?'
- About the apparent movement of the sun – 'Suppose the Earth was turning and the sun was in the same place . . . where would we see of the sun at different times?'

The teacher need not be the source of the information, which could come from books or other source. For example, models of the solar system can be used to introduce explanations of the apparent movement of the sun and moon which can override the naïve interpretations of direct observations. But whatever the source of information, it is the teacher's role to bring the ideas to the children in a way that allows them to try them out, rather like trying on new clothes for size. The analogy is quite apt, since new clothes for growing children are always chosen to be just a little larger, but not too much.

A warning has to be given about scaffolding, however. Research on the effects of introducing scaffolding in professional development, by Askew, Bliss and Macrae (1995, p. 216) found that 'teachers could "talk scaffolding", but appeared to implement it only marginally'. Similarly Scott warned that 'Casual use of this term is common' before going on the point out that the notion of scaffolding was initially 'in the context of a tutor working with a single child; this is a rather different situation to that of the school teacher working with thirty children' (Scott, 1998, p. 69). So we should be wary of assuming that an idea that is a good fit for one child will 'fit all'.

Moreover, scaffolding is not an excuse for telling children the 'right answer'. It enables children to advance their ideas but it remains essential that they work out for themselves that these ideas make sense of their experience.

Promoting communication and reflection

Language, thought and knowledge

Different schools of thought exist about the relationship between language and thought. On the one hand is the view that speaking is a means of communicating thoughts which have been developed through actions and interaction with things in the world around. On the other hand is the view that thinking and speaking are virtually the same, that language and social interaction have key functions in *developing* ideas not just in communicating them. This is taken further in the view that regards picking up language and ways of representing things from a community of learners to be an important part of learning.

Piaget's view of intellectual development lays less emphasis on the verbal interaction between child and adult than do the views of Bruner, Vygotsky and Ausubel. For Piaget, the development of knowledge is tied to physiological development of the brain and learning is brought about by direct physical activity with things around. Thoughts are internalised actions not words, and language a means of sharing thoughts, not of developing them. Construction of ideas is within the individual; this is 'personal constructivism'. Until the child reaches the stage of formal operations (Piaget, 1964), usually after the age of 13, the role of the teacher is seen mainly as facilitating firsthand interaction with materials and social interaction with peers.

Bruner emphasises the role of language in translating experiences into a symbolic form in the mind. The development of language in the child opens up the possibility of direct input into a child's thinking through language and the reordering by the child of experience by using language 'as a cognitive instrument' (Bruner, 1964b, p. 12). Vygotsky shares this view that language is a means of reinterpreting the world: 'Speech . . . does not merely accompany the child's activity; it serves mental orientation, conscious understanding; it helps in overcoming difficulties' (Vygotsky, 1962). In this view ideas are constructed through social interaction rather than by the individual alone.

In Ausubel's theory of 'meaningful learning', the role of firsthand activity is subordinated to the role of giving meaning to verbal statements. Ausubel, like Bruner, believes that any scientific idea can be made accessible to children in some form. He does not believe that learners invent ideas but learn them from others. What is needed is that the idea or theory to be learned is broken down and expressed in language appropriate to the learner, then illustrated by practical activity. The significant point is that he regards verbal statements as the source of knowledge and the role of practical activity as giving meaning to them (Ausubel, 1968).

In recent thinking about learning there has been a perceptible shift away from the view that ideas are formed by individuals in isolation, that is, personal constructivism, towards social constructivism, which recognises the impact of others' ideas on the way learners make sense of things. This means that there is greater emphasis than before on communication through language, on the influences of cultural factors and on linking in to a 'community of learners'.

Thinking in different languages

Before turning to the subject of discussion more directly, the relationship between language and thought should not be left without reference to learning contexts where there is a difference between a child's language of instruction and the language used in the home. This situation arises not only in the case of immigrants but also in those countries where there is a change from the indigenous language to an official language used in the school, often from about the third year of primary school.

Studies of learning in countries where the home language differs from the language of instruction have produced varying findings. Where the teachers are themselves less competent in the second language (of instruction) than in the home language, it appears that children learn best in the latter. This is providing the language is rich enough to express the scientific ideas and the essential tentativeness of scientific knowledge. If children can form ideas with understanding in one language, these ideas are not damaged by later translation, but if subtle ideas cannot be formed, then learning clearly suffers. This can be either because the home language is limited or because of uncertain knowledge of the official language.

Developing shared understanding

It is through language that we develop a shared understanding of ideas. The ideas that we may form from direct experience have to be

communicated and this involves trying to find words that convey our meaning to others. In this process our own ideas often have to be reformulated in ways that are influenced by the meaning that others give to words. This is not the same as saying that learning science is learning the 'language' of science, or just the commonly accepted definitions of words. But it does mean that an important element of learning is 'negotiating meaning'.

In the case of children in school, negotiation provides children with assurance that they have reached a way of understanding something that is shared by their teacher and other children (Sutton, 1992). The process requires some 'give and take' as children reflect on and reconstruct their own ideas in response to others'. When ideas are changed, it is important for there to be some review of how earlier experience was understood. Without this there may be a residue of naïve ideas which are still used to explain previous experience. For example, we can all probably recall believing in something like 'the man in the Moon', but recognise that this belief was overtaken by more rational views. It would be illogical to believe both in a man in the moon and the moon as understood more scientifically. To avoid the equivalent in children's growing ideas the teacher should help them to reflect on previous experience in terms of new ideas. It is helpful to be quite explicit about 'how your ideas about . . . have changed' for this legitimises changing ways of understanding things, which is essential for the continued development of ideas.

The role of discussion

Discussion plays a central role in both negotiation of meaning and reflection on thinking. Douglas Barnes drew attention to this role through studying children's speech when involved in group tasks. Barnes showed how individuals contribute to an understanding of an event (or process or situation). An idea of one child is taken up and elaborated by another, perhaps challenged by someone else's idea and leads them back to check with the evidence or to predict and see which idea stands up best to a test. With several minds at work there is less chance of ideas being tested in a superficial manner than there is if one child does so with no one to challenge it. The challenge can only be made if the thinking is made open and public through the use of language.

Thus Barnes argues that talking is essential to learning. By 'talking' he does not, however, mean the formal reporting or answering of teachers' questions which in some classrooms is the only speech officially sanctioned. Barnes lays particular emphasis on the value of talk among children with no adult authority present. In such situations children with a problem to solve use non-formal speech: they interrupt each other, hesitate, rephrase and repeat themselves. Barnes sees this hesitant or 'exploratory' talk as signifying the openness of the situation and constituting an invitation to all involved to throw in ideas.

The opportunity for exploratory talk of this kind comes only when the children are in charge of the situation. Generally, this does not happen when the teacher is present, for his or her presence provides an authority which children expect to be greater than their own views. As Barnes says:

> the teacher's absence removes from their work the usual source of authority; they cannot turn to him to solve dilemmas. Thus . . . the children not only formulate hypotheses, but are compelled to evaluate them for themselves. This they can do in only two ways: by testing them against their existing view of 'how things go in the world', and by going back to 'the evidence'.
>
> (Barnes, 1976, p. 29)

It is not difficult to see that learning through talking is exposing children not only to different ideas but compelling them to think about how those ideas relate to previous and new experiences. In other words they are finding better ways of dealing with ideas and checking them against evidence; they are developing the mental process skills. Hence what Barnes has to say, while relevant to all learning, is particularly significant for science. In making this point, he goes further in proposing a role for language in helping children to reflect on the way in which they have processed the ideas and information available to them:

> Much learning may go on while children manipulate science apparatus, or during a visit, or while they are struggling to persuade someone else to do what they want. But learning of this kind may never progress beyond manual skills accompanied by slippery intuitions, unless the learners themselves have an opportunity to go back over such experience and represent it to themselves. There seems every reason for group practical work in science, for example, normally to be followed by discussion of the implications of what has been done and observed, since without this what has been half understood may soon slip away. Talk and writing provide means by which children are able to reflect upon the bases upon which they are interpreting reality, and thereby change them.
>
> (Barnes, 1976, pp. 30–1)

It is possible that by following the ideas of Piaget, mediated through educators who have translated his views of learning into classroom experiences, there has been an overemphasis in primary classrooms on activity at the expense of discussion. Moving from one activity to another without pause for thinking and reflection is not an effective learning experience. Children need not only to have direct experience but to develop their understanding of it through negotiation – exchanging views with others. The alternative is not direct verbal instruction but planning time for discussion into practical work. It also helps to structure that time so that ideas are shared and used to take the understanding of all beyond what each could achieve individually.

Introducing scientific words

Some of the questions that concern teachers of 5–12-year-olds revolve around the use of a scientific vocabulary: when should teachers introduce the technical language of science and expect children to use it correctly? Should this be done, as it were, from the beginning? Or should we allow children to describe things in their own words even though more precise terms are available? What do we do about those words which have both an 'everyday' and a 'technical' meaning, such as 'work', 'force', 'power', 'condensation'? These are not separate but interconnected problems and opinions differ as to how to deal with them.

Words used in science label a related set of ideas or characteristics. But the same word can be used with a 'big' meaning or with a meaning that is locally applicable, or 'small'. For example, take the word 'solution':

- Big meaning: for the scientist a solution means a system in which one substance is distributed at the molecular level in another without being chemically combined with it. It includes the solution of solids in solids as well as in liquids, liquids in liquids and gases in liquids.
- Smaller meaning: for the secondary school pupil the meaning will be much less extensive, probably being restricted to solids in liquids but still bringing with it the notion that there is a limited amount of solute that will dissolve in a given amount of a solvent, that solutions are clear but may be coloured and are different from suspensions.
- Small meaning: for younger children it will have an even more restricted meaning. It may not include a coloured solution or a solution in which some solid remains undissolved.

For all, however, a solution is also the answer to a puzzle or crossword clue!

It would be unreasonable to insist that the word 'solution' should only be used with its full scientific meaning (indeed, it would never accumulate this meaning without being used in a more restricted sense first). But it is equally unreasonable for the word to be used the first time a child experiences a solid disappearing into a liquid.

There is probably no single guideline that can be used for all children and all words. The decision about introducing a special word depends on:

- whether the child needs the word, that is, has had relevant experiences that require a label
- whether it would add to the understanding, for example by linking to other experiences and ideas.

If these things apply it may be the right time to introduce an appropriate word. A simple example is of supplying the word 'sinking' to a young child who is describing an object as 'falling to the bottom' of the bowl of water. The word 'solution' might be offered to the older child with plenty of experience of putting various solids in water who wanted to describe how the liquids 'that you can see through' are different from the liquid before any solid was put in. Feasey (1999) proposes that teachers scaffold the use of new words by using both the everyday and the scientific word together (for example, 'see-through' and 'transparent') until the new word can be used confidently.

The most persuasive argument for waiting until the child seems to need the word before introducing it is that there is then more chance that the 'package of ideas' that it represents to the child will not be too far away from what it represents for the teacher or the author of the books the child might read or other people with whom the child may communicate. It does children no service to provide words which they cannot use to convey meaning because they do not realise what meaning the word has. Of course, we cannot prevent children collecting words, like stamps, and showing off their trophies by talking about black holes, radioactivity, cloning and such. But we accept this for what it is, mere imitation of adult language, not intended for communication.

The same argument can be the guideline for the words that are used not only in science but have a more precise meaning when used as a scientific term than when used in everyday life. It is pointless to try to prevent the word 'work' being used for occupations, like thinking, which involve no 'work' in the physicist's understanding of the word. When the word is required in its scientific meaning, that is, when children have some notion of the concept, then is the time to say 'the word "work" is used for this in science and not for other things that are called work'. The everyday use of the word can be discussed as well as the scientific use to clarify the distinction (cf. the suggestion about the meaning of 'animal' on p. 42). Thereafter, the teacher should be careful to notice how the children are using the words, by listening and reading what they write, so as to find out the concept that is conveyed by the children in the words they use.

Concern about the special vocabulary of science should not take all the attention. Normal non-scientific words can also present a barrier to communication if they are put together in complex structures. When we say warm air is 'rising' (instead of going up), light is 'travelling' (when we could say that it is going from one place to another), a balloon is 'expanding' (rather than getting bigger), we should stop to ask ourselves: do we really need to use these words? Do they help the children's understanding or are they just another layer of verbal wrapping paper?

When a new word is introduced it will be necessary to spend some time discussing with children their view of where it fits their experience. Asking for examples and non-examples is a useful way to approach this. For instance, in the context of introducing the word 'dissolve' where children had been using 'melt', can they give examples of things dissolving and examples of things becoming liquid which are not dissolving? Children need time and encouragement to reflect on earlier ideas and to ask themselves, for example, 'is this, that I used to call melting, what I now know to be dissolving?' Reflection on earlier experience is necessary so that this is taken into ideas as they expand and so that ideas called forth by words bring with them all the relevant experience.

Summary

This chapter has made a start on looking at the teacher's role in helping children to develop their understanding, by looking at helping development of ideas. The theme is continued in the next chapter since understanding depends not only on developing children's ideas but also on their ways of thinking and of inquiry.

Actions that the teacher can take have been considered under three broad headings:

- *Helping children to test their ideas*: through exposure to new experience as well as using existing experience that they may have ignored. Also included here is linking ideas used in other situations to a new event that may be explained by them. In all these ways ideas become 'bigger' by being applied to a wider range of experience.

- *Providing access to alternative ideas*: which may come from other children, from the teachers, from books or from other sources. The teacher's role is to ensure that these ideas are tested and not just accepted. This may involve 'scaffolding', i.e. helping the children to 'try out' ideas to see if they help their understanding of events, and gradually withdrawing this support once the children have made the ideas their own.
- *Promoting communication and reflection*: which involves developing understanding through exchanging ideas with others and arriving at a 'negotiated' meaning. Discussion, both with the teacher and among groups without the teacher, is important in this process and lesson planning should ensure that there is opportunity for it to take place. Words have an important part in this and words with a specific meaning in science can be introduced when the children have the experience that requires the use of certain words and when they help in linking together ideas from different experiences.

Points for reflection

- In what ways might teachers help children to become aware of the ideas that can be developed through their activities, without 'telling them what to learn'?
- Are some approaches to developing ideas more appropriate to some ideas than to others? Can specific approaches be 'matched' to ideas, for example, about living things, about the Earth in space, about energy transformations?
- Are some approaches to developing ideas more suitable for children at particular ages or stages?

Further reading

Detailed descriptions of teachers' interactions with children are given in:

Frost, J. (1997) *Creativity in Primary Science*. Buckingham: Open University Press.
Qualter, A. (1996) *Differentiated Primary Science*. Buckingham: Open University Press.

Many ideas for linking literacy development and learning in science are set out by R. Feasey in the ASE (1999) publication *Primary Science and Literacy*, Hatfield, Association for Science Education.

12

Helping the development of process skills and attitudes

Here we continue the theme, begun in the last chapter, of the teacher's role in helping children to take the next steps in their learning. What role should the teacher have if the intended learning is to take place? What will he or she be doing to encourage progress and development? It is worth emphasising that in reality actions in relation to developing ideas and actions for developing skills and attitudes are not separated. They are part of a complex whole, but breaking this down helps in showing how each part contributes to children's learning.

This process of analysis is taken further in this chapter, where we consider action in relation to process skills by first taking each one separately. In this way actions relating to specific skills can be exemplified. Following this, the strategies common across all the skills are drawn out.

The final part of the chapter deals with what teachers can do to help children develop attitudes that support their learning.

Promoting the use of process skills

We begin by considering action in relation to each of the process skills which were identified as goals of science education in Chapter 2 and briefly defined in Chapter 6:

- raising questions (distinguishing ones that can be answered through inquiry and investigation from those that cannot)
- developing hypotheses (suggesting possible explanations by applying existing ideas)
- predicting (saying what is likely to happen before it is known, based on an hypothesis or pattern in findings)
- gathering evidence: planning (including making decisions about and setting up opportunities to gather evidence)

- gathering evidence: making observations (including comparisons and measurements)
- interpreting and drawing conclusions (including finding relationships and comparing results with predictions)
- communicating and reflecting (giving information in an appropriate form and understanding information in various forms).

Raising questions

The concern here is to help children identify the kinds of questions that can be answered through scientific inquiry. This is a key factor in developing an understanding of the nature of scientific activity and it is important to lay a foundation for this in the early years. Children come to realise the distinction between questions that can or cannot be answered by inquiry by considering their own questions. So an important role for the teacher is to encourage children to raise all kinds of questions and, through discussion of these questions, to help them realise which can be answered by information obtained in different ways.

Children can be encouraged to raise questions by providing interesting and thought-provoking material to explore, time to handle, examine and wonder about them, encouragement to ask questions and opportunities to discuss ways of finding the answers. Displays with a notice 'what would you like to know about these things?' and perhaps a box for questions, help to make explicit the invitation to question. At other times children can be asked to explore and given time in small groups to think of questions before pooling them in whole-class discussion.

When children do ask questions, however, how does the teacher respond to them? It helps to begin by identifying various kinds of questions that children commonly ask. It is also useful to remember that children sometimes ask questions for motives other than curiosity. Sometimes they are seeking attention and sometimes seeking approval or hints about what the teacher expects.

Types of children's questions
Children's questions can usually be identified in terms of four common types. Most are represented in this list of questions asked by children whilst handling pieces of rock (quoted in Osborne *et al.*, 1982):

- What are rocks made of?
- How do they get their colour?
- Why are they hard?

- How do rocks get their shape?
- Why do rocks have holes in them?
- Why are some rocks different weights than others?
- Why are rocks sometimes smooth and flat?
- Is gold a rock?
- Why is diamond the most valuable rock?

1 *Questions expressing wonder or interest*. Some of these questions are ways of expressing interest rather than asking for information. The researchers who reported this list collected questions from separate classes of children and found 'Why are they different colours?' sometimes and 'How do they get their colours?' in other cases. The exact words used are not carefully chosen and so we should not read too much into them. 'How do rocks get their shape?' could easily be expressed as 'Why are rocks different shapes?' Questions such as these are a way of saying 'Look at all the different shapes' or 'I've just realised that rocks are not all the same colour'. An appropriate response to such questions is therefore to share the children's interest and perhaps take it further: 'Let's see how many different shapes/colours there are.' A teacher will be able to judge from the children's reaction whether there is particular interest in the shapes and colours or whether these were passing comments expressed as questions.

2 *Questioning for information*. Children's questions always include some of a second kind, asking for straight information: 'Is gold a rock?', 'Why is diamond the most valuable rock?' or perhaps one that well might have been in the list 'Where were these rocks found?' The answers to these can be given directly, if the teacher knows, or the children can be referred to a source of the information. They are facts, some a matter of definition; they add to children's knowledge, which is important to their understanding of the world but is by no means all of it.

3 *Complex and philosophical questions*. Questions of a third type are the ones that often give teachers most difficulty because they require complex, not factual, answers. Many teachers may not know the answers and those who do will realise that the children's existing concepts are not sufficient to enable them to understand the answer. 'Why are they hard?', 'Why do they have holes in them?', 'Why are rocks sometimes smooth and flat?' are examples of these. They ask for an explanation, but in fact if the children were to be given the explanation they would probably not understand it, and might well be deterred from asking such questions in future. So teachers should not feel inadequate at not

answering such questions from their own knowledge; in most cases it would be the worst thing to attempt.

Some of these questions can be turned into investigable ones, the fourth type and the ones that are especially valued in science education. So, instead of presenting a problem to the teacher these questions actually present the opportunity to help children define investigable questions, ones which they can answer from investigations. 'Why are rocks sometimes smooth and flat?' could be used to lead to an investigable question by asking:

- Where do you find rocks that are smooth and flat?
- What is the same about places where smooth flat rocks are found?
- What is different about places where rocks are not smooth and flat? Could these differences account for the shapes of the rocks?
- Could we make a rough rock into a smooth one?

The end point may be a series of questions such as: 'Does rubbing one rock against another make them smooth?' 'Does putting them in water make any difference?' 'Do you need a harder rock to rub against a softer one to make it smooth?' Once children embark on answering any of these questions, inevitably others will occur. And since the further questions are generated in the context of activity, it is likely that many of them will be framed by the children in terms of things they can do themselves. Thus once begun the process of defining questions is self-generating.

4 *Investigable questions.* These are the questions most readily answered by exploration or investigation by children. If the children had asked 'Which is the hardest?' this could have been directly investigated by the children. In the activity with the ice cubes, the children could directly answer the question: where do they melt most quickly? or, what is the best way of keeping ice from melting? In some cases the teacher is likely to know the answer but has to resist the urge to give it and instead to let the children investigate and try out their ideas.

Handling children's questions

The techniques for handling each type, some of which have been hinted at in discussing children's questions can be summarised as follows:

1 *Questions which are comments or expressions of interest* (e.g. Why is it raining today?). Children do not pause for an answer when they ask questions of this kind. They require only sharing of interest.

There may be an opportunity to develop this interest into an investigable question, by asking, for instance: 'How many days this week has it rained?' 'How can we keep a record of the weather?'

2 *Questions asking for information* (e.g. Does it rain more often in England or in Wales?). Here an answer is expected and if it requires only factual information, the teacher may supply it directly, or suggest a source where the child may find it or undertake to find out at a later time. Factual information is useful in testing ideas and there is no reason to withhold it or to insist that children must find out everything for themselves. Learning to use sources of information helps children to expand the evidence on which their ideas are based.

3 *Complex and philosophical questions* (e.g. Why is the soil brown?). These questions often require some clarification in discussion with the child. They may be philosophical questions, if, for example, the intention was 'Who made the soil brown?' These kinds cannot be answered and are best treated as expressions of interest. But if the question is one that can be answered but only with a complex answer it may be necessary to say that 'the reason is too complicated for me to explain, but we can find out more about it'. The question need not be dropped, however, for it would be possible to turn it into an investigable one, for example, by finding out if all soils really are brown. What different colours can be found? Where are they found? What is the same and different about soils which vary in colour? Soon this leads to several investigable questions from which the children may find the answers at the level which satisfies their interest for the moment.

4 *Questions which are investigable by the children* (e.g. What happens if we plant the bean seeds the other way up?). Children's questions of this kind are not often expressed in a form which is already investigable, but can readily be made so. There may be a difficult decision for teachers as to whether to supply the simple answer or whether to devote the time needed for children to investigate the question for themselves, in which case they will learn more than the simple answer. The opportunity to find the answer from the things themselves by their own actions gives children valuable experience of scientific activity and not just the information about whether the bean will or will not grow upside down.

Children soon realise from experience what kinds of questions they can and cannot answer from investigation and what kinds require a different approach. Ten-year-old Stephen, looking at a giant African land snail, wanted to know why it grew bigger than other snails he had seen, how long it was and what it could eat. He set about answering the last two questions for himself and when asked how he thought he could find out the answer to the first said 'I suppose I'd have to read a lot of books'. Knowing how to answer different kinds of questions is more important to children than knowing the answers, but it comes only through experience of raising questions and discussing the process of answering them.

The teacher's role in the development of raising questions can be summarised as:

- Providing opportunities for children to study things which can provoke questions and be used to answer some of them through inquiry.
- Responding to children's questions according to whether
  - they require an answer or just an encouraging comment
  - they require a brief factual answer that children can understand
  - the children could find the answer for themselves by inquiry
  - the question could be turned into one that is answerable by inquiry.
- Discussing with children how questions can be answered.
- Making sources of information available.

Hypothesising

As defined in Chapter 6, this process skill includes the application of concepts and knowledge in the attempt to explain things. The difference between application of something already learned to explain a new phenomenon and generation of an explanation from hunch or imagination is not as great as it may at first seem. Both ways of attempting to explain should be encouraged for, although it is important to help children to use information or ideas learned previously in making sense of new experience, it could give them a closed 'right answer' view of science if this were the only approach used. The question put to children in asking for an explanation should more often be 'What *could be* the reason?' rather than 'What *is* the reason?' For instance, what could be the reason for:

- some pieces of wood floating higher in the water than others?
- apples turning red when they ripen?
- pigeons sometimes puffing out their feathers?
- snow melting on the footpath before it does on the grass?
- Julie's salt dissolving more quickly than David's?

To all of these questions there could be more than one answer. A worthwhile task for children to undertake in small groups is to think of all the possible answers they can. Their combined ideas will be richer than those of any individual. Furthermore, in groups, the children are less worried about contradicting each other and turning down far-fetched ideas or ones that would not explain the phenomenon. For example (about the snow melting on the path):

John: People walk on the path and not on the grass, so that took it away.
Peter: But it was on the path as well at the start and went before anyone walked on it, didn't you see? Can't be that. I reckon the path was wet – wet sort of dissolves the snow . . .
Mary: They put salt on roads . . .
John: Yes, that's it.

Peter's idea, too, was later challenged but he stuck to it because there was no convincing evidence against it so it went down on their list of possibilities. It was noteworthy that as this discussion went on the children began to talk in terms of what *might* be happening instead of the more certain earlier claims of what was happening. Another feature of the situation was that what they were trying to explain was a shared experience and one which provided the chance for them to check some of their hypotheses. Other ideas needed information from further observations or tests, depending in this case on the co-operation of the weather. The important thing was that they were not trying to advance grand theories to explain a whole range of phenomena (e.g. energy is needed to cause a change of state), but making sense of particular things in their immediate experience. Success and enjoyment in doing this would help the development of the ability to hypothesise which might well serve them well later when they might have to entertain alternative bigger ideas.

   As well as the ideas generated within a group the children should have access to ideas from others outside the group. As noted in Chapter 11, listening to what other groups have proposed is one way, but they should also be able to consult books and other information sources. Part of the teacher's role is to make relevant books, posters and pictures available, selected so that the children can easily find ideas in them. For younger children it helps to place appropriate books next to the aquarium or the display or have them ready when a particular topic is to be discussed. Older children might be expected to find books for themselves.

The provision for development of hypothesising therefore involves the teacher in:

- selecting or setting up phenomena which children can try to explain from their past experience
- organising groups to discuss possible explanations
- encouraging the checking of possibilities against evidence to reject those suggestions which are inconsistent with it
- providing access to ideas for children to add to their own, from books and other sources (including the teacher and other children).

Predicting

Predictions can be based on hypotheses or on patterns in observations. In either case, using hypotheses or patterns predictively is important to testing them. The question 'does this idea really explain what is happening?' is answered in science by first predicting a so far unknown event from the explanation and then seeing whether there is evidence of the predicted event taking place. For children the explanation may be in terms of associated circumstances rather than mechanisms, but the same applies. For example, the appearance of a misty patch after breathing on a window pane may be explained 'because my breath is warm and the window is cold'. Although there is much more to the explanation than this, it is still possible to use this idea to make a prediction about what will happen if the window is warm and not cold. Investigation of 'breathing' on surfaces of difference temperatures would test predictions based on this hypothesis.

It is not easy to encourage children to make genuine predictions, as opposed to guesses, on the one hand, or a mere statement of what is already known, on the other. At first it is useful to scaffold the process by taking the children through the reasoning which connects the making of a prediction to the testing of an idea: 'according to our idea, what will happen if . . . ?' and so 'if that happens, then we'll know our idea is working so far. Let's see.' It is also important to check whether 'we already know what will happen'; only if the answer is not already known is it a real prediction and a genuine test of the hypothesis or pattern.

The prerequisite for this kind of interaction is that the children are engaged on activities where they can generate hypotheses to test or observe patterns. Such activities include those where an explanation can arise from the observations, as in the behaviour of a 'Cartesian diver', or why footsteps echo in some places but not others, or why moisture forms on the outside of cold containers taken from the fridge into a warm room.

So the teacher's role in helping children to make predictions includes:

- providing opportunities where children can investigate their ideas through making and testing predictions
- discussing with them how to make a prediction and test it (scaffolding)
- helping them to recognise the difference between a prediction and a guess by asking them to explain how they arrived at their prediction
- expecting them to make predictions of something that is not already known in order to test their ideas.

Gathering evidence: planning

Gathering evidence involves planning what evidence is needed and how to gather it as well as making the observations needed to gather it.

Planning is a complex skill requiring experience and ability to think through to the possible outcomes of actions. In practice it does not always precede carrying out an investigation. It is characteristic of young children that they think out what to do in the course of doing it; they do not anticipate in thought the results of actions, unless the actions are already familiar to them. So children need to be introduced to planning gradually, starting with simple problems which make no greater demand than just 'tell me what you're going to do'. By about the third year, more can be expected, such as the planning of a fair comparison, supported by a series of questions, orally or on a work sheet, such as:

- What are we trying to find out?
- What are we going to change?
- What are we going to look at or measure?
- How will we make sure it is a fair test?

The teacher can 'scaffold' more detailed planning by identifying steps to be thought through. For a fair test, these steps are:

- defining the problem in terms of what is to be investigated
- identifying what is to change in the investigation (the independent variable)
- identifying what should be kept the same so that the effect of the independent variable can be observed (the variables to be controlled)

- identifying what needs to be observed (measured or compared) when the independent variable is changed (the dependent variable)
- considering how the evidence is to be used to solve the original problem.

Although they should have the chance to plan an investigation quite frequently, children do not have to plan out every activity for themselves. It is particularly useful to provide guidance in planning in those investigations where they have only one chance to make the observations and mistakes cannot be easily rectified by starting again (such as in gathering information during visits or using materials that are strictly limited in availability).

Development of this skill can be aided by reviewing the steps after the investigation has been carried out, whether or not the children planned the investigation for themselves. This is best done during discussion when the equipment is still at hand. Questions which probe how decisions were made, whether fair comparisons were made, how measurements or observations could have been made more accurately, etc., can be asked without implying criticism. The supporting structure the teacher provides can be gradually reduced as children grasp what is involved in investigating. Children will gradually be able to take over responsibility for reviewing their work if the teacher introduces it as a regular part of the discussion that should follow any practical activity.

The role the teacher takes in developing skill in planning and carrying out investigations therefore consists of:

- providing problems but not instructions for solving them, thus giving children the opportunity to do the planning
- supplying a structure (scaffolding) for the planning appropriate to the children's experience (questions to take them through the steps of thinking about variables to change, to control and to observe)
- sometimes reviewing what is being done during an investigation in relation to what was planned, recognising that not everything can be anticipated beforehand
- always discussing activities at the end to consider how the method of investigation could have been improved with hindsight.

Gathering evidence: observing

The main purpose of developing children's skill of observation is so that they will be able to use all their senses (appropriately and safely) to gather relevant information from their investigations of things around them.

Development of observation is fostered by opportunities for children to make wide-ranging observations. This means:

- providing interesting materials or objects to observe and appropriate aids to observation (such as magnifiers)
- allowing sufficient time to observe them
- giving invitations to observe
- holding discussions about what is observed.

Materials that can potentially interest children abound in their surroundings and can be brought into the classroom for closer inspection and for display. The way in which these are displayed can increase the information children can gather from their observations:

- Shells and pebbles might be displayed not only dry, but in water, so that their colours show more clearly.
- Snail shells of different sizes but of the same type provide a chance for children to find out through observation how the shell 'grows'.
- Children can also get some idea of mechanisms from observation of objects that can be taken apart, like a bicycle bell, torch or clock (preferably one made for this purpose).

When new material is gathered or provided to start a new topic it is always worth while to allow a period of time for them just to look, touch, smell and perhaps listen, before suggesting a task. Time is also an important element at later stages in an investigation, so that observations can be checked, refined and extended. By watching a group of children with new materials it is interesting to see how they often appear to observe very superficially at first. This may well be just a first quick run through; however, given time and encouragement they start again, more carefully, sometimes using measurement to decide whether or not differences they think they have seen are real. If the teacher stops the activity after their quick tour of what there is to see, then the only observations they make are the superficial ones and they are prevented from going into depth.

Some children need few 'invitations to observe' but others are more reluctant and may be easily distracted after a superficial glance. There can be many reasons for this; likely ones include the effective discouragement of detailed observation by allowing insufficient time, or the teacher plying them with questions too soon. Reluctant observers can be helped by a teacher making a comment that might encourage observation rather than a question, which can seem threatening. For example, 'Look what happens to the pebbles when you put them in water' is more of an invitation than 'What happens to the colour of the pebbles when you put them in water?'

Discussion plays a major part in encouraging observation at all stages. In the early stages of development, talking about their own observations and hearing about what others have observed helps children to make some sense of what they have found, to fit it into their understanding of the things just observed and of the others like them which they may have encountered previously. They may find that what others report differs from their own view, so they may want to return to observe more carefully, focusing on the particular feature that will decide the issue.

The move towards focusing is a sign of progress in developing observation skill. It is then appropriate to help this development with questions: do the snail shells all have the same number of turns? Is there any connection between the size and the number of turns? These questions encourage the children to focus the observations for themselves. Problems in which objects or events have to be placed in some sequence are useful for this purpose, for they demand that the children find and focus on the feature that determines the sequence.

The narrowing effect of focused questions should be moderated by more open ones: what else is different about the shells of the same type of snail? What things are the same about shells of different types? Answering these questions helps children to realise that their focused selective observation uses only part of the information that is available. It can prevent them becoming blinkered by existing ideas which lead them to observe only what they expect.

In summary, the teacher helps the development of ability to gather evidence through observation by:

- providing opportunity (materials and time) and encouragement for children to make wide-ranging *and* focused observations (by comments and questions)
- enabling children to talk informally about their observations, to each other and to the teacher (discussion)
- arranging for observations made in small groups to be shared in a whole-class discussion.

Interpreting evidence and drawing conclusions

Although this process is the key to children learning from their investigations, it is often neglected. Sometimes time runs out and the important discussion after practical work is not held. Children go on to the next activity without bringing together what they have already found (cf. Douglas Barnes's comment on p. 168).

One of the important aspects of this process skill is looking for patterns which relate together observations or data which might otherwise remain disconnected from each other. The ability to do this enables children to make sense of a mass of information which would be difficult to grasp as isolated events or observations. But not all patterns are easily detected, they may be obscured by features which vary unsystematically. So it is useful in helping children to search for patterns to provide some activities where the patterns can be easily picked out. For example:

- the distance a toy car rolls before it stops when started on a ramp at different heights
- the pitch of a plucked stretched string when its length is changed
- the pitch of different notes made by striking bottles with different amounts of water in them.

Those who have difficulty will be helped by discussion and hearing what others have found, so arranging for children to talk about the patterns they find in their results is important. The way in which they refer to pattern may indicate whether they are taking account of all the information. For example, children often describe the relation between the length and pitch of a plucked string in these ways:

- The longer the string the lower the note.
- The longest string gives the lowest and the shortest the highest.
- A long string gives a low note.
- If you change the length the note changes.

Each is correct, but the last three give less information than the first. The teacher's problem is to find out whether children who give an incomplete account of the pattern have actually grasped it as a whole but cannot express it as a whole, or whether they do not see the pattern that links all the information, as done in the first statement. There have to be opportunities therefore for a great deal of talking about patterns and about different ways of describing them. Generally, much too little time is used in this way.

Checking predictions against evidence is an important part of 'pattern-finding' work, as well as contributing to an attitude of respect for evidence. So the organisation of this work has to allow for toing and froing between making observations or finding information and discussing it. Children might also be encouraged to speculate about the patterns they expect to find, before gathering data and checking carefully to see if there is evidence to support their ideas.

As children's ability to detect and express straightforward patterns becomes established their experience can be widened, taking in situations where the relation between two quantities is not an exact pattern. For example, there may well be a general relation between the size of people's feet and their height but there will be people who have larger feet than others who are shorter than they are. Discussion of these cases is useful in encouraging caution in drawing conclusions from patterns. Clearly, with foot size and height there is no cause–effect relation; the pattern shows only that these are features which tend to go together, though not invariably. This is probably because they are both related to other features, ones which determine growth. It often happens that a pattern is found between two things which both relate to a third variable, or a string of other variables, but have themselves no direct cause–effect relation. (Success in school and month of birth is an example, winter-born children tending to be more successful than summer-born children, until about the age of 11 or 12. There is nothing about the time of year that itself makes any difference; it may be related to time in school which in turn is related to measured success in school.)

This digression has been made to show that there are good reasons for resisting the temptation to draw conclusions about cause and effect from observed relations. Causes have to be established through controlled experimentation. Children cannot be expected to realise this but when interpreting findings or information they can, and should be expected to, make statements which keep to the evidence.

It requires a delicate touch on the part of the teacher to encourage children, on the one hand, to try to relate together different pieces of information but on the other hand not to assume a type of relation for which there is no evidence. We also want children to try to explain the patterns and associations they find but to realise that when they do this they are going beyond the interpretation of evidence and making use of previous knowledge, or imagination, in their hypotheses.

Summing up, the teacher's role in encouraging children to interpret evidence and draw conclusions involves:

- providing opportunities in the form of activities where simple patterns or more general trends can be found (practical work)
- enabling children to talk about their findings and how they interpret them (by questioning and listening)
- expecting them to check interpretations carefully and to draw only those conclusions for which they have evidence (discussion and practical work)
- organising for interpretations of findings to be shared and discussed critically.

Communicating and reflecting

The dual role of communicating, as a means of giving or gaining information and as an aid to thought, makes it a particularly important skill. But the fact that communication may be going on all the time may mean that no special effort is made to promote it. Recent re-emphasis on developing literacy has drawn attention to the fact that communication is going on all the time and that each subject area has a contribution to make. So we have to be concerned with two complementary aspects of communication in science:

- using it to develop general literacy skills
- using literacy skills to develop children's scientific understanding.

The way in which science activities can contribute to general literacy skills is well illustrated by Feasey (1999). She sets out examples of how science activities can be used in language lessons (including the 'literacy hour') to encourage skills such as oral retelling of experiences, the use of labels and captions, using new vocabulary, using dictionaries, sequencing events, asking and answering questions, making notes and writing for various purposes and audiences. In the case of making notes, for example, the suggested science activity (based on an idea from the Nuffield Primary Science unit on Materials) is as follows:

Give children a sheet of paper divided into 6–8 sections. Ask them to tell, in a set of pictures, the story of an object, such as a spoon or a glass, from the origin of the material or materials of which it is made to the finished product.

Discuss with children their ideas on how a particular object was made, looking for similarities and differences. Ask them to justify what they have put, where possible drawing on evidence they might be able to offer, such as personal experience.

Provide children with access to either non-fiction books of an appropriate level or video or CD-ROM material. Ask them to use the reference material to find out the key stages in making the material under discussion.

(Feasey, 1999, p. 44)

In many such activities learning science and literacy skills are combined, although there may be a greater emphasis on one or the other. In this activity the discussion is particularly valuable to the development of ideas, as we have noted in Chapter 11. Equally strong arguments are made for the value of writing to learning. But, as with talking, the fact that some kind goes on all the time does not necessarily mean that children have opportunities for the kind of writing that is most useful for their learning in science.

The use of a personal notebook and keeping a diary are devices for encouraging children to use writing to aid their memory and to help sort out their thoughts. For this purpose it is best if they are regarded as personal and not 'marked' by the teacher. The teacher, however, can make suggestions about what might go into the notebook – observations and particularly measurements which may be quickly forgotten. Teachers who wish children to use these things have to arrange to supply not just the materials, but the incentive and the time to use them.

More formal written communication in science often involves use of non-verbal forms: graphs, charts and tabulated numbers. The techniques of using these are usually not difficult to learn; what is more difficult and more important is the selection of the appropriate form to suit particular purposes and types of information. Skill in selecting among possible symbolic representations comes with experience, but experience is more likely to bring development if it is discussed. The critical review of activities could, with advantage, include discussion of the form of presentation of findings. The teacher can also help in this matter by displaying in the classroom good examples of information appropriately and clearly presented.

From these points the teacher's role in developing communication and reflection skills can be summarised as:

- organising the class so that children can work and discuss in groups
- providing a structure in the children's tasks that encourages group discussion and the keeping of informal notes
- introducing a range of techniques for recording information and communicating results using conventional forms and symbols
- discussing the appropriateness of ways of organising and presenting information to suit particular purposes.

Common strategies

Looking back now over what has been said about the role of the teacher in regard to the development of process skills a great deal of repetition is apparent. There are certain things the teacher has to do to enable children to use and develop all the process skills.

Actions that teachers can take to help children to develop process skills include:

- providing opportunity for children to encounter materials and phenomena to explore at first hand
- arranging for discussion in small groups and in the whole class about procedures that are planned or have been used, so as to identify ways in which they might be improved
- providing access to alternative procedures through discussion, books, etc.
- setting challenging tasks whilst providing support (scaffolding) so that children can experience operating at a more advanced level
- teaching the techniques needed for advancing skills, including the use of equipment, measuring instruments and conventional symbols
- encouraging children through comment and questioning to check that their ideas are consistent with the evidence available
- encouraging critical reflection on how they have learned and how this can be applied in future learning
- using questioning to encourage the use of process skills, for example:
  - What would you like to know about . . .?
  - Why do you think x is growing better than y?
  - What do you think will happen if . . .?
  - What will you do to find out . . .?
  - What differences do you notice . . .?
  - Have you found any connection between . . .?
  - What is the best way to show what you found?

The common factors in the approach to teaching for development of all the process skills constitute both an advantage and a disadvantage. The advantage is that if the teacher does put all these things into practice then the conditions exist for the various skills to be developed in step with each other. Observation advances at the same time as interpretation and communication, for example. Each activity therefore contributes to several areas of development, though to each one only in a small degree. Gradually, the cumulative effect of successive activities builds up the skills. This creates the case for what might be considered by some to be the disadvantage, that opportunities for process skill development have to be provided frequently, if not continuously. It is no use allocating one or two sessions to developing 'raising questions' or 'planning investigations' and then forgetting about these process skills. Not only will the skill drop out of use but it will probably be actively discouraged if an approach to teaching is adopted which excludes children raising questions and doing their own planning.

Table 12.1 attempts to bring together the components of the teacher's role in developing process skills and some of the purposes that each serves. It highlights the close interplay of development of ideas and process skills since these roles echo those which help children to develop their ideas.

Helping the development of scientific attitudes

Attitudes are more generalised aspects of people's behaviour even than process skills. They can be said to exist only when a general pattern of reacting in certain ways to certain types of situation has been established. One observation of a child spontaneously checking a suggested conclusion by seeking more evidence is not a sufficient basis for assuming that he has developed 'respect for evidence'. But if he or she did spontaneously check so often that one could confidently predict that he would do so in further instances, then he or she might well be described as having this attitude.

The nature of attitudes means that there is a great deal that is common in encouraging their development. They cannot be taught, for they are not things that children know or can do; rather they are 'caught', for they exist in the way people behave and are transferred to children by a mixture of example and selective approval of behaviour that reflects the attitude. Indeed, quite frequent reference has already been made to the encouragement of certain attitudes during the discussion of opportunities for process skill development and it must already be obvious that there is

Table 12.1 Components and purpose of the teacher's role in process-skill development

Role	Purposes
Providing the materials, time and physical arrangement for children to study and interact with things from their environment	For children to have the evidence of their own senses, to raise questions, to find answers to them by doing things, to have concrete experience as a basis for their thinking and to be able to check ideas they develop against the behaviour of real things
Designing tasks that encourage discussion among small groups of children	For children to combine their ideas, to listen to others, to argue about differences and to refine their own ideas through explaining them to others
Discussing with children as individuals and in small groups	For children to explain how they arrive at their ideas; for teachers to listen, to find out the evidence children have gathered and how they have interpreted it, to encourage children to check findings and to review their activities and results critically
Organising whole-class discussions	For children to have opportunity to describe their findings and ideas to others, to hear about others' ideas, to comment on alternative views and to defend their own; for teachers to offer ideas and direct children to sources that will extend the children's ideas
Teaching the techniques of using equipment and conventions of using graphs, tables, charts and symbols	For children to have available the means to increase the accuracy of their observations and to choose appropriate forms for communication as the need arises
Providing books, displays, visits, visitors and access to other sources of information	For children to be able to compare their ideas with those of others, to have access to information that may help them to develop and extend their ideas, to raise questions that may lead to further enquiry

much in common in the approaches required to foster attitudes and skills. In general terms these are:

- showing an example
- creating a classroom climate that gives approval to the behaviour that signifies the attitude
- providing opportunity for the attitude to be shown
- making allowances for individual differences
- providing time.

The following are some examples of teachers' actions that show what these might mean in practice for each attitude.

Curiosity

- Sharing in the excitement and questioning about things; 'wondering why' with the children.
- Welcoming children's questions and comments that show curiosity, storing these questions if they cannot be dealt with straight away and making sure of returning to them later.
- Providing new stimuli that will encourage curiosity; refreshing displays.
- Encouraging those who show fleeting curiosity as well as those whose interest is more sustained.
- Providing time for curiosity to be satisfied rather than frustrated.

Respect for evidence

- Teachers providing the evidence for the statements they make; not expecting children to accept them without evidence.
- Asking children to say what is behind their claims and statements; encouraging them to question each other and ask for evidence.
- Ensuring plenty of time for interpreting evidence and considering how sure they can be about conclusions drawn.
- Reminding children of evidence that they may have ignored.
- Providing time for discussion when findings are being reviewed so that alternative interpretations can be considered.

Flexibility in ways of thinking

- Participating in discussions about ideas that have changed, being prepared to say 'I used to think that . . . but now . . .'.
- Avoiding associating ideas with individuals ('Daniel's idea') so that children do not defend ideas in order to protect self-esteem.
- Planning opportunities for children to think of alternative ideas; introducing new ideas to try.
- Providing ways of dealing with conflicting views that support the separation of ideas from their sources and treat all as open to test.
- Providing time for thinking about problems in different ways.

Critical reflection

- Starting a discussion about whether a better way of doing something could be found.
- Expecting children to reflect on what they have learned from an activity.
- Adopting as routine the discussion of how an investigation might be improved if it were to be repeated.
- Letting children work in groups to combine ideas about how their investigations could be improved and problems avoided in the future.
- Providing time for reviewing the way activities have been carried out as well as what was found.

Sensitivity in investigating the environment

This attitude is more obviously linked to particular concepts and understanding than those we have considered so far, though one of our main themes is that all attitudes, concepts and skills are interrelated to some degree. It is more likely that someone with an understanding of, say, the effect on wild flowers of over-picking, will look and not pick than someone without such understanding who may pick the flowers innocently. There is no certainty about this; the knowledge helps but it is not enough to create the attitude. The converse is also true, fortunately, that lack of understanding is not an inevitable barrier to forming these attitudes. Thus, although many of the concepts relating to care of the environment are too complex for very young children to grasp (air pollution and ozone depletion, for instance), and some are controversial (the need to preserve endangered species, seal-culling, even fox-hunting), it is still possible to begin the development of attitudes towards the environment by example and rules of conduct.

The teacher's role here is to:

- provide opportunities for children to look after living things, including invertebrates, and become aware of their needs
- show, by checking frequently on any living things in the classroom, the importance of regular and appropriate care
- ensuring that living or non-living material (e.g. rocks) taken from the environment for study are returned to where they were found
- discussing and agreeing simple rules for protecting the environment, both living and non-living when they are studying it or using it for recreation.

Summary

This chapter has continued the discussion, begun in Chapter 11, of actions that can be taken to help children take the 'next steps' in learning, once these have been identified by gathering and interpreting evidence of their current achievements. The focus here has been on process skills and attitudes. In relation to process skills, the action appropriate to the various skills has been considered for each one separately. This has revealed a degree of commonality across the skills in relation to the need to provide:

- opportunity to use the skills, which includes time to do this thoroughly
- access to others' ideas about procedures
- help in operating at a more advanced level (scaffolding)
- guidance in techniques needed for advancing skills, such as using equipment and the conventions of drawing graphs and tables
- a structure that supports checking that conclusions are consistent with evidence
- encouragement to reflect on procedures and identify how they might be improved
- questions that require children to use process skills.

The development of attitudes that support scientific inquiry has been discussed in terms of action relevant to encouraging curiosity, respect for evidence, flexibility in ways of thinking, critical reflection and sensitivity in investigating the environment. In each case attention has been drawn to:

- the importance of the example provided by the teacher
- the classroom climate that gives opportunity for and approval to behaviours relating to the attitude
- making allowances for children at different points in development of the attitude
- providing time for observation, discussion, review and reflection.

Points for reflection

- Attention to developing and using process skills takes time. How can this be reconciled with the need to develop children's knowledge and understanding across the basic scientific concepts?

- To what extent might children be made aware of the process skills they are using and recognise when, for example, they are hypothesising, or drawing conclusions, rather than just doing it?

Further reading

Discussion of questioning can be found in two chapters in W. Harlen (ed.) (1985) *Primary Science: Taking the Plunge*. London: Heinemann: S. Jelly, 'Helping children raise questions – and answering them' and J. Elstgeest, 'The right question at the right time'.

Ideas for using science in developing children's literacy can be found in:

Feasey, R. (1999) *Primary Science and Literacy*. Hatfield: Association for Science Education.

13

Gathering and interpreting evidence for summative assessment

Here we pick up from Chapter 8 the thread of assessment for summative purposes. These purposes require information on each child's achievement to be available at certain times and in forms that make it useful to other teachers and meaningful to parents and to the children themselves. For these purposes, evidence has to be judged by the same criteria for all children, since comparisons between children may be made. The information also needs to give an overall picture of achievement and so much of the detail has to be summarised. This will inevitably mean bringing together aspects of achievement that are best kept separate for formative assessment purposes. A further difference from formative assessment is that those receiving the report on achievement generally want to know where a child has reached in relation to expectations set for all children, indicated by standards or levels.

Figure 8.2, in Chapter 8, outlined the procedures for summative assessment. It indicated that the evidence collected by the teacher is interpreted and summarised in terms of achievement of goals. There are three ways of doing this depending on the type of evidence gathered:

- using evidence gathered during regular activities
- using special tasks or tests
- a combination of both the above.

These form the foci for the first three sections of this chapter. Making and using records is the subject of the fourth section. The final part discusses records and the role of children in summative assessment. Our concern in this chapter is essentially assessment for use in reporting and supporting the learning of individual children. The use of this information in other ways, such as in school evaluation, in discussed in Chapter 15.

Interpreting evidence from regular activities

Under this heading we consider the use for summative assessment of evidence obtained using methods discussed in Chapter 9. This is evidence that the teacher has gathered for formative assessment, to help day-to-day teaching and learning. It is very detailed, specific to particular activities and probably too voluminous to be used for summative purposes. It will, hopefully, have been used in feeding back judgements to children and involving them in decisions about next steps. In this process it is interpreted in relation to the expectations and recent achievements of the children and not just in terms of progress towards goals.

For summative assessment, however, interpretations differ from those for formative assessment in three main ways:

- They are often expressed in terms of how a child's achievement compares with levels or standards which indicate expectations for particular stages or ages.
- They indicate children's progress towards the same goals in the same way for all children.
- They are less detailed and give an overview of progress.

We now look at the practical implications of these features.

Comparing achievement with expectations

Since 1988 in the UK and perhaps earlier in the USA and other countries there has been a move away from using class 'norms' for interpreting children's performance in summative assessment in favour of national standards. These standards are indicated in various ways. For example in the National Curriculum for England they are indicated by descriptions of performance at eight levels (DfEE, 1999). Levels are roughly two years apart and the first four apply to the primary school (up to age 11). The level labels provide a shorthand for indicating the nature of achievement and enable pupils to be compared with one another. Although these levels are not expressed in terms of ages, the expectations are that level 2 is reached by the average 7-year-old and level 4 by the average 11-year-old.

A similar system (except with the levels labelled A to F) is used in the Scottish 5–14 curriculum and the levels are defined explicitly in terms of year levels, but allowing for a range within each year:

- Level A should be attainable in the course of P1–P3 by almost all pupils.

- Level B should be attainable by some pupils in P3 or earlier, but by most in P4.
- Level C should be obtainable in the course of P4–P6 by most pupils.
- Level D should be obtainable by some pupils in P5–P6 or earlier, but certainly by most in P7.
- Level E should be obtainable by some pupils in P7–S1 but by most in S2.

(Here P1 is the first class of the primary school (age 4–5) and S1 the first class of the secondary school (age 12–13).)

In the USA, the American Association for the Advancement of Science (AAAS) set out Benchmarks for Science Literacy, which are the expected outcomes at particular grade levels (AAAS, 1993). Figure 13.1 shows the expected outcomes for the grade 2 and grade 5 in relation to understanding the structure of matter.

End of 5th grade (all students should know that:)
- Heating and cooling cause changes in the properties of materials. Many kinds of changes occur faster under hotter conditions.
- No matter how the parts of an object are assembled, the weight of the whole object made is always the sum of the parts; and when a thing is broken into parts, the parts have the same total weight as the original thing.
- Materials may be composed of parts that are too small to be seen without magnification.
- When a new material is made by combining two or more materials, it has properties that are different from the original materials. For that reason, a lot of different materials can be made from a small number of basic kinds of materials.

End of 2nd grade (all students should know that:)
- Objects can be described in terms of the materials they are made of (clay, cloth, paper, etc.) and their physical properties (color, size, shape, weight, texture, flexibility, etc.).
- Things can be done to materials to change some of their properties, but not all materials respond in the same way to what is done to them.

Figure 13.1 AAAS Benchmarks: outcomes relating to the structure of matter
Source: AAAS (1993)

These standards or benchmarks are created by groups of people with relevant professional expertise from classroom experience or research data. They go about this task in one of two ways. The first, more common, is to start with children of different ages or school grade levels in mind and to identify what are the expected levels of achievement for these children. In some cases this is expressed in terms of average expected performance (as in the case of the

National Curriculum) or in terms of what all children should be able to do (as in the AAAS Benchmarks). The second way is to begin from maps of development, described in Chapter 10. The task is then to label certain parts of this development as appropriate achievement at certain ages or stages. This second approach makes it rather easier to interpolate between levels.

Summarising the evidence on the same basis for all children

When evidence from regular activities is used for summative assess-ment it is important that it is the *evidence* that is reviewed, not the *judgements* made for formative purposes. This important distinction was also made in Chapter 8 (p. 117). The teacher should review the child's work and the private notes on it and decide how it compares with criteria, indicators or level descriptions. This should be done in the same way for all children so that the resulting judgements have the same meaning.

In practice this is not as easy as it sounds. For it is not enough to be aware of the criteria but for those using them to share a common interpretation. No criteria in a list of manageable length can be so specific that they can be used with total agreement. Useful criteria have to be couched in general terms so that they can apply in the wide variety of contexts in which learning takes place and this means that they are inevitably ambiguous to some extent. For example, it could be said that 'notices patterns in findings', could apply as equally to a research scientist as to an 8-year-old. The same could be said of almost any statement that uses the word 'appropriate' or 'relevant'. In using such statements, therefore, there must be some consideration of what it is reasonable to expect of children at certain ages. Thus an element of norm-referencing intrudes into a criterion-referenced judgement.

Clearly it is essential for there to be as near uniformity as possible in the interpretation of criteria if they are to be useful in practice. Ideally one teacher's judgement of whether a child has achieved, say, level 2 or the standard expected at 5th grade must be the same as another's. In practice it is very difficult to achieve this and even to find out the extent to which there is agreement. However, there are various steps that can be taken to help to align, or moderate, teachers' judgements. Among these are:

- Collecting examples of work, which can be judged against the criteria by several teachers independently. This has the disadvan-tage that such examples rarely evoke the context, background and conditions in which the work was done – all of which influence judgements in real situations.

- Discussing published exemplars. This can be valuable as a basis for helping teachers to adjust their judgements to be in line with official views on the meaning of standards. The exemplification of standards published by SCAA and the Performance Standards for the New Standards published in the USA are examples.
- Individual teachers can use the examples given in some curriculum materials which are designed to help teachers to summarise achievement in terms of national standards (e.g. Nuffield Primary Science, Teacher's Guides, 1995).

It is important in such examples that it is the work that is described in terms of the levels and not the child, since a child's level should be judged from a number of pieces of work. The examples give guidance as to what to look for.

Summarising the detail

When a summary is created, there is always some loss of information. The alternative is to retain the full detail and lose the potential to grasp the information as a whole. So with summative assessment, it is necessary to lose detail that is essential for formative assessment in order to gain an overall picture. So we need criteria that help to bring together different kinds of information. Standards and level descriptions are one way of doing this, but not the only way.

Figure 13.2 illustrates an approach to summarising achievement of process skills in a way that acknowledges the unevenness of development for individual children. It brings together statements relating to all the process skills into three broad stages.

Achievement could then be described in terms of expectations at different ages, if this was required, in terms of expectations, such as:

Age   Statements for which there is evidence of achievement
5   None or one from early list
6   2 or 3 from early list
7   More than half from early list
8   Almost all from early list + at least 2 from middle list
9   More than half from middle list
10   Almost all from middle list + at least 2 from later list
11   More than half from later list
12   Almost all from later list

So if two or three statements from the early list apply then the child could be described as operating at the level expected of a 6-year-old.

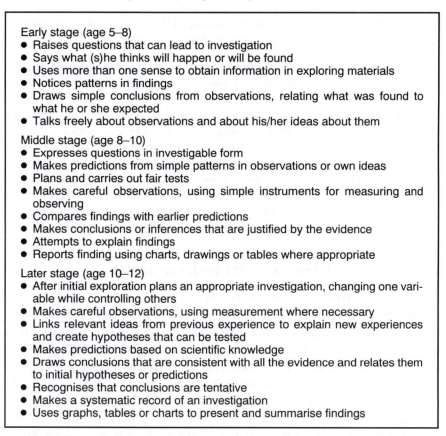

Early stage (age 5–8)
- Raises questions that can lead to investigation
- Says what (s)he thinks will happen or will be found
- Uses more than one sense to obtain information in exploring materials
- Notices patterns in findings
- Draws simple conclusions from observations, relating what was found to what he or she expected
- Talks freely about observations and about his/her ideas about them

Middle stage (age 8–10)
- Expresses questions in investigable form
- Makes predictions from simple patterns in observations or own ideas
- Plans and carries out fair tests
- Makes careful observations, using simple instruments for measuring and observing
- Compares findings with earlier predictions
- Makes conclusions or inferences that are justified by the evidence
- Attempts to explain findings
- Reports finding using charts, drawings or tables where appropriate

Later stage (age 10–12)
- After initial exploration plans an appropriate investigation, changing one variable while controlling others
- Makes careful observations, using measurement where necessary
- Links relevant ideas from previous experience to explain new experiences and create hypotheses that can be tested
- Makes predictions based on scientific knowledge
- Draws conclusions that are consistent with all the evidence and relates them to initial hypotheses or predictions
- Recognises that conclusions are tentative
- Makes a systematic record of an investigation
- Uses graphs, tables or charts to present and summarise findings

Figure 13.2 Summary of achievement in process skills at early, middle and later stages for the 5–12 age range

Alternatively achievement could be described more broadly in terms of the progress towards what is expected at each stage. It should be noted that these are *suggested ways* of going about summarising achievement; they are not validated instruments.

As acknowledged earlier, this loses information – we would not know which process skills were better or less well developed. But it gives a general idea of the level of development of the skills of inquiry. Since these skills should all have been used and developed in a number of investigations, it is not unreasonable to expect them all to have been developed together.

For achievement in relation to ideas, however, it makes less sense to combine them into an overall indication of development of understanding. Achievement in this respect in any period of time will depend on the topics that have been covered in that time. So it is best to report on the understanding of key aspects of those topics that have been covered. This can be done in terms of the specific

areas of understanding given in Chapter 10 (pp. 152–155) or using a
general framework of development. For example:

Early stage (5–8)	Has acquired basic information about (living things . . , forces . . . , rocks . . . , the Earth in space . . .)
Middle stage (8–10)	Can use ideas that link different experience of (living things . . . , forces . . . , rocks . . . , the Earth in space . . .) to give explanations of new experiences within the topic
Later stage (10–12)	Can use ideas that link experience of (living things . . . , forces . . . , rocks . . . , the Earth in space . . .) to other topics to explain a range of relevant phenomena

Using special tasks or tests

One of the differences in characteristics between formative and
summative assessment, noted in Chapter 8, was that the needs of
formative assessment were for greater emphasis on validity than
on reliability, whilst the reverse applied to summative assessment.
Thus there would appear to be attractions in using special tasks or
tests for summative assessment since they appear to provide reliable measures and equal opportunities for children to show what
they can do at a particular time. However, giving children the
same tasks is not the same as giving them the same opportunities
since learning opportunity implies a match between the activity
and the child's ability to engage with it. Moreoever, if this degree
of apparent 'fairness' is to be gained then the children have to be
treated in the same way and placed in a test situation. This has
other disadvantages:

- The tasks are restricted to those which can be done in the test
  context.
- There is a restricted range of skills and ideas that can be included,
  partly because of the practical limitation on length of a test and
  partly because some skills are only revealed in extended
  activities.
- Tests require considerable teacher time for organisation and
  marking.
- They take up learning time.
- They can induce anxiety in children.

Many of these disadvantages are avoided when teachers who
wish to check up on children's progress through giving special tasks

try to present these to children as part of their usual work rather than as formal tests. Examples of such tasks have been provided by the work of the Science Teaching Action Research Project (STAR) and published in Schilling *et al.* (1990). The materials devised and used in the STAR project take the form of a small class project about an imaginary 'walled garden'. The children are introduced to various features of the walled garden – water (in a pond with a fountain), walls, wood, minibeasts, leaves, bark, sundial. For each of these seven features a poster was produced which could be displayed in the classroom, giving suggestions for activities and posing some questions. Pupils work on one poster at a time and answer the questions in the answer booklet linked to the activities for that feature. Pupils can carry out the activities in any sequence and so a whole class can be working at the same time without interfering with each other's work. The questions were designed for written answers, but the element of active exploration in arriving at the answers extends the range of skills which can be tested. The questions are process based and the different content provided by the seven features creates opportunities for the skills to be used in different contexts and so avoids to some extent the problem of validity which arises when skills are used on limited content. Since the activities are well designed, attractively presented and intriguing to children there is no problem in children engaging with the tasks as if they were normal work. Thus in various ways, many of the disadvantages of tests are avoided. As examples, the questions on leaves are reproduced in Figure 13.3.

The approach embodied in the 'walled garden' materials can be readily adapted in the classroom, perhaps avoiding the expensive individual pupil booklet. Other questions and tasks could be designed using the original material as a pattern. For example, more questions could be added that require children to show understanding of science concepts relevant to their activities.

In checking on children's developing ideas the important aim is to ensure that children are *applying* their ideas, working out their answer from their own thinking rather than simply recalling it. The decision as to what children are likely to be able to recall and what they will have to work out depends on the experiences of the children. For some, an answer to the question 'How would you try to stop an ice cube from melting for as long as possible without using a fridge?' may require application of ideas about the need for heat to bring about melting and transfer of heat through different materials. For others, however, who may have undertaken such an activity, it may be a matter of recalling what was done and the reasons put

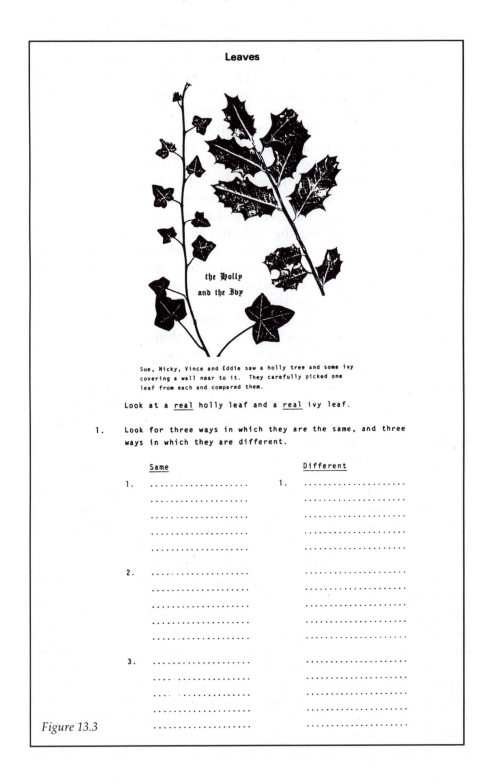

Leaves

the Holly
and the Ivy

Sue, Nicky, Vince and Eddie saw a holly tree and some ivy
covering a wall near to it. They carefully picked one
leaf from each and compared them.

Look at a <u>real</u> holly leaf and a <u>real</u> ivy leaf.

1.   Look for three ways in which they are the same, and three
     ways in which they are different.

     Same   Different

1.   ....   1.   ....
     ....
     ....
     ....
     ....

2.   ....
     ....
     ....
     ....
     ....

3.   ....
     ....
     ....
     ....
     ....

Figure 13.3

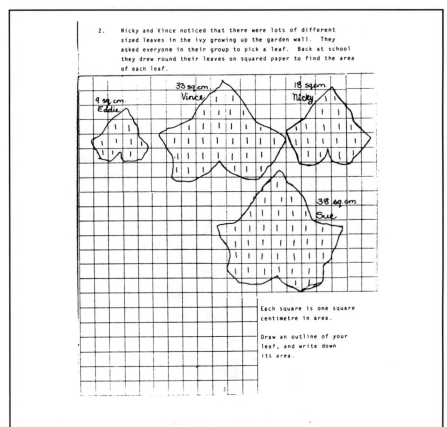

2. Nicky and Vince noticed that there were lots of different
    sized leaves in the ivy growing up the garden wall. They
    asked everyone in their group to pick a leaf. Back at school
    they drew round their leaves on squared paper to find the area
    of each leaf.

Each square is one square centimetre in area.

Draw an outline of your leaf, and write down its area.

Sue wondered, "Are holly leaves different sizes?"

They asked their teacher to cut a holly twig for them. There
is a picture of it in the project folder.

The holly leaves were too prickly to draw round so the children
decided to measure the length of each leaf instead.

leaf position	leaf length
1	7 cm
2	9 cm
3	10 cm
4	9 cm
5	cm
6	6 cm
7	5 cm

Figure 13.3

3.   a)   The children had found that the IVY leaves were larger the further they were from the tip of the twig.

Are HOLLY leaves arranged that way? What do you notice about the length of the leaves and the distance from the tip of the twig?

....

....

....

b)   What do you <u>think</u> the length of leaf 5 might have been?

.... cm.   (The picture is NOT the right size.)

The leaves are numbered in order from the tip of the twig.

Sue and Jack were interested in the holly tree. They planned to find the area of some holly leaves but the leaves were too prickly.

The prickles were such a nuisance that they decided to count how many were on each leaf. They made a table of their results.

leaf length	number of prickles
10 cm	17
9 cm	16
7.5 cm	14
6 cm	12
5 cm	10

Figure 13.3

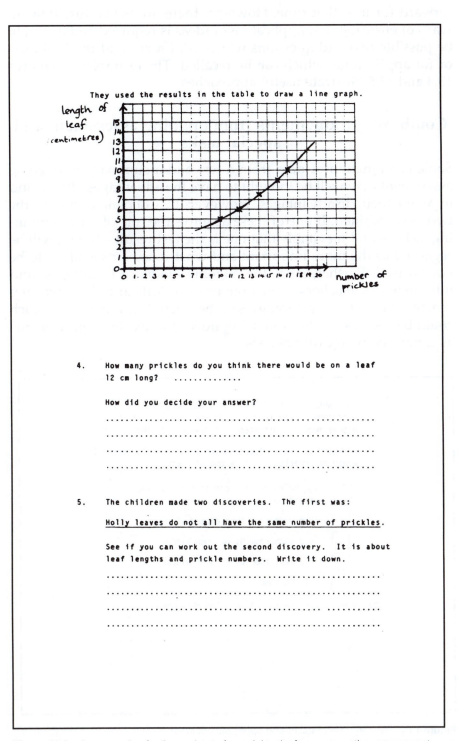

They used the results in the table to draw a line graph.

length of leaf (centimetres)

number of prickles

4. How many prickles do you think there would be on a leaf 12 cm long? ....

How did you decide your answer?

....
....
....
....

5. The children made two discoveries. The first was:

<u>Holly leaves do not all have the same number of prickles</u>.

See if you can work out the second discovery. It is about leaf lengths and prickle numbers. Write it down.

....
....
....
....

Figure 13.3 An example of a themed set of special tasks for a summative assessment

forward for it at that time. However, there are many variations in ways of ensuring that application of ideas is required and it should be possible to avoid questions which ask for straight recall of facts or for applications which can be recalled. The examples in Figures 13.4 and 13.5 illustrate useful approaches.

Combining judgements from ongoing assessment and special tasks

Some combination of data from a test and a summary of ongoing assessment may well be thought to have the advantages of each and to avoid their disadvantages. However, this depends on how the two are combined. If one of these acquires the role of the determining factor – and inevitably that one is the test result – then it will be regarded as the more important and what it assesses is likely to be emphasised. Further, since the ongoing evidence is gathered and interpreted by teachers, whilst the tasks or tests and their marking schemes are usually externally set, the relative value given to each could be seen as a reflection of confidence in teachers' judgements as compared with external tests.

John washed four handkerchiefs and hung them up in different places to dry. He wanted to see if the places made any difference to how quickly they dried.

a) In which of these places do you think the handkerchief would dry quickest? Tick one of these:

☐ In the corridor where it was cool and sheltered
☐ In a warm room by a closed window
☐ In a warm room by an open window
☐ In a cool room by an open window
☐ All the same

b) What is your reason for ticking this one?

. . . .
. . . .
. . . .
. . . .
. . . .

Figure 13.4 Written task for assessing application of ideas 1
Source: DES (1984)

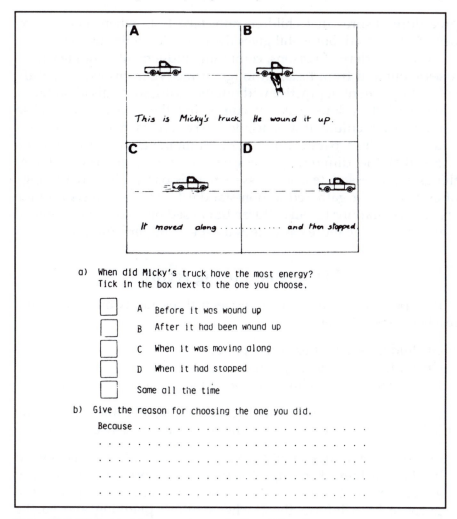

Figure 13.5   Written task for assessing application of ideas 2
Source: DES (1983)

In some systems the two are combined in a given proportion (e.g. 50:50 or 30:70) to give the overall result. Numerical scores are needed to make such calculations and the result lacks meaning in relation to criteria. An alternative way, that preserves this meaning, is used in the Scottish system. Teachers use their accumulated evidence to decide when a child has achieved what is specified at a certain level. The teacher then administers an externally produced test for that level. If the test is passed (i.e. a cut-off score achieved) the child is confirmed as having reached that level. If not, then the teacher uses the test results to identify weaknesses and, after a minimum period of 12 weeks, can retest the child using a parallel form of the test. This procedure ensures that children only take tests when they are expected to succeed, but it still gives the test a determining role.

So, for a variety of reasons, combining judgements from teachers' assessment and from tests, although attractive in principle, is difficult to implement in practice without incurring some disadvantages. Having tried various ways of combining the two in the English National Curriculum, it was decided to report teachers' assessments and test results separately and not to combine them. This acknowledges that the different procedures mean that slightly different things are assessed: teachers' assessment is based on a broad range of evidence, but gathered in non-standard situations; tests provide standard situations for all children but based on a narrower range of evidence and the more easily tested aspects of performance.

Making and using records

It is important to distinguish between three kinds of records that teachers need to keep:

1 Of children's activities and experiences.
2 Of children's day-to-day achievements.
3 Of what individual children have achieved at certain points.

The guiding principles in keeping records are that the information should have clear purposes and that it is used for those purposes.

1 Records of activities should not be confused with records of what has been achieved through them. These records are not part of assessment and so we will not dwell on them at this point. The purpose is to inform the teacher's future planning and so the record of what children have experienced is often kept by annotating teachers' short-term plans (see Chapter 15).
2 Information about day-to-day achievements is used formatively by the teacher. Any records that are made are essentially for the teacher to remind him or herself of children's progress, and the amount of detail and the exact form are individual matters. Circumstances and experience as well as personal preference influence the amount of information teachers can keep in their heads and what it is essential to put down on paper. Unnecessary recording and transcribing from one form to another should be avoided.
3 Summary records are made for communication with others and so it is usual for the format and structure to be agreed within the school. Records of what children have achieved may attempt to capture the richness and variety of their performance through

description and collection of examples of work, or it may take the form of symbols representing the achievement in relation to certain criteria. This is where it is important for any symbols or summary phrases that are used to be interpreted in the same way by the teacher who makes the record and others who will receive and use it. The form of record is an integral part of an assessment. It is in making the record that the actual performance is replaced by some representation of it.

Most teachers now include intended outcomes as well as experiences in their scheme of work and these form a focus for recording achievement. The scheme of work for key stage 1 and key stage 2 science published by the DfEE (see p. 94) makes a distinction between learning outcomes for specific activities and 'end of unit expectations'. For example, in a unit of work on 'using electricity' (for year 2, or 6–7-year-olds) there are six activities, each with identified learning outcomes, extending over about eight hours of work. It would probably be unnecessary as well as far too time-consuming for teachers to record achievement for each child in relation to each activity. Notes about any child with particular problems would be sufficient as a reminder to give help later in the unit.

It is at the end of the topic or unit of work that it is helpful to make a record since that topic may not be revisited before the end of the year or the time when reports are given to parents. This could be done in relation to the 'unit expectations'. However, in the DfEE scheme these refer only to the knowledge developed in the unit and a more comprehensive record of progress would include process skills and attitudes. Figure 13.6 gives an example of how a cumulative record might be kept using the indicators of development at the end of Chapter 10. Each number represents a particular indicator. Some achievements could be represented by a single line across the appropriate box, with a second line being added when there is more evidence leading to greater certainty about what the child can do. Such records create a summary automatically.

Many teachers keep records of their summary judgements by making reference to the level descriptions of the National Curriculum (or their equivalent in national guidelines or standards). By using different signs for 'approaching', 'attempted', 'achieved' or similar, more discrimination can be made than only whether a level has been reached or not. While this may be appropriate for within school records, where usually teachers have taken steps to make their judgements consistent, it is not a friendly form for a report to parents, who need help in interpreting levels. It is more helpful for

Child's name ....
Dates of records ....

Raising questions	Hypothesising	Predicting	Gathering evidence: planning	Gathering evidence: observing	Interpreting and drawing conclusions	Communicating and reflecting
1 ☐ 2 ☐ 3 ☐ 4 ☐ 5 ☐ 6 ☐	1 ☐ 2 ☐ 3 ☐ 4 ☐ 5 ☐ 6 ☐	1 ☐ 2 ☐ 3 ☐ 4 ☐ 5 ☐ 6 ☐	1 ☐ 2 ☐ 3 ☐ 4 ☐ 5 ☐ 6 ☐	1 ☐ 2 ☐ 3 ☐ 4 ☐ 5 ☐ 6 ☐	1 ☐ 2 ☐ 3 ☐ 4 ☐ 5 ☐ 6 ☐	1 ☐ 2 ☐ 3 ☐ 4 ☐ 5 ☐ 6 ☐

Curiosity	Respect for evidence	Flexibility in thinking	Critical reflection	Sensitivity towards the environment
1 ☐ 2 ☐ 3 ☐ 4 ☐ 5 ☐ 6 ☐	1 ☐ 2 ☐ 3 ☐ 4 ☐ 5 ☐ 6 ☐	1 ☐ 2 ☐ 3 ☐ 4 ☐ 5 ☐ 6 ☐	1 ☐ 2 ☐ 3 ☐ 4 ☐ 5 ☐ 6 ☐	1 ☐ 2 ☐ 3 ☐ 4 ☐ 5 ☐ 6 ☐

Living things & life processes	Interaction living things & their environment	Materials	Air, atmosphere & weather	Rocks, soil & materials from the Earth	The Earth in space	Forces and movement	Energy sources and use
1 ☐ 2 ☐ 3 ☐ 4 ☐ 5 ☐ 6 ☐ 7 ☐	1 ☐ 2 ☐ 3 ☐ 4 ☐ 5 ☐ 6 ☐	1 ☐ 2 ☐ 3 ☐ 4 ☐ 5 ☐	1 ☐ 2 ☐ 3 ☐ 4 ☐ 5 ☐ 6 ☐	1 ☐ 2 ☐ 3 ☐ 4 ☐ 5 ☐ 6 ☐ 7 ☐	1 ☐ 2 ☐ 3 ☐ 4 ☐ 5 ☐ 6 ☐	1 ☐ 2 ☐ 3 ☐ 4 ☐ 5 ☐ 6 ☐ 7 ☐	1 ☐ 2 ☐ 3 ☐ 4 ☐ 5 ☐ 6 ☐ 7 ☐

Figure 13.6   Using the indicators of development for recording achievement

parents for the meaning of levels to be stated in words and for progress between levels to included. It is also widely agreed that reports to parents should indicate the teacher's personal knowledge of the child, be expressed positively to encourage motivation and identify the next steps in learning.

Children's participation in summative assessment

The characteristics of summative and formative assessment (Chapter 8) bring out the greater need for reliability and judgements against common criteria in summative compared with formative assessment. This suggests that there might be less room for children to assess themselves for summative than for formative purposes. Some attempts have, however, been made to involve children and to express the criteria in terms that children are likely to understand. For example, the Association for Science Education has published a document designed to be used with children. It comprises a series of statements relating to attainment of the knowledge targets of the National Curriculum, expressed in language easily understood by children. For example: 'I have made a circuit with a bulb and a switch to control it. I can put the switch in different places in the circuit. I can make a circuit diagram containing a battery, bulbs and wires' (Willis, 1999, n.p.). The statements are arranged as 'bricks' in a wall and a brick is coloured in when the teacher and child feel that it has been achieved. This is a cross between a record of activities and a record of achievement and it only relates to the knowledge outcomes of the curriculum. However, it does allow children to take part in building a record of their work and is something they could show to and talk about with their parents.

The participation of children in reviewing their work and recognising progress is central to the creation of their own individual records of achievement. The National Record of Achievement was intended to have a dual role of providing a record to be used by others (the product) and providing children with the experience of self-assessment and target-setting (the process). It has now been replaced by the Progress File, which has the primary aim of supporting self-assessment and improving motivation for learning. Although introduced first in secondary schools, the aims, if not the procedures, are relevant to the 5–12 age group. By becoming involved in self-assessment it is intended that children gradually take more responsibility for future learning.

The London Record of Achievement team did much to pioneer records of achievement for 5–12-year-olds. Using this record requires 'a special time set aside for individual children to talk privately with their teacher about their achievements, hopes and concerns' (Johnson, Hill and Tunstall, 1992, p. 11). During this time the teacher might start by talking about a particular piece of work, or an activity the child has enjoyed. Open and person-centred questions (see p. 124) are used to encourage the child to talk and take a leading role in the discussion, moving from what the child enjoys about the work to what he or she would like to be able to do and what help he or she thinks is needed.

> As children begin to reflect on what they would like to be able to do, what they think they are good at and what kinds of help they have needed, this gives you the basis for considering in a practical way how each child's work in class might be improved and the support needed to bring this about. These considerations are formalized in the setting and writing down of agreed targets.
>
> (Johnson, Hill and Tunstall, 1992, p. 16)

The process is thus very similar to that described in Chapter 9 for involving children in formative assessment. Indeed there is little difference from the child's point of view, except that the process ends with a more formal identification of targets. Johnson, Hill and Tunstall emphasise that, as in the case of formative assessment, self-assessment flourishes within a supportive class ethos which recognises everyone's need for recognition. The suggestions made in Chapters 6 and 12 for fostering positive attitudes in science are consistent with this approach described in more general terms both by Johnson, Hill and Tunstall and in the Schools Examinations and Assessment Council's booklet on *Records of Achievement in the Primary School* (SEAC, 1990).

Within such an ethos children can also have a role in creating reports on their progress and in reporting to their parents. The national guidelines on reporting in Scotland suggest three ways of involving children:

> First, pupils might be invited to consider their progress to date and to comment on it, perhaps in response to specific questions, for example:
> What have I done well this year?
> What particular part of my work would I like to be able to do better?
> What am I going to work particularly hard at next term?
> What can I do to improve my work?
> Secondly, pupils might be asked to react to comments in the teacher's record of their individual progress, by responding, in writing or discussion, to questions such as:
> What did the teacher say about my work which pleased me?
> Was there anything in the teacher's comments which concerned me?
> Did the teacher suggest anything that I need to work on?
> What should I try to do?
> Is there anything I would like to talk about with the teacher?
> Thirdly, pupils might be invited to work with teachers to identify their own Next Steps and to discuss which strategies might be most successful in addressing these.
>
> (SOED, 1992, p. 22)

These suggestions tend to emphasise the children's participation in using the report for helping future learning. They perhaps serve to confirm that the children have a greater role in formative assessment than in making the kind of judgements about their work needed for summative assessment.

Summary

This chapter has discussed the gathering, interpreting, recording and use of evidence for summative assessment. The purposes of summative assessment require:

- information about how a child's achievement compares with agreed standards or levels of achievement at certain stages or ages

- systematic and uniform interpretation of evidence
- a manageable volume of information
- an overview of achievement.

Ways of meeting these requirements have been discussed which use information already available from ongoing assessment of regular activities, from special tasks or tests, or a combination of these. Reference has been made to various ways of establishing levels of achievement that are embodied in national curricula, guidelines or benchmarks.

In summative assessment, the form of record is an integral part of the assessment. It is in making the record that the actual performance is replaced by some representation of it. The design of a record has also to take into consideration the use to be made of it. Detail useful to teachers can be retained in summative records by using symbols to refer to lists of criteria or descriptions set out in national standards or curricula. For reports to parents, however, such short-hand is inappropriate.

Finally some ways in which children can have a role in their own summative assessment have been noted. Whilst it is not expected that young children can apply criteria expressed in the form as used by teachers, they may be able to take part in reviewing what they have done against simplified statements, or comment on the teacher's judgement of their work. However, the value is in the process rather than the product and, as such, is more formative than summative.

Points for reflection

- Far more attention is given to *making* records rather than to using them. What difference would it make to records passed from teacher to teacher if the *receiver* decided what information was required?
- A positive tone of reports to parents is generally advised, but does this enable teachers to give a frank account of children's performance?

Further reading

New Standards (1997) *Performance Standards: New Standards* Vol. 1, Elementary Science. National Center on Education and the Economy and the University of Pittsburg.

SCAA (1995) *Exemplification of Standards: Science at Key Stages 1 and 2, level 1 to 5*. London: Schools Curriculum and Assessment Authority.

Schilling, M., Hargreaves, L., Harlen, W. with Russell, T. (1990) *Assessing Science in Primary Classroom: Written Tasks*. London: Paul Chapman.

14

Choosing and using resources

In Chapters 11 and 12 the experiences needed to help children develop their scientific ideas, skills and attitudes were discussed in terms of providing opportunities for them to: test their ideas; extend their experience of scientific aspects of the world around; have access to alternative ideas; and communicate and reflect on what they have found through inquiry and discussion. Certain things, such as books, equipment and materials for investigation, are essential for children to have these opportunities. Other things are highly desirable and often enhance the value of direct experience. These include visits, non-book sources of information such as posters, photographs, television, CD-ROMs, and other computer-based information technology for collecting and handling data.

Material in these forms is also produced to help teachers plan and provide children's learning experiences and to support professional development. These will be discussed in Chapter 15, whilst here the focus is on materials for use with and by children during science activities. We look at these under four main headings:

- resources for firsthand study
- information and communications technology (ICT) for supporting firsthand study
- information sources such as books, television and CD-ROMs
- visits, links and use of out-of-school resources.

Resources for firsthand study

Both tools to use in inquiry and objects for study or experimentation are essential at some time. These living and non-living resources for children to use in their learning take some effort to obtain, organise and store. Fortunately there are many publications which provide help with this in the form of lists of equipment, advice about obtaining and maintaining it and useful addresses. These include several publications from the ASE, such as *Primary Science Resources* (Feasey, 1998b), *Be Safe* (ASE, 1990) and *Safety in Science in Primary Schools* (INSET pack) (ASE, 1995). Curriculum materials invariably list the equipment needed for the units or activities they suggest (e.g. Nuffield Primary Science *Teachers' Guides*, 1995) and the *Scheme of Work for Science, Key Stages 1 and 2* (DfEE, 1998), produced by the Qualifications and Curriculum Authority (QCA) lists the materials and resources needed for each unit.

When children are testing their own ideas, however, their activities will not be standard ones but ones devised to test particular ideas or solve problems. Most such activities can be anticipated from accumulated experience and research for, as noted in Chapter 4, children's ideas and what follows from them bear a remarkable similarity across the globe. However, it is the essence of helping children to develop *their* ideas that activities are open-ended rather than 'following the book'. Unexpected problems will occur and the overriding consideration at such times should be safety. So we consider this first.

Safety first

Children's natural curiosity may lead them to try certain things which could be dangerous or to pick up objects outside the classroom which may harm themselves, as well as collecting things which may harm the environment. So it is essential for teachers to be aware of potential dangers, and, without confining children's activities unnecessarily, to avoid situations which could lead to injury. There is comprehensive advice available in the excellent booklet *Be Safe* published by the ASE (1990). This covers use of tools, sources of heat, chemicals, suitable and unsuitable animals for keeping in the classroom, poisonous plants and work out of doors. It contains several safety 'codes' which usefully summarise precautions that teachers should take in certain situations. It suggests that children should be taught to recognise and observe warning symbols, and be encouraged to consider safety when they plan and carry out investigations and 'arising from their awareness of safety in their own environment . . . should develop a concern for global issues which affect the safety and well-being of all living things' (ASE, 1990, p. 5).

Working safely should not be presented in a way that controls children but as a positive aim of science education. Conscious attention to behaving safely enables children to recognise dangers in other areas of their experience, at home and in the playground and street. Helping children to act responsibly in matters of safety is part of helping them to take responsibility for their learning.

Choosing equipment

Rarely does a school have the task of drawing up a shopping list of requisites for science starting from scratch. Almost always it is a matter of augmenting an existing collection which has often been assembled in an unplanned way. However, listing and keeping a catalogue of equipment is essential and, with the help of a simple computer database, is not as arduous a matter as it used to be. Whenever the school programme for science is revised it is important for there to be a review of equipment to support it. Unless the school policy is to follow a particular set of curriculum materials, it will be necessary for the school to draw up its own list of resources to support its own programme.

Equipment requirements fall into two categories:

- materials and equipment that are generally available in every classroom (glue, Plasticine, string, scissors, rulers, etc.) plus some items used mainly in science but which are of the 'everyday' kind, such as transparent plastic containers, rubber bands, boxes
- science specific equipment such as magnifiers, measuring instruments for mass, time, temperature, and bulbs, wires, etc.

The list of science-specific equipment is not in fact very long, for many activities can be carried out with materials already in the classroom. For example, no specialised equipment is required for the wide range of activities young children can engage in that help their awareness that there is air all around. They can 'feel' air moving as they rush through it or fan it on to each other, make paper gliders, parachutes, kites, windmills, make bubbles in water, try blowing a pellet of paper into an 'empty' bottle – all without using any materials other than those which can be collected at school or brought from home. Similarly, there are many activities concerning sound and hearing which make use of everyday objects or containers, rubber bands and any musical instruments already in the school.

There is virtue in keeping the specialised equipment to a minimum and not merely on grounds of economy. As mentioned in Chapter 7, special equipment that is used only in science and not found in other parts of children's school or everyday experience can isolate science from the 'real' world around children. If a special set of instruments has to be used for weather observations, for example, the impression may be given that useful measurements depend on that set. It can come between the things being measured and the child. Research has shown that this is often the case in secondary science (Woolnough, 1997). A better understanding of what is being measured may come from a home-made rain gauge, a windsock made from a stocking and an anemometer made with yoghurt containers rather than from more sophisticated equipment. These will be designed by the children to do the job that they have defined; they will not be starting with an instrument whose function they have to learn. The more children help in designing the ways they interact with their surroundings the more they will realise that they can investigate and learn about the world around through their own activity.

Storing equipment

Storing equipment centrally in the school is an obvious way to make best use of items which have to be purchased. Items such as hand lenses, mirrors and magnets need only be obtained in sufficient quantities for one class, or for two in a large school. The disadvantages of keeping equipment in a central store can be overcome by systematic labelling and indexing, keeping records and providing easy access and ways of transporting equipment.

The organisation of equipment in the store depends to some extent on how science is organised in the school. The notion of 'topic boxes' has been adopted in some schools, particularly where the work is organised round workcards or units of work used throughout the school. It seems wasteful, however, for materials to lie in boxes when they could well be of use in topics other than that for which they are earmarked. Further, this organisation would not suit more open-ended activities where equipment demands cannot be anticipated. The opposite extreme is to have all items stored in separate sets and for the collection needed at any time to be gathered by the teacher. This could be wasteful of time, too, since it could be anticipated that bulbs, bulb holders, wires and batteries would probably always be used together.

A compromise is probably possible, in which some equipment is kept in topic collections and other more general equipment kept in separate sets. Careful cataloguing is the key to the success of this, or indeed any other, system. A listing of every item should be available to all staff showing where it can be found, if stored as general equipment, or in which topic box it is stored.

When boxes are used for storage, the contents and storage position of each topic box should be listed. This may seem a great deal of cataloguing but this is no problem once a computer database has been set up. The database can be designed to enable items to be viewed alphabetically, by shelf or whatever variable is appropriate. It should be accessible to all teachers and in some cases, children, who can help to organise the equipment. In large schools the computer may also be used to 'book' equipment at certain times, so that a planned lesson involving the microscope, for instance, is not frustrated by finding it already in use in another classroom. The database would also have a section for ICT hardware, where this is shared among classes and for software, such as CD-ROMs and videos.

For transporting equipment a trolley, or preferably more than one, is almost a necessity. If several can be obtained, some can be converted as the permanent and mobile store for certain commonly used materials, or for particularly heavy topic equipment. Most often, though, a teacher will load the trolley with the collection needed at a particular time. When a chosen collection is in use in a classroom for a few days or longer, details of what is there should be left in the store.

In setting up a store it is as well to remember that collections of material generally grow quite rapidly, they rarely diminish. Items brought to school to add to a display or to the range of materials being investigated are generally donated. In this way useful items such as an old camera, clock, clockwork or battery-driven toys, metal and wood off-cuts are added to the store and room has to be available for them. The store should also house a range of containers and other general equipment that is extra to that required in each classroom for activities other than science.

This collection can swell quite quickly, too, once parents are aware that squeezy bottles, yoghurt pots, foil pie-tins and plastic bottles are all useful for school activities.

Display

A great deal of attention has been given to storing equipment and materials tidily away, but not all of it should be always out of sight. As mentioned in Chapter 12, displays can provide starting points for activities and give children a useful way to pass odd moments. Displays can feature anything from a collection of tools, measuring instruments, or materials taken from the store, to special items on loan from the museum, local craft centre or industry. There should always be information provided about the exhibits in a suitable form and, if possible, invitations for children to handle and explore them or to inquire further in other ways.

Living things

Animals kept in the school for an extended period of time require specialised housing and regular care. It is worth while planning the provision of these non-human members of the school so that they make the most contribution to children's experience of the variety of living things. In one school there were salamanders in one classroom, fish in another, gerbils in another and so on. Each year the children changed classroom, so that they lived with each type of animal in turn. In other cases an agreed rota for exchanging classroom animals might be more appropriate, with teachers planning children's activities to suit the animals in residence at different times.

As well as captive animals in the classroom it should be possible to provide access to animals in natural habitats set up in the school grounds. Many schools are now using a small part of the grounds for an outdoor study area, where plants are grown and where birds, insects or other 'minibeasts' can find food and shelter. Few schools are unable to find the few square metres where plants can be grown, even if it is only in a chequer-board garden formed by taking up one or two patio slabs. Generally, much more can be done, so that nesting boxes can be provided, shrubs planted to attract butterflies, a bed for planting seeds with larger areas of garden for planting out seedlings and, quite important, a semi-wild area where wild flowers and grass can grow up round a pile of stones, giving shelter to a range of insects and other invertebrates. An outdoor resource area provides a valuable opportunity for children to study creatures without disturbing them too much. But if brought into the classroom for further study, temporary housing can be improvised from a variety of clear plastic containers.

Safety aspects of keeping and studying living things are well covered in *Be Safe* (ASE, 1990), which advises on suitable plants for growing in the classroom and on poisonous ones that should be avoided when exploring outside. With regard to animals in the classroom there are, in addition to *Be Safe*, a number of guides produced by animal welfare organisations.

Using ICT to support firsthand investigation

One of the criticisms of practical work in science, at pre-secondary as well as at secondary level, has been that the procedures of handling equipment and of recording results, particularly drawing graphs or charts, often assumes the main focus of attention, whilst the meaning of the results assumes a minor role. For example, the simple investigation of the cooling of warm water in different containers involves using a thermometer (and so knowing how to read it), taking down readings at particular times (and remembering to do this – or risk dubious results) and then drawing a graph or displaying the results so that comparisons can be made. This takes much time and energy and although it is useful to learn how to do these things, if the purpose is to understand something about cooling, there is too much activity intervening between asking the question and obtaining the answer.

The use of sensor probes and data-logging using a computer removes these intervening steps and enables children to focus on their results. Portable and hand-held (pocket-book) computers enable this kind of work to be carried on outside as well as inside the classroom. There are also data-loggers that can be used in the field and then connected to a computer on return to the classroom.

Two teachers described the effect this had on a project involving taking various measurements in a woodland (Baume and Gill, 1995). Some children (10- and 11-year-olds) had to use conventional instruments whilst others used a portable computer and temperature and light probes. The teachers reported:

> Those using the probes were able to gather data and very quickly see a graph, or graphs, appearing on the computer screen. Without any prompting, the children commented on what appeared on the screen and immediately began to ask questions such as, 'What would happen if?' The emphasis changed from collecting data to working in the field, analysing, predicting, moving probes and testing what we had discussed. Dynamic thought and action had replaced mundane recording. Science sprang to life.
>
> (Baume and Gill, 1995, p. 14)

They also reported that the children were motivated to test ideas about temperature and light levels in other locations such as the stream, the football pitch and the playground. 'The tools were in our hands. Ideas could be quickly tested. We were in charge' (ibid., p.15).

Using computers not only takes the drudgery out of some practical work, but can extend the range and sensitivity of information that pupils can use in their science investigations. Sensitive and rapidly responding detectors of temperature, light, sound, rotation, position, humidity and pressure, linked to the computer via a universal interface, can become the means for pupils to investigate phenomena to which the tools previously available to them were quite insensitive. For example, a probe that can measure temperature precisely can be used to test the idea that dark surfaces heat up more quickly than light ones when exposed to sunshine, or to find out whether the skin on different parts of the body is at the same temperature, or whether metal objects that feel cold really are at a different temperature from their surroundings. Light-sensitive probes can be used to compare intensities associated with changes in the size of the pupil of the eye, to investigate regular and irregular reflection from surfaces, the effect of placing a filter between a light source and the probe, etc. In all cases the measurements can be displayed in numerical, symbolic or graphical form.

These are just some examples of the wealth of possibilities opened up by using the computer to extend the senses, to help in measurement and recording data. Such uses increase dramatically children's ability to use evidence in testing ideas, both their own and others'. The speed with which the computer accomplishes the drudgery of measurement, tabulation and display enables children's attention to be focused on the interpretation of data, on making sense of what they are finding. This is just the aspect of investigating which is neglected in the absence of this help, when obtaining results seems an end in itself, the climax of the work rather than the beginning of thinking, as should be the case. The construction and testing of ideas by children can become more central to their scientific activity when they control the technology and are not confined by it.

Of course, children have to become used to using the technology – although one suspects that this is far easier for them than their teachers. Moreover, a warning has to be sounded in relation to ensuring that the 'real world' is not replaced by the vision on the computer screen. This is less likely to happen when computers programs are used for data-logging and display, where the sensor is clearly in touch with the situation being investigated, than when a progam is used to simulate reality. Simulations enable children to investigate situations which they may not be able to explore directly. They enable users to test out the effect of changing certain variables, but only the ones built into the program. Even with older children, there is a danger that simulations give the impression that variables in physical process can be easily and independently controlled, and can represent a caricature of reality rather than a representation of it. Thus computers are probably best used as tools in children's investigations of the real world rather than as a replacement of the real world.

Information sources for children

Children's experience can be extended not only through direct interaction with the world around but through information provided in books, CD-ROMs, television, video and film. These may provide information about the natural world, scientific ideas, suggestions for inquiry and, in some cases, data that can be used by children to test their own and alternative ideas. Some of these resources are used individually by children and some in groups. In all cases it has to be emphasised that these resources have an important role in learning science, but they must be regarded as supporting and not replacing children's first-hand inquiry.

Books for children

Children need access to reference books for information beyond that which a teacher can supply, to satisfy their curiosity and sometimes their appetite for collecting names and facts. Information books for young children are difficult to write. Finding a way to present information in simple understandable terms requires an expert in the subject-matter; the best such books are written by scientists or doctors (for example, the award-winning books by Balkwill and Rolph, 1990a and 1990b). Introducing fantasy as a vehicle for telling 'the story of a meal' or 'the life of a drop of water' does not necessarily aid understanding.

In choosing reference books for children the criteria are not very different from those for good reference books for adults – large, clear, coloured photographs, with straightforward text and an easily used index or other way of locating information. Reference books can usefully be kept together in a central school library and borrowed by classes, perhaps for an extended time such as half a term, on those occasions when they are likely to be in constant demand for the topic in hand. With this type of use in mind it may be preferable to purchase smallish books restricted to one topic (such as Observer's Books published by Warne) rather than large encyclopaedic volumes.

Not all reference material is in book form. Wallcharts, although less durable than books, have some advantages over them. Several children can consult them at one time and each can see all the information available: useful either for identifying a specimen by matching or for seeing the parts of a process linked together in a large flow diagram.

Children's books which are published as part of a programme of curriculum materials combine the purposes of providing information, extending experience (through photographs), showing applications of science in the world around and relating science to other areas of the curriculum, through, for example, stories, drawings and poems. Such books can be least successful when they suggest activities, since these are often a matter of confirming information given rather than testing children's own ideas.

Recently the popularity of 'big books' has grown, particularly for use with the youngest children. These are large-format books, usually on board and about 600 by 450 mm, with large print and illustrations which can be seen by a group of children. The most effective use is as part of discussion between the teacher and a small group of children. The teacher may cover some of the written information at the start and question children about what is shown in the illustrations to gather ideas and gradually reveal the text so that there is not too much to take in all at once. Used in this way they can provide a stimulus to investigation, but without an active follow-up there may be little scientific understanding developed.

CD-ROMs

More and more information is being provided in CD-ROM form, some including video, sound and animation as well as text and graphics. Navigation through such a resource may absorb much of children's attention when they first use it and teachers need to ensure that this is not so demanding that little thought is given to the subject-matter. In general, if the CD-ROM is well chosen for the children, they quickly become adept at exploring the material. The chief problem then becomes selection, since there is so much information available, and so it is particularly important to ensure that the children have a clear purpose in mind and are able to use the resource selectively. The criteria for choosing CD-ROMs will include the reading level, the ease of exploring and the extent of interactivity that is possible.

By providing information in a visual and easily accessible form, CD-ROMs allow children to seek answers to their own questions, test hypotheses and make connections between different pieces of information. A good example of hypothesis testing was described by Govier (1995). Some children new to using CD-ROMs chased down information to test their hypotheses about the position of the eyes of various animals. Some, like lions and cheetahs, have forward-facing eyes, whilst others, like horses and deer, have side-facing eyes. Having rejected the idea that this difference was associated with the speed of the animals, the children considered the predator–prey difference. The CD-ROM helped them to test their suggestion that the predators have eyes at the front and the preyed-upon have eyes at the sides:

> Even before they had looked at lots of examples to test this hypothesis, some of the children were postulating an explanation. The hunted animals need side-facing eyes so that they can keep a good look out all around. Explaining the eye position of the hunters was more difficult. But a few experiments on binocular vision, in particular the difficulty of judging distances or looking at stereoscopic pictures with only one eye open, pointed to a possible answer. Several video clips on the CD-ROM showed predators making a kill, and the importance of being able to gauge distance accurately could clearly be seen.
>
> (Govier, 1995, p. 16–17)

Television, video and film

The widespread use of video recorders has extended the flexibility of use of television programmes in primary schools and many schools make some use of science programmes. Suitable equipment for using video is more readily available than computers to play CD-ROMs, although this is likely to change in the near future. Meanwhile in the UK, both the BBC Education and the commercial Channel 4 Schools service produce science programmes which are well supported by written notes suggesting ways of using the material and possible follow-up work. The programmes use only very carefully selected and tried activities, and audience-reaction evaluation during development of a series is used to ensure that both the content and its treatment will be interesting to children. Furthermore, the television programmes can, and often do, show children engaged in investigations, so they can indicate methods of working as well as content.

The programmes are generally designed to be recorded and shown on video and so used flexibly, with only short sequences being shown at a time and allowing for discussion or for the children to conduct investigations before the next section. This helps to prevent science becoming a spectator sport. However, there is much less opportunity for individual children or small groups to interact with the materials at their own pace or to explore their own ideas, as is the case with CD-ROMs. Together, CD-ROM and video-recorded television programmes have taken over from the use of radio and film, which have ceased to have a role in science education in schools.

Visits, links and out-of-school resources

Visits out of school

The overall aim of science activities is to help children understand the world around them, and so getting out into that world has an important part to play. This is not to deny that the classroom and school and all that is in them are part of the child's environment, but this is a selected and controlled part and to make connections between children's activities in school and the larger environment it is necessary regularly to observe and interact with parts of it at first hand.

There are good practical reasons for taking children out of school. Visits are highly motivating to children, who bring back to school many vivid impressions which sustain follow-up work and often persist over several weeks.

These visits contribute, of course, to work in other areas of the curriculum and this is not being forgotten in concentrating here on the science work. A most successful teacher of primary science always began every topic with a visit; he said it was the equivalent to charging a battery, giving energy and vitality to the work for the next five or six weeks. Each visit was chosen to suit the programme planned and to provide opportunities for children to develop science concepts during follow-up investigations. It is not difficult to select a site for a visit in this way since most venues provide opportunities for development of any of a whole range of ideas. Figure 14.1 illustrates this, showing just some of the links between the possibilities for visits and the main areas of basic science concepts. The list in Figure 14.1 does not include museums or special exhibitions which could relate to any or all of the concepts; these have a valuable role in children's learning in addition to and not as a substitute for visiting places which are more a part of everyday life.

A considerable amount of work for the teacher is involved in planning and organising a visit but this is rewarded several times over by the quality of the ensuing work of the children. The necessary preparation varies according to whether the visit will be entirely under the control of the teacher (as in fieldwork at a pond or in a wood) or whether people at the site will be involved in giving access and information (as in a visit to a workplace).

Where the teacher is the sole person involved in planning (even if helping parents or others accompany the party) the preparation must involve an initial survey of possibilities, having in mind the characteristics of the children who will be visiting. For example,

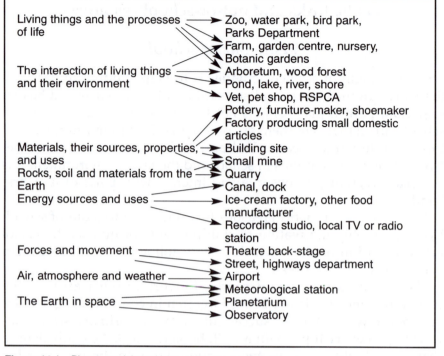

Figure 14.1   Places to visit and ideas that can be developed

5–8-year-olds will want things to watch, touch, smell, handle and so there should be plenty of opportunity for being able to do these things safely; children need to be shown very clearly any dangerous plants or objects that should not be touched. Eight to 10-year-olds will not be satisfied with just looking and feeling; they will want to explore how things are related, to make more systematic observations in which patterns can be detected. Ten to 12-year-olds are capable of concentrating on a particular question and can use the visit to gather evidence systematically, for example, about the different communities of plants and animals to be found in different habitats.

Finding local sites to visit

Some useful ideas for exploring possibilities in the environment near the school are given by Elstgeest and Harlen:

  1 Which landscape or elements of landscape do you find around your school?
      A landscape is a piece of earth, small or large, that can be recognized as a complex whole. There are many kinds and many sizes. We

think of the large rural, agrarian, mountainous, forested or prairie-type landscapes, not forgetting seascapes. Landscapes may be wild like moors, or cultured like a park. But there are small landscapes, too. Think of your own playground and its surrounding shrubbery as a landscape. Or take a footpath and its verge, or a piece of wasteland; the village green, or town square, or a front garden; a hill side, a brook, a bank or a copse, a lawn or a flowerbed. These are all land-scapes, each forming a complex entity, each recognizable by its own particular characteristics.

On a still smaller scale, look for minilandscapes, such as an over-grown wall, a mouldered, mossy stump of treetrunk, a hollow tree such as an ancient pollard willow. Anything might raise questions about what grows and flourishes (or not), about what is happening or what has recently happened, about what has been erected, con-structed or put in order. Don't just look for green or bloom; non-living things also speak a language. Notice, for instance, the pattern of the bricks in the buildings or the paving slabs in the streets.

2 Don't only search at ground level. Look up! A tree, a hedge, a shrub in the shrubbery already takes the eye upward, but let it go further; there is so much to explore above eye level. There are colours and shapes and constructions of many kinds; kites fly, as do birds, aero-planes, flies and other winged creatures. The sky, with its clouds and rainbows stretches above, and the whole world is filled with sounds and fragrances. Feel changes in temperature as the winds veer in new directions; watch how the sun seems to move, and how the moon changes place and face.

3 If your school is near the coast, there may be a beach nearby where the high water mark is full of treasure. Or a sandy plain where the wind moulds wave patterns, or where the rains leave little river systems and patterns of erosion.

4 If your school has a farm nearby, this can be an enormously rich experience and it is very worthwhile to cultivate the friendship and interest of the farmer so that children can visit and investigate. What grows in the fields? Did the farmer intend all of it to grow in the field? Does only grass grow in the meadows? What else grows there? If it is a dairy farm, what animals are kept? How? Where? What animals does the farmer keep? Cattle? Sheep? Goats? Are there more animals belonging to the farm? Pigs? Fowl? Turkeys? Rabbits? Dogs? Cats? Which other animals walk, fly, scurry, and sneak about the farm? Does the farmer want those? And . . . ? One can keep asking and looking and finding out on a farm.

5 If there is an interesting industry, suitably small and safe, it will be valuable for children to visit and to observe how things are manufac-tured, or investigate the raw materials that are delivered, stored and used. Visits to industry offer many other opportunities for education in other areas of the curriculum . . .

6 If houses are being built in the neighbourhood, make use of this whenever you can. Not only are there many skilled people working together (which can be observed from a safe distance), but many problems of space and construction are actually being solved right there! It isn't difficult to obtain (by showing interest) samples of the interesting materials to be found there: cement, bricks, wood, metals, plastics and so on, for the children to investigate in the classroom.

7 Is there a garage, car-works, repairshop, bus station, airport or railway station with a shunting yard?

8 Are there other interesting structures such as a swing bridge, or a lift bridge, a sluice or a lock, a pier or a ferry-boat installation? Is there a belfry or a carillon?

In the search for potential in the environment, don't ignore tourist guides or local and national societies which exist to study, protect and preserve the environment. These often produce posters, pamphlets and brochures, and sometimes produce other valuable learning materials to buy or borrow, such as books, films and videotapes.

(Elstgeest and Harlen, 1990, p. 24)

Once the site for a visit has been selected the particular aspects to be observed or investigated have to be fully planned, possibly involving another visit. A few selected places for working and talking are better than a tourist guide approach. The teacher needs to think out questions for children to answer actively in relation to what can be found at the selected spots.

Where the visit will involve those at the site, then the preparation must involve correspondence and close communication between the school and those who will be involved in the visit. A prior visit by the teacher is essential, not only for the teacher to find out what the children may experience and what safety precautions need to be made beforehand, but to tell those in the place to be visited who may be acting as guide, demonstrator or informer, something about the children. In some cases those involved may have little idea of the level of background knowledge, length of attention span and interests of primary school children. The teacher can help them with their preparation by suggesting some of the questions the children might ask and the sorts of things that will need to be explained in simple terms.

Links with industry

Schools for children of all ages are being encouraged to create links with industry, which are seen as having advantages for both partners. Some of these are:

- Children develop an informed view of modern industry, which often contrasts with an old-fashioned, even Dickensian, view of industry as dull, dangerous and dirty that they gain from stories and hearsay.
- Children realise how familiar things that they use every day are produced.
- Children can relate some of the things they learn in school to the world outside.
- Those in industry gain knowledge of what and how science is taught in schools.
- Both those in industry and those in schools identify ways in which industry can help schools.

However, fruitful partnerships do not occur without effort and Feasey (1998a) gives some good advice on developing successful science-industry links. Among the variety of forms that the links can take are:

- a scientist or industrialist having an extended relationship with a school, so that they are able to visit classrooms, talk to children and teachers and help to plan lessons and visits
- teacher placements in industry, so that teachers can experience for themselves how industry works, for as short a time as one day or for a week or two
- the production of materials for classroom use, in partnership with teachers
- a supply of unwanted material that the school can use, for example, off-cuts of wood or metal, paper, plastic sheeting
- children communicating with industry through fax, e-mail and letters
- visits.

Although visits are perhaps the most common form of relationship between schools and industry, they are more successful if they are part of a more sustained partnership. Useful points about setting up a visit are that:

- it should not be an isolated event, but the centrepiece of extended work which begins beforehand and continues afterwards
- the type of industry visited should preferably be one producing something which children recognise and relate to, for example bicycles, toys or domestic utensils. Complex processes involving huge machinery, often very noisy, do not make for successful visits
- groups of about six to eight children seem to work best, so a class needs to be broken down into groups of this size and the help of

parents or staff from the industry being visited used to escort each group.

The question of worksheets for the children to use during the visit is likely to arise. If these are detailed and require children to look for specific things, they may end up focusing their attention too narrowly and spending their time with their head buried in their notebooks. It is, however, important for the children to be prepared beforehand so that their attention will be focused on the main areas of interest and inquiry. If questions are identified beforehand, the children should help in framing them, and they may also think beforehand of what information they should aim to collect, in whatever form, so that they can discuss and review it afterwards. It may also be helpful to invite someone from the industry back to the school to talk to the children some time after the visit. This gives the children an opportunity to pose questions which have occurred later during reflection on the visit. The double benefit here is that the representative from the industry has the chance to learn about the children's work and the school environment, which can improve school–industry communication to the good of later visiting groups.

Other links

There are other schemes which, for example, link individual scientists with schools. Feasey notes benefits for both in this relationship:

The research scientists offer:
- Up-to-date information, resources and expertise
- Classroom support and ideas
- Role models which can help to dispel the usual stereotypes.

The teachers and children offer the research scientists an opportunity to:
- Share their ideas and interests
- Develop interpersonal skills
- Develop communication skills
- Gain insight into primary children's ideas.

(Feasey, 1998a, p. 109)

Other links that are fruitful in relation to science education include links with schools in other parts of the world. Children can communicate from school to school electronically and sometimes via video-link. They can exchange data about, for example, the weather, the locality, what they eat and wear and, most importantly, undertake collaborative investigations, pooling data and adding to what each class could achieve alone.

Summary

This chapter has considered the range of resources that can broaden children's experience, extend their opportunities to investigate and develop their understanding of the world of work as well as the physical world.

In relation to resources for investigations in the field and in the classroom, consideration has been given to safety, selecting, storing and displaying equipment and keeping living things. The use of probes and data-logging devices for collecting information and computer programs for displaying data help to ensure that children reach the point of interpreting their findings and are not held up by the mechanics of collecting data manually. Sensors also extend the range of data that children can collect to test their ideas.

Children need information sources to answer some of their questions and test their hypotheses and these can be provided in the form of books, CD-ROMs and people – people visiting the classroom or at places visited by the children. Visits also provide further opportunities for inquiry and motivation for continued study later in the classroom. The particular value for learning science of links with industry, scientists and other schools have also been mentioned.

Points for reflection

- To what extent is there a conflict between using everyday equipment in the pre-secondary years and preparing children for using more scientific apparatus in the secondary school?
- How might the balance between firsthand experience and experience and information at second-hand – through books, video and computers – change across the 5–12 age range?

Further reading

ASE (Association for Science Education) (1990) *Be Safe*, 2nd edn. Hatfield: ASE.

Feasey, R. (1998) Science and industry partnerships. In *Association for Science Education Guide to Primary Science Education*. Cheltenham: Stanley Thornes.

Frost, P. (1999) *IT in Primary Science: a Compendium of Ideas for Using Computers and Teaching Science*. Hatfield: ASE.

Hollins, M. (1998) Resources for teaching science. In *Association for Science Education Guide to Primary Science Education*. Cheltenham: Stanley Thornes.

15

The whole-school role

In a relatively short time, schools for 5–12-year-olds have changed from being collections of classes each planning its own programme of work with only light central prescription, to organisations where a great deal of planning is done centrally and collaboratively. Consequently decisions made at the whole-school level now have a greater impact on the learning of individual pupils. These decisions extend beyond planning to evaluation of the implementation of plans and of their outcomes. The evaluation undertaken within the school should have a formative role in developing science education and raising the standards of teaching through professional development of the staff.

Although described as the 'role of the school', the work involved in planning, implementing and evaluating provision for science falls upon the teacher with special responsibility for science – who may be called the science subject leader or co-ordinator – in collaboration with the head teacher or principal. The role of the subject leader has dramatically grown in extent and importance since the later 1980s and in England is now underpinned by the specification of national standards (Teacher Training Agency [TTA], 1998). This chapter is, therefore, in one sense, all about the role of the science subject leader, since all the topics discussed relate to the tasks that are likely to be part of this role. Thus in the first section, the responsibilities and tasks of the science subject leader are reviewed. In the sections that then follow, aspects of the role which have not been covered in earlier chapters are discussed; these are:

- curriculum planning at the school level
- record-keeping at class and school levels
- school self-evaluation and development planning in relation to science
- self-evaluation at the class level
- provision for professional development in science.

In discussing evaluation the concern here is limited to evaluation for formative purposes, for improving science education in the school. The concern is not with evaluation by external agents such as inspectors. Inspections of science are described by Oakley (1998), whilst the role of the subject leader in preparing for such external evaluations are discussed by Bell and Ritchie (1999).

The role of the science subject leader

In schools where all teachers teach all, or almost all, subjects to their own classes, and there is no specialist teaching, the responsibility for co-ordinating the teaching of particular subjects is generally assigned to particular teachers. There has been a change in the title of the teacher who takes such responsibility, from co-ordinator to subject leader. This change signifies a change in the range of tasks undertaken and, to some degree, of emphasis within them. As Bell and Ritchie (1999) point out, when described as a 'co-ordinator', the role is reactive, whilst the title of 'subject leader' is associated with a more proactive role. The latter may extend to appraising other staff in relation to their teaching of the subject and involves greater emphasis than before on monitoring, evaluation and target-setting.

The National Standards for Subject Leaders, set out by the Teacher Training Agency in England, are couched in terms that can apply to any subject. Interpreted in relation to science, they describe a set of responsibilities set out in Table 15.1.

Table 15.1   The responsibilities of the science subject leader

Key areas	Responsibilities	Tasks
Strategic direction and development of science in the school	• Develop and implement a science policy • Create and maintain a climate of positive attitudes and confidence in teaching science • Establish a shared understanding of why teaching science is important and of its role in children's education • Identify and plan support for underachieving children • Analyse and interpret appropriate data, research and inspection evidence • Establish short, medium and long-term plans for developing and resourcing science in the school • Monitor progress in implementing	• Auditing provision for children's learning in science • Analysing and evaluating audit evidence • Communicating information about science teaching in the school to management and other staff • Seeking advice as necessary • Agreeing aims, targets, criteria for success and deadlines

continued over

Table 15.1   (continued)

Key areas	Responsibilities	Tasks
	plans and achieving targets and evaluate effects to inform further improvement	• Preparing actions plans in relation to science • Documenting policies and plans
Teaching and learning	• Ensure science curriculum coverage, continuity and progression for all children • Ensure teachers understand and communicate objectives and sequences of teaching and learning • Provide guidance on teaching methods to meet the needs of all children and the requirements for understanding science • Ensure that science contributes to the development of literacy, numeracy and ICT skills • Establish and implement policies and practices for assessing, recording and reporting learning in science • Set expectations for staff and children and evaluate achievement • Evaluate teaching, identify good practice and act to improve the quality of teaching in science • Establish partnership and involvement of parents • Develop links with the community, business and industry	• Preparing and documenting schemes of work, assessments, records and reports for science • Advising colleagues on science activities and lessons, and providing ideas and starting points • Helping colleagues to develop their own understanding in science • Mounting displays relating to science • Keeping up to date with new ideas in the teaching of science • Checking links with other areas of the curriculum • Being the link between the school and outside contacts, such as zoos, museum services, industry
Staff management	• Audit staff needs for professional development in science • Co-ordinate provision of professional development • Ensure that trainees and newly qualified teachers are supported so that they reach appropriate standards in teaching science • Work with the school co-ordinator for special needs to develop individual plans for some children	• Planning, arranging and running professional development • Working with colleagues in classrooms • Keeping the schools in touch with new thinking and developments in science
Resource management	• Establish needs for resources of all kinds for teaching science • Ensure effective organisation and	• Selecting and ordering materials and equipment

Key areas	Responsibilities	Tasks
	use of resources for science including ICT • Maintain existing resources and find out about new ones • Create a stimulating and safe environment for learning science	• Organising storage and efficient access for resources • Finding out about new equipment and materials for teaching science • Making proposals for enriching the school environment as a resource for scientific investigation • Assessing risks in using equipment and ensuring safety precautions are observed.

Source: Based on TTA (1998).

Research by Ritchie (1997) indicated that in practice, science subject leaders are most frequently involved in developing the school policy, preparing schemes of work, obtaining and managing equipment and materials and giving advice to colleagues. Few were teaching science to other teachers' classes or worked in other classes to provide support for colleagues. The latter, whilst highly desirable, is limited by opportunity, since it would require the subject leader to be released from teaching his or her own class to help others.

Curriculum planning at the school level

Planning at the school level should provide a framework within which each teacher can produce his or her class programmes of work with confidence that there is progression and no unintended overlap across the years. Schools may not wish to adopt, in its entirety, an official scheme of work such as that proposed by the Qualifications and Curriculum Authority (DfEE, 1998) but such documents do provide useful examples of what needs to be set out in a school's scheme if it is to provide a basis for continuity and progression. The QCA document is also helpful in defining three levels of planning:

Long-term planning for science is undertaken in the context of each school's overall curriculum plan which reflects the needs of all children.

All staff need to agree which parts of the programmes of study are drawn together to make coherent, manageable teaching units. The long-term plan shows how these teaching units are distributed across the years . . . in a sequence that promotes curriculum continuity and progress in children's learning. The units for each year should reflect the balance of the programme of study. They may be linked with work in another subject.

A medium-term plan identifies learning objectives and outcomes for each unit and suggests activities enabling these to be achieved. A medium-term plan usually shows a sequence of units that will promote progression and an estimate of the time each unit will take. In many schools all staff are involved in the production of the medium-term plan, with the science co-ordinator ensuring there is consistency within the units and that they promote progression.

Short-term planning is the responsibility of individual teachers, who build on the medium-term plan by taking account of the needs of the children in a particular class and identifying the way in which ideas might be taught to the children in the class.

(DfEE, 1998, p. 12)

The overall long-term plan for the school should set out how the parts of the curriculum are divided across the years so that there is a balance of topics within each year and progression from year to year. How the topics are designated may vary according to the school's decision about the extent of integration of science activities with other learning. General topics (such as 'transport', 'clothing', 'festivals') combine objectives of learning science with those of other subjects. Science-focused topics (such as 'water', 'the sky', 'the weather', 'stopping and starting') concentrate on the objectives of learning science and are usually designated as science lessons or science activities. There are values in both forms of curriculum organisation. Integrated topics or themes allow work to follow children's interests and can extend across timetable and subject boundaries. Science topics, on the other hand, have the advantage of providing opportunities for in-depth study of particular ideas, explicit attention to process skill development whilst children test their own ideas and identify science activities as such.

In practice, the integration of science with other subjects is extremely difficult. When not done well it has been criticised by school inspectors for leading to fragmentation of the subject and comprising activities that do not justify the label of 'science activities'. Integrated topics that do lead to good science require 'outstanding knowledge, expertise and insight from the teacher' (DES, 1989, p. 18). In the past the publication of the work of the few outstanding teachers may have given the impression that this approach to science is much easier than is really the case.

It is common for schools to identify science topics in their long-term plan by titles such as 'ourselves', 'forces and movement' or 'making sounds'. These are readily turned, through medium-term planning, into science-focused topics, whilst still leaving open the possibility of weaving them into broader topics if preferred. But in either case, medium-term planning should result in setting out the learning goals and types of activity so that the meaning of the topics is clear enough to prevent repetition or gaps across children's experiences. These medium-term plans are often worked out by the class teacher and science subject leader together.

Record-keeping at class and school levels

Part of the science subject leader's responsibility, often shared with the head teacher, is to devise a system of keeping records that enables the school management to evaluate the implementation and effects of the school's programme for science. Such records should, however, not add to the burden of teachers but draw on the ones that class teachers need to keep to for their own purposes.

Separate records are needed of the activities undertaken by children and the summative assessment of their learning. The record of activities could be a simple tick-list of the activities set out in the medium-term plan, indicating what have been completed by each child. The class teacher will want to maintain such a list to assist his or her short-term planning. A copy of this record can be made for the school records at the end of a term or year.

A record of achievement of each child can be made either in terms of the extent of achievement of the goals of each unit of work or by using one of the ways of reporting summative assessment described in Chapter 13. The latter would provide assessment for each child based on common criteria. They could, for example, be recorded in terms of national performance standards or levels. From these records a class summary could be created of the numbers of children achieving various levels. Such records are necessary at the school level as part of self-evaluation, where they may help, for example, in identifying classes where progress meets or falls short of expectations and so focusing attention on where help may be needed.

It is, of course, necessary to ensure that records based on teachers' assessment are dependable and some means of moderating or aligning teachers' judgements are required. As mentioned in Chapter 13, this can be done by discussing with the subject leader examples of the work of particular children and/or using published materials such as *Exemplification of Standards: Science at Key Stages 1 and 2, Levels 1 to 5* (SCAA, 1995).

School self-evaluation and development planning

The process of evaluation

Evaluation is the process of gathering and using information to help in making decisions or judgements. The distinction between the *information* and the *criteria* used in judging it is important, although the two are connected, as discussed later. Making explicit the criteria on which the judgement is based identifies evaluation as quite different from passing an opinions which does not need to be justified.

Nevertheless evaluation is by no means the value-free process that some might have supposed and others would wish it to be. The selection of criteria, the kind of information and the way the two are brought together will all affect the judgement that is made. Indeed it might well be said that understanding the nature and limitations of evaluation is essential to its usefulness. Naïve assumptions as to what can be achieved by evaluation, what faith can be placed in its results, have to be avoided.

There is a close parallel between the process of assessment of learners' achievement, in which evidence is judged in relation to criteria (see Chapter 8), and the process of evaluation. There is also a parallel in relation to the different purposes of making the judgements, which can be formative or summative. The concern here is with formative evaluation, conducted for the purpose of improving the educational provision. Nevertheless, to be useful the process has to be carried out with rigour and this means identifying the criteria to be applied in making judgements and using them systematically.

School self-evaluation

Evaluation at the school level is a cyclical process in which information is gathered and used in deciding whether, and if so what, action is needed, followed by planning and taking action and then collecting further information about the implemented plans, as in Figure 15.1. The links between the criteria and gathering and evaluating information reflect their role in determining what information is needed as well as being used in judging it.

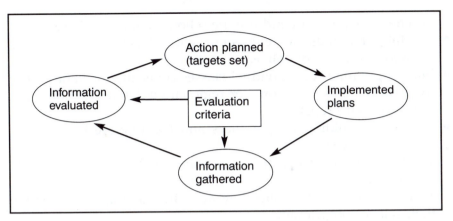

Figure 15.1   Formative school evaluation cycle

The information gathering and action planning can be about any aspect of a school's programme. It could be about, for example:

- science provision for children with special educational needs
- use of ICT in science
- children's achievement of process skills
- teachers' understanding of objectives of teaching science, etc.

Since all aspects of the school science programme cannot be evaluated every year, it is usual for schools to plan to evaluate a 'core' set of activities and outcomes and then to select, as part of school development planning, one or more aspects for action in a particular year. Information collected from the class-level records will enable review of such core aspects as the time spent on science in each class and the relationship of each class programme to the overall school plan for science and the extent to which the intended goals were achieved. A specific audit relating to science might supplement this information with the following:

- the nature and use being made of the school's policy for science
- the extent of continuity in pupils' experience from class to class
- the progress being made in learning by pupils from class to class
- the adequacy of resources and equipment
- the support and development of staff
- assessment and record keeping in science.

Evaluation criteria

Criteria used in evaluation at the school level will depend on the particular focus of the evaluation. Such criteria might include:

- Teachers are aware of and use the school policy on science.
- Teaching methods are consistent with those agreed and expressed in the school policy.
- The programmes of individual classes cover the relevant part of the requirements of national or regional guidelines without gaps or unnecessary repetition.
- Records of children's experiences and learning are kept consistently in every class.
- Teachers are satisfied with the amount, quality and accessibility of equipment.
- Teachers can find the help they need in planning and teaching their science programmes.
- Teachers are satisfied with provision for professional development within and outwith the school.
- Children's performance shows regular progress at the levels expected.
- Children are enthusiastic about science.
- Parents are satisfied with their children's experiences and performance in science.

Sources of information are signalled in these criteria. Teachers are clearly a major source. Their records and opinions need to be collected and reviewed systematically. In addition, their views on the adequacy of support, equipment, professional development, etc. can be sought by questionnaire or interview. Documents provide a second source of information. School programmes and procedures and national or regional curriculum standards and assessment requirements or guidelines have to be analysed and compared. Then there are the perceptions of pupils, parents and others, such as governors, local inspectors or advisers, which can be elicited by questionnaire or interview. Where time allows, semi-structured interviews held with a well-selected sample are probably most helpful, since they can probe reasons for satisfaction or dissatisfaction and so suggest action to be considered. The science subject leader has a key part in collecting these data and in evaluating how well the criteria are met.

Using the criteria

Some measure of the extent to which the criteria are met is needed in deciding whether action is required. In some cases information will come from several sources, and so it is probably best to take the criteria one at a time and to scan across all the relevant information in order to make the judgement. This procedure may seem rather rough and subjective, as indeed it is, but in practice greater refinement is not needed for the purpose being considered. It is usually the case that in the areas where there is a gap between what we would like to be happening (as represented by the criteria) and what is happening (evident in the information gathered) it is likely to be large and obvious. Evaluation in this context is not intended to produce fine judgements of the extent of success, but to the make the work of the school more effective. The process of gathering information and sifting it systematically is likely to be of more value in bringing shortcomings to the attention and in suggesting ways of improvement than the end product. Indeed the end product is only the beginning of the next cycle in what should be an ongoing review.

Ideally these are tasks that science subject leaders should be able to undertake, since the process would add to the richness of their overview of science provision in their schools. However, this is clearly time-consuming and also depends upon subject leaders acquiring the necessary skills.

Self-evaluation at the class level

Whilst evaluation at the school level can improve overall provision for science, the quality of individual children's experience is ultimately dependent on their teacher. Self-evaluation by teachers, with the support of the subject leader, is a process that should be directed at answering the question: how can the children's learning opportunities be improved? The intention is formative, for the teacher to judge how well he or she is doing and what changes might be made. It is not so that others can judge how well the teacher is doing.

Information about the children's activities and what they have achieved will in any case be recorded, as suggested above. To find out how to improve learning this needs to be supplemented by information about how the children go about their activities and what they feel about them. For example, have the children:

- talked to each other and listened to others' ideas?
- talked freely to the teachers about what they think?
- explained certain words they have used?
- suggested ways of testing ideas?
- used sources of information to gain information or test ideas?
- been absorbed in their work or shown in other ways that it is important to them?
- shown understanding by readily linking new ideas to previous experience or applying ideas to new situations?

To answer these questions (which are criteria in a different form, embodying value judgements about how children best learn) teachers will need to gather information during lessons which can be reviewed later. Ways of doing this include making brief notes during lessons, holding discussions with groups of children about their preferences and how they feel about certain activities and sometimes tape-recording discussion among children during their group activities. There is perhaps more value, however, in having the help of a colleague, particularly the science subject leader, to give an alternative view and advise on change that may improve the quality of the children's learning experiences.

Professional development

Evaluation at both class and school levels is likely to identify staff development needs, particularly for improving teachers' own understanding of science. Research studies provide ample evidence that 'increasing teachers' own understanding is a key factor in improving the quality of teaching and learning in science' (Harlen, 1999, p. 80). Classroom observations by inspectors (OFSTED, 1994) and by researchers (Osborne and Simon, 1996) show a close relationship between teachers' own understanding and the understanding of the children they teach. It is, however, important to recognise the role of teachers' subject knowledge in teaching science, which is not so that teachers can convey factual information didactically to pupils. Rather it is so that:

- they can ask questions that lead children to reveal and reflect on their ideas
- they can avoid 'blind alleys'
- they can provide relevant sources of information and other appropriate resources
- they can identify progress and the next steps that will take their children's learning further.

These things cannot be done if teachers do not understand the ideas they are aiming for. At the same time, knowledge of the scientific ideas is not enough. As Shulman (1987) has pointed out so effectively, teachers also need:

- general pedagogical knowledge – about classroom management and organisation
- curriculum knowledge – about national requirements and materials that are available

- pedagogical content knowledge – about how to teach the subject matter, including useful illustrations, powerful analogies and examples
- knowledge of learners and their characteristics
- knowledge of educational contexts
- knowledge of educational goals, values and purposes, including the history and philosophy of education.

So it is important that subject knowledge is acquired as part of a wider discussion of children's learning and how to facilitate it. Recent publications that do this rather than presenting science in a testbook style have been produced by Wenham (1995) and the Nuffield Primary Science Project (1997).

Opportunities for staff development can be provided at other centres or institutions, in-school, or through using ICT. Out-of-school workshops and courses are generally well prepared and led by well-informed tutors, but they are not, by definition, tailor-made for the particular needs of individual schools or teachers. Moreover, they are available only at certain times at certain locations. In-school workshops or meetings can be better tailored to the help needed by a school, but provide less opportunity for sharing ideas and solutions across schools. However, good material is available as input to school-based sessions and subject leaders do not have to rely only on their own resources. For example, the *Making Sense of Science* materials (SPE, 1995) comprise ten programmes on videotape which cover the teaching of basic concepts and provide examples of different teaching styles for discussion.

Unique opportunities for teachers to experience science at first-hand were provided by the Primary Teachers as Scientists project. Teacher undertook an extended scientific investigation with support from academic and research institutions. The questions investigated were those that the teacher could talk to their children about and in some cases involve them. Positive outcomes were reported by Hobden and Reiss (1999), although they pointed out that not all teachers had completed their study because of competing demands on their time.

The Internet has been used to enable teachers to access information and share ideas with others at any time and from any location with an internet link. For example the 'Science On-Line Support Network', developed in Scotland, provides teachers with four facilities:

- an e-mail connection to science educators who act as 'helpers' and respond to questions put to them by teachers

- a 'library' of selected documents which can be read on the screen or down-loaded as required
- a 'notice board' where messages and information (about new sources of equipment, for example) can be posted and which provides the facility for teachers to add comments to notices
- a 'preparation room' where teachers can share schemes of work, children's work and methods of assessment.

No doubt, as schools gain access to the National Grid for Learning, opportunities for time-independent access to professional development will extend. Use of ICT will also enable the science subject leader to have access to information about available resources of all kinds and to the professional development that they need to spearhead the development of science education in their schools.

Summary

In this final chapter we have been concerned with the structure and context that the whole school provides for science work in individual classrooms. The role of a member of staff given responsibility for science in the school – the subject leader – is a key one and has been vastly extended in the 1990s. The aspects of this role which have been given attention in this chapter are those concerned with long-term and medium-term planning, keeping records and gathering and using information for evaluating the effectiveness of the school's provision for science.

Evaluation has been discussed as a process used at the school and class level to improve provision for teaching and learning. At the school level the science subject leader has the task of collecting information and judging how well what is being done matches the criteria of quality and effectiveness. It has been suggested that the process of evaluation, quite apart from the outcome, is itself of considerable benefit in identifying areas where improvements need to be made. Action taken is then evaluated as the cycle of school evaluation continues.

At the class level, teachers can also improve the effectiveness of their teaching through self-evaluation. This involves collecting information about how children go about and how they feel about their learning and then comparing what is found with the criteria that reflect intentions. Involvement of the science subject leader can help in deciding on any action needed to narrow the gap between intentions and practice.

Finally the provision of professional development opportunities has been considered. It has been suggested that greater use of ICT for this purpose will free teachers from time-bound and place-bound courses, and provide access at any time to information and to a community of teachers who are also learners.

Points for reflection

- How might central medium- and long-term planning of school programmes be reconciled with the need for teachers to have room to respond to children's interests as well as to accommodate their own strengths and limitations?
- To what extent does the evidence of the significance of teachers' own understanding of science on their teaching influence decisions about specialist teaching of science in pre-secondary schools?

Further reading

Bell, D. and Ritchie, R (1999) *Towards Effective Subject Leadership in the Primary School.* Buckingham: Open University Press.

Hargreaves, D. H. and Hopkins, D. (1991) *The Empowered School: The Management and Practice of Development Planning.* London: Cassell.

Ritchie, R. (1998) From science co-ordinator to science subject leader. In *Association for Science Education Guide to Primary Science Education* Cheltenham: Stanley Thornes.

References

AAAS (1993) *American Association for the Advancement of Science Benchmarks for Scientific Literacy*. New York: Oxford University Press.

ASE (1990) *Be Safe* (2nd edn). Hatfield: Association for Science Education.

ASE (1995) *Safety in Primary Science* Inset Pack. Hatfield: Association for Science Education.

ASE (1997a) *Gender and Science Education: Policy*. Hatfield: Association for Science Education.

ASE (1997b) *Race, Equality and Science Teaching: Policy*. Hatfield: Association for Science Education.

ASE (1997c) *Access to Science Education: Policy*. Hatfield: Association for Science Education.

ASE (1998) *Primary Science*, No. 56. Hatfield: Association for Science Education.

Askew, M., Bliss, J. and Macrae, S. (1995) Scaffolding in mathematics, science and technology. In P. Murphy, M. Selinger, J. Bourne, M. Briggs (eds), *Subject Learning in the Primary Curriculum: Issues in English, Science and Mathematics*. London: Routledge.

Atkinson, H. and Bannister, S. (1998) Concepts maps and annotated drawings. *Primary Science Review*, **51**, 3–5.

Ausubel, D. R (1968) *Educational Psychology: A Cognitive View*. Holt, Rinehart and Winston, New York.

Balkwill, R. and Rolph, M. (1990a) *Cell Wars*. London: Collins.

Balkwill, R. and Rolph, M. (1990b) *Cells Are Us*. London: Collins.

Barnes, D. (1976) *From Communication to Curriculum*. Harmondsworth: Penguin.

Baume, J. and Gill, D. (1995) IT puts the children in charge. *Primary Science Review*, **40**, 14–16.

Bell, B. (1981) *Video: Animals*. Working Paper No. 51, Science Education Research Unit, University of Waikato, Hamilton, New Zealand.

Bell, B. and Barker, M. (1982) Towards a scientific concept of 'animal'. *Journal of Biological Education*, **16**, (3), 197–200.

Bell, D. and Ritchie, R. (1999) *Towards Effective Subject Leadership in the Primary School*. Buckingham: Open University Press.

Biddulph, F. and Osborne, R. (1984) Pupils' ideas about floating and sinking. *Research in Science Education*, **14**, 114–24.

Black, P. J. and Wiliam, D. (1998a) *Inside the Black Box*. London: School of Education, King's College.

Black, P. J. and Wiliam, D. (1998b) Assessment and classroom learning. *Assessment in Education*, **5** (1), 7–74.

Brown, A., Campione, J. C., Metz, K. E., Ash, D.B (1997) The development of science learning abilities in children. In K. Harnqvist, and A. Burgen (eds), *Growing up with Science*. London: Jessica Kingsley.

Bruner, J. S. (1960) *The Process of Education*. New York: Vintage Books.

Bruner, J. S. (1964b) The course of cognitive growth. *American Psychologist*, **19**, 1–15.

Bruner, J. S., Goodnow, J. J. and Austin, G. A. (1966) *A Study of Thinking*. New York: Wiley.

DES (1983) *Science in Schools. Age 11*. APU Report No. 2, DES Research Report. London: DES.

DES (1984) *Science in Schools. Age 11*. APU Report No. 3, DES Research Report. London: DES.

DES (1989) *Aspects of Primary Education. The Teaching and Learning of Science*. London: HMSO.

DES (1991) *Your Child's Report – What it Means and How it Can Help*. London: HMSO.

DfEE (1998) *Science. Teacher's Guide: A Scheme of Work for Key Stages 1 and 2*. London: Department for Education and Employment.

DfEE (1999) *Science in the National Curriculum*. London: HMSO.

Einstein, A. (1933) Preface to M. Plank, *Where is Science Going?* Allen and Unwin, London.

Elstgeest, J. (1985) The right question at the right time. In W. Harlen (ed.), *Primary Science: Taking the Plunge*. London: Heinemann.

Elstgeest, J. and Harlen, W. (1990) *Environmental Science in the Primary Curriculum*. London: Paul Chapman Publishing.

Feasey, R. (1998a) Science and industry partnerships. In *Association for Science Education Guide to Primary Science Education*. Cheltenham: Stanley Thornes.

Feasey, R. (1998b) *Primary Science Resources*. Hatfield: Association for Science Education.

Feasey, R. (1999) *Primary Science and Literacy*. Hatfield: Association for Science Education.

Forster, M. and Masters, G. (1997) *Assessment Methods*. Camberwell, Victoria: Australian Council for Educational Research.

Frost, J. (1997) *Creativity in Primary Science*, Buckingham: Open University Press.

Glover, J. (1985) Case Study 1. Science and project work in the infant school. In Open University, *EP531: Primary Science – Why and How?* Block 1 Study Book. Milton Keynes: Open University Press.

Goldsworthy, A., Watson, R. and Wood-Robinson, V. (1998). Sometimes it's not fair! *Primary Science Review*, **53**, 15–17.

Govier, H. (1995) Making sense of information handling. *Primary Science Review*, **40**, 16–18.

Gunstone, R. and Watts, M. (1985) Force and motion. In R. Driver, E. Guesne and A. Tiberghien (eds), *Children's Ideas in Science*. Milton Keynes: Open University Press.

Hargreaves, D. H. and Hopkins, D. (1991) *The Empowered School: The Management and Practice of Development Planning*. London: Cassell.

Harlen, W. (ed.) (1985) *Primary Science: Taking the Plunge*. London: Heinemann.

Harlen W. (1999) *Effective Teaching of Science: A Review of Research*. Edinburgh: Scottish Council for Research in Education.

Harlen, W. and Jelly, S. (1997) *Developing Science in the Primary Classroom*. London: Longman.

Harlen, W. and Malcolm, H. (1999) *Setting and Streaming: A Research Review*. Edinburgh: Scottish Council for Research in Education.

Harlen, W. and Osborne, R. J. (1985) A model for learning and teaching applied to primary science. *Journal of Curriculum Studies*, **17** (2), 133–146.

Harlen, W., Macro, C., Schilling, M., Malvern, D. and Reed, K. (1990). *Progress in Primary Science*. London: Routledge.

Hawking, S. W. (1988) *A Brief History of Time*. London: Bantam Press.

Hobden, J. and Reiss, M. (1999) The primary teacher as a scientist project. *Primary Science Review*, **56**, 1–2.

Hodson, D. (1993) Teaching and learning about science: considerations in the philosophy and sociology of science. In D. Edwards, E. Scanlon and R. West (eds), *Teaching, Learning and Assessment in Science Education*. London: Paul Chapman Publishing and Open University Press.

Hollins, M. (1998) Resources for teaching science. In *Association for Science Education Guide to Primary Science Education*. Cheltenham: Stanley Thornes.

Howe, C. (1990) Grouping children for effective learning in science. *Primary Science Review*, (13), 26–7.

Jelly, S. J. (1985) Helping children to raise questions – and answering them. In W. Harlen (ed.), *Primary Science: Taking the Plunge*. London: Heinemann.

Jenkins, E. W. (1997) Towards a functional public understanding of science. In R. Levington and J. Thomas (eds), *Science Today*. London and New York: Routledge.

Johnson, C., Hill, B. and Tunstall, P. (1992) *Primary Records of Achievement: A Teacher's Guide to Recording and Reviewing*. London: Hodder and Stoughton.

Keeves, J. (1995). Cross-national comparisons of outcomes in science education. In B. J. Fraser and H. J. Walberg (eds). *Improving Science Education*. Chicago: National Society for the Study of Education.

Layton, D. (1990) *Inarticulate Science?* Occasional Paper No. 17, University of Liverpool, Department of Education.

Masters, G. and Forster, M. (1996) *Progress Maps*. Camberwell, Victoria: Australian Council for Research in Education.

Masters, G. and Forster, M. (1996a) *Development Assessment*. Camberwell, Victoria: Australian Council for Research in Education.

Match and Mismatch (1977) Materials include three books: *Raising Questions, Teacher's Guide* and *Finding Answers*. Edinburgh: Oliver and Boyd.

Millar, R. and Osborne, J. (1998) *Beyond 2000, Science Education for the Future*. London: King's College London, School of Education.

Morris, R. (1990) *Science Education Worldwide*. Paris: UNESCO.

National Research Council (1996) *National Science Education Standards*. Washington: NRC.

New Standards (1997) *Performance Standards: New Standards*, Vol. 1, Elementary Science. National Center on Education and the Economy and the University of Pittsburg.

Nuffield Primary Science (1995) 11 Teacher's Guides and 22 Pupils' Books for Key Stage 2, *Teacher's Guide for Key Stage 1, Science Co-ordinator's Handbook* and INSET Pack. London: Collins Educational.

Nuffield Primary Science Project (1997) *Understanding Science Ideas*. London: Collins Educational.

Oakley, D. (1998) Inspection and the evaluation cycle. In *Association for Science Education Guide to Primary Science Education*. Cheltenham: Stanley Thornes.

OECD (1999) *Measuring Students Knowledge and Skills, A New Framework for Assessment*. Paris: OECD.

OFSTED (Office for Standards in Education) (1995) *Science: A Review of Inspection Findings 1993/4*. London: HMSO.

Ollerenshaw, C. and Ritchie, R. (1988) *Primary Science: Making it Work*. London: David Fulton.

Osborne, R. J. (1985) Children's own concepts. In W. Harlen (ed.), *Primary Science: Taking the Plunge* London: Heinemann.

Osborne, R. J. and Freyberg, P. (1985) *Learning in Science: The Implications of 'Children's Science'*. Auckland: Heinemann.

Osborne, J. and Simon, S. (1996) Primary science: past and future directions. *Studies in Science Education*, **27**, 99–147.

Osborne, R. J., Biddulph, F., Freyberg, P. and Symington, D. (1982) *Confronting the Problems of Primary School Science*. Working Paper No. 110, Science Education Research Unit, University of Waikato, Hamilton, New Zealand.

Piaget, J. (1929) *The Child's Conception of the World*. New York: Harcourt, Brace.

Piaget, J. (1964) Cognitive development in children: Piaget papers. In R. E. Ripple and D. N. Rockcastle (eds), *Piaget Rediscovered: Report on the Conference on Cognitive Studies and Curriculum Development*. Ithaca, NY: School of Education, Cornell University.

Qualter, A. (1996) *Differentiated Primary Science*. Buckingham: Open University Press.

Ratcliffe, M. (1998) The purposes of science education. In *Association for Science Education Guide to Primary Science Education*. Cheltenham: Stanley Thornes.

Reiss, M. J. (1998) Science for all. In *Association for Science Education Guide to Primary Science Education*. Cheltenham: Stanley Thornes.

Ritchie, R. (1997) The subject co-ordinator's role and responsibilities in primary schools. Proceedings of the 3rd Primary Science Conference, Durham University.

Ritchie, R. (1998) From science co-ordinator to science subject leader. In *Association for Science Education Guide to Primary Science Education*. Cheltenham: Stanley Thornes.

Schilling, M., Hargreaves, L., Harlen, W. with Russell, T. (1990) *Assessing Science in the Primary Classroom: Written Tasks*. London: Paul Chapman Publishing.

SCAA (1995) *Exemplification of Standards: Science at Key Stages 1 and 2, Levels 1 to 5*. London: Schools Curriculum and Assessment Authority.

Scott, P. (1998) Teacher talk and meaning making. *Studies in Science Education*, **32**, 45–80.

SCRE (1995) *Taking a Closer look at Science*. Edinburgh: SCRE.

SEAC (1990) *Records of Achievement in the Primary School*. London: SEAC.

Shulman, L. S. (1987) Knowledge and teaching: foundations of the new reform. *Harvard Educational Review*, **7** (1), 1–22.

SPE (1995) *Making Sense of Science*. Ten programmes for Inset. London: SPE.

SOED (Scottish Office Education Department) (1992) *Using Performance Indicators in Primary School Self-Evaluation*. Edinburgh: SOED.

SPACE Research Report (1990a) *Evaporation and Condensation*. Liverpool: Liverpool University Press.

SPACE Research Report (1990b) *Growth*. Liverpool: Liverpool University Press.

SPACE Research Report (1990c) *Light*. Liverpool: Liverpool University Press.

SPACE Rsearch Report (1990d) *Sound*. Liverpool: Liverpool University Press.

SPACE Research Report (1991a) *Electricity*. Liverpool: Liverpool University Press.

SPACE Research Report (1991b) *Materials*. Liverpool: Liverpool University Press.

SPACE Research Report (1992) *Processes of Life*. Liverpool: Liverpool University Press.

SPACE Research Report (1993) *Rocks, Soil and Weather*. Liverpool: Liverpool University Press.

SPACE Research Report (1996) *Earth in Space*. Liverpool: Liverpool University Press.

SPACE Research Report (1998) *Forces*. Liverpool: Liverpool University Press.

Sutton, C. (1992) *Words, Science and Learning*. Buckingham: Open University Press.

TTA (1998) *National Standards for Subject Leaders*. London: Teacher Training Agency.

Thurber, J. (1945) *The Thurber Carnival*. London: Hamish Hamilton.

Tobin, K. and Garnett, P. (1993) Exemplary practice in science classrooms. In D. Edwards, E. Scanlon and R. West (eds), *Teaching, Learning and Assessment in Science Education*. London: Paul Chapman Publishing and Open University Press.

Vosniadou, S. (1997) On the development of the understanding of abstract ideas. In K. Harnquist, and A. Burgen (eds), *Growing up with Science*. London: Jessica Kingsley.

Vygotsky, L. S. (1962) *Thought and Language*. Massachusetts: MIT Press.

Wenham, M. (1995) *Understanding Primary Science: Ideas, Concepts and Explanations*. London: Paul Chapman Publishing.

White, R. and Gunstone, R. (1992) *Probing Understanding*. London: Falmer Press.

Willis, J. (1999) *National Curriculum Science: Walls*. Hatfield: Association for Science Education.

Woolnough, B. (1997) Motivating students or teaching pure science? *School Science Review*, **78** (283), 67–72.

Index